D1733821

To Defend Our Water with the Blood of Our Veins

Sonya Lipsett-Rivera

To Defend Our Water with the Blood of Our Veins

The Struggle for Resources in Colonial Puebla

The University of
New Mexico Press

Albuquerque

HD
1696
. M63
P845
1999

·1 1 3629864

40545482

© 1999 by The University of New Mexico Press
All rights reserved.
First edition

Library of Congress Cataloging-in-Publication Data

Lipsett-Rivera, Sonya, 1961–
To defend our water with the blood of our veins: the struggle for
resources in colonial Puebla / Sonya Lipsett-Rivera. — 1st ed.
p. cm.
Includes bibliographical references and index.
ISBN 0-8263-2034-1 (CL : alk. paper)
1. Water-supply—Political aspects—Mexico—Puebla (State)—History.
2. Water resources development—Political aspects—Mexico—Puebla
(State)—History. I. Title.
HD1696.M63 P845 1999
333.91'00972'48—dc21
98-58046
CIP

Contents

Figures

Preface

This book is about water and power. Water is the prism through which I examine the political transformation of Puebla, a central highlands region of Mexico. By focusing on water I explain how environmental change over the long term caused alterations in the politics of the Poblano countryside. At the same time I show the importance of the natural cycle of wet and dry seasons in shaping the lives of Poblano farmers. This book attempts to mediate two levels of inquiry; on the one hand, the larger picture of long term transformation and on the other, the daily struggle for water and its impact on the local societies.

The case of Puebla is particularly interesting because the region is semi-arid and therefore different from the vast majority of examples already explored within the realm of water studies. Although a literature of water studies exists and these works are varied in terms of locale and focus, they tend to focus on the extremes—either arid places or regions where water is overly abundant. Few water studies are focused on semi-arid regions such as Puebla. By doing so, I examine a region where the contrasts are not so sharply delineated and where the processes are more subtle though not less critical for the political structures under which societies of farmers lived.

My work focuses on the hydrological regimes of Puebla and thus differs from the majority of literature on Mexican agriculture. Since François Chevalier's landmark study of the great estate, there is a long tradition within Mexican historiography of studies of land tenure and the *hacienda*. Many scholars have provided important regional studies of the countryside and show variations in the pattern of land acquisition according to locale. But, generally, these studies present static visions of the environment. Land—the ultimate prize—is unchanging because the environmental factor is missing from their analyses. The impact of environmental change on institutions has been forcefully shown by Elinor Melville who studied the effect of sheep on the Valle de Mezquital.

Land, plants, and water, as a rule, do not figure as actors in the story which most historians explore. Some notable exceptions are Elinor Melville and Alfred Crosby. Juan Carlos Garavaglia and Bernardo García Martínez deal with the environment but not over the long term. Some historians of Puebla are conscious of the role of the environment, such as Carlos Paredes and Luis Henao, but do not perceive much change.

Other historians—principally Michael Meyer and Michael Murphy—focus on water exclusively although for different regions (the U.S. Southwest and the Bajío, respectively). These works examine arid and moderately arid regions. Murphy is most interested in how water systems worked in the Bajío, while Meyer emphasizes the law and human adaptation to natural conditions. My approach differs. Although the same themes are present in my book, my primary interest is to place the environment at the center of the history of social change in the Poblano countryside.

The documents serving as the foundation of my research were located primarily in the section called "Tierras" in the Archivo General de la Nación (Mexican National Archives). Lawsuits of varying length and detail provided the most valuable source of information. These cases supplied data regarding farming practices, stream water levels, and legal and nonlegal means of guaranteeing control over water. Another section, "Indios," holds the complaints of indigenous communities lodged in the Indian Court and yielded a sense of some of the internal politics of these towns. Other parts of the archives also served to complete the picture. The National Library's Colección Tenencia de la Tierra en Puebla (Puebla Land Tenure Collection) is an extensive depository of manuscripts, many of which documented the regularization of irrigation rights, among other topics. The Archivo Judicial de Puebla (Puebla Judicial Archives) allowed me to complete the picture for some of the lawsuits found in the National Archives and locate others which I had not previously encountered.

Theoretical concepts help to explain trends and alterations in social structures surrounding irrigation and water usage. For the persons involved in a daily struggle for access to water, however, these ideas might seem far-fetched, although the notion that control of water could be a source of power would not. The focus on conflicts, although limited and limiting, does shed new light on social institutions in the colonial countryside. Alterations in the environment caused major social problems and eventually transformed the map of an agrarian society. This study is further evidence that the environment must be taken into account in order to understand changes within a rural society.

Acknowledgments

"We never miss the water till the well runs dry." So says an eighteenth-century Scottish proverb. My twentieth-century version is "Don't write a book about water in a land of lakes and rivers." Indeed, I have spent many years thinking and writing about water in places where it is abundant, and it was a leap of imagination for many of those around me to see the significance of my work. Many others simply believed me foolish. For those who supported and encouraged me, therefore, I owe even more than the usual debt of gratitude.

First of all, I wish to thank Richard Greenleaf, who directed the thesis which was the kernel of this book. He shared his knowledge of Mexican archives and life unstintingly. Jacques Barbier started me on this road when his lectures sparked my interest in the region. Gertrude Yeager and Ralph Lee Woodward were insightful teachers who went beyond the role of professor in their kindness and assistance.

When I embarked on my professional career, Donald Wright read all my first articles and guided me along the path to publication. I still think of him whenever I use a gerund. Rod Phillips advised me on the perils of presses and helped me over many hurdles, usually with a glass of shiraz in hand. I have also benefited from colleagues who encouraged me as a scholar, and in particular, David Craven and Robert Goheen.

Much of the most important work for any historical study is done in archives. I am particularly grateful to those who made my time studying documents so much more pleasant: the staffs of the Archivo General de la Nación, Archivo Judicial de Puebla, Archivo del Ayuntamiento de Puebla, and the Biblioteca Nacional, as well as the Latin American Library at Tulane University. I also benefited from researchers who shared their expertise with me, especially David Marley and Jonathan Amith.

Funding is a most important component. Research for this book was made possible by generous grants from the Social Sciences Research Council of Canada, the Mesoamerican Ecology Institute, and the State University of New York.

While in Mexico many people made life more enjoyable and accentuated my already devoted affection for the country. I am particularly grateful to my in-laws, Amalia Ayala Figueroa and Francisco Rivera Aguilar, as well as their children, with whom I live regularly and who have truly made me feel part of the family. In Puebla, I have a second family, Rosalva Loreto López and Francisco Cervantes Bello, as well as their children Pablo and Alba, whose company is as enchanting and intellectually stimulating as their city.

I am also grateful to many colleagues whose interest or simple good cheer has helped me: Lyman Johnson, Bill Beezley, Linda Curcio-Nagy, Linda Hall, Don Stevens, Betsy Smith, Jeff Pilcher, Stephen Webre, Juan Carlos Garavaglia, and Susan Kellogg. In Mexico, Carlos Paredes, Teresa Rojas Rabiela, and Miguel Angel Cuenya Mateos were water enthusiasts. I also salute those who were not interested in water matters but were still good company: Norma Helsper, Marshall Thrailkill, Marilou McLaughlin Wright, Sandy Gutman, and Linda Myers, Jutta Goheen of the wonderful dinners, and Jill St. Germain of the wonderful lunches.

Elinor Melville read this manuscript twice, and because of her perspicacity it is a much better book. Over many glasses of tequila or sitting in the theater at intermission, her passion for ideas was always apparent and I was very grateful for her capacity to explain me to myself. David Holtby, my editor, stuck with me through a long process and was ever a gracious friend. Of course, all mistakes are mine despite all this fine assistance.

The last word, as tradition seems to dictate, goes to my family. My parents, Fred and Elizabeth Lipsett, took me to Mexico at the age of four and instilled in me a passion for books and travel. Sergio, my husband, is my greatest supporter and always makes me laugh even when I am in a bad mood. What more could a historian with writer's block ask for? This book is dedicated to Fred, Elizabeth, and Sergio.

ONE

Going to the Stream

Twelve-year-old Rafaela Antonia fell into a ravine and died on August 9, 1743. For the Indians of the village of San Rafael, her death was one consequence of a long-term struggle to recover water rights for both their fields and public fountain. Crossing two very deep ravines, Rafaela fetched water every day for her household at the Atlatlapachucan spring located about a quarter of a league from her village. Along with most of the other young women of the surrounding villages, Rafaela made the trip for several years before her fatal accident. Even before her death, the town officials of San Rafael were quite concerned about the daily expedition because while the men were busy in the fields and married women were engaged with their household work, young girls had to perform this task. The isolation of the ravines contrasted with the safety at the edge of the communal fountain, and officials reported that cattle drovers and other transients who frequented these out-of-the-way places deflowered the young women.[1] The town officials presented the water shortage as a moral problem affecting the women's security. Yet, in a more profound sense, the absence of water unbalanced the community and threatened its continued existence.

The people of San Rafael were not alone in their complaints nor in their understanding of the central place that water occupied in the lives of colonial Mexicans. Where rain fell regularly and bodies of water abounded, it remained a necessary but often underappreciated daily companion. Yet, without water, humans could not survive. Agrarian societies were doubly vulnerable because their sustenance also came from their crops and these plants only flourished with either adequate rainfall or the substitute of irrigation.[2] Many peoples in Mexico appealed to deities such as Tlaloc or Chac to ensure precipitation while others asked for the intervention of the Virgin to end droughts. But, on a more day-to-day basis, less divine entities controlled the available water and could cause artificial crises such as the one of which the people of San Rafael complained. In fact, their

1

problem was not an extraordinary drought, but rather that farmers upstream used too much water which reduced the amount available to them. The people of San Rafael suffered from an artificial shortage.

The enforced drought in the village of San Rafael was part of a larger struggle for resources in the eighteenth century. During the eighteenth century access to water for irrigation and other uses became more difficult in Puebla and conflicts over water use rose sharply. Thus the problem facing the people of San Rafael must be inscribed into a larger framework: that of a widespread struggle for resources. This book is focused on the upsurge in conflicts over water in eighteenth-century Puebla, and attempts to explain the increase in conflicts, but also to explore the effects of this phenomenon upon the social and political structures of the region.

The state of Puebla provides an interesting framework for the study of an irrigation governance system. Many monographs already deal with arid climates where water allocation is fraught with much more severe tensions, while others examine centralized systems rather than decentralized ones.[3] Puebla's climate is mostly semi-arid (with a few arid and humid niches) and its environment is not generally as harsh as many of the regions which have already been examined within the context of water studies.[4] As a result, the relationship between control of water and political power is much more subtle than it seems in arid regions. Individuals or communities did not derive their political power solely from total control over water. Instead, they accumulated power in different manners and built up both irrigation rights and political power.

In Puebla—like most of central Mexico—the year is divided into a wet season (from about May or June to September or October) and a dry season for the rest of the year. As such, irrigation was only vital in the period before the daily rains of the wet season began and over the dry season. Farmers in the region used irrigation to increase their yields and lengthen the growing season long before the Conquest. Therefore, the Spanish who acquired lands in the fertile valleys around Puebla de los Angeles could build upon existing canal networks and a tradition of manipulating streams and rivers. With such a strong base the Spanish were easily able to harness these resources. Wheat flourished under these conditions and Poblano estates became the motor for one of New Spain's first commercialized agricultures.

Puebla wheat was exported and served as the backbone of local markets. Because the prosperous agriculture of the early colonial period depended upon irrigation, control over water in such a society was vital. Yet, despite traditions of centralized control over irrigation in both Spain and the indigenous nations in Puebla, the colonial period was marked by a decentralized system of irrigation management—that is, one without a strong local bureaucracy. Centralization occurred in eighteenth-century Puebla, at first informally and unofficially, and then was finally imposed by the large landholders who had amassed the greatest quantities of water. This centralization in Puebla did not come about as a result of communal consent but rather because it was to the advantage of a few of the most important actors in the Poblano countryside.

If Puebla's system of water governance was not centralized, how can it be characterized? Donald Worster argues that an inverse phenomenon—decentralization—can also occur. If societies can move towards a centralizing bureaucracy they can also choose to reject such consolidations of power. Worster's corrective is most applicable to Puebla where the early period of settlement and the beginnings of Spanish agriculture were marked by an absence of the creation of any bureaucratic system to regulate and adjudicate water rights. Instead of replicating the Spanish model of irrigation societies or replacing the Indian conception of communal authority over water, the control of water was vested in normal judicial channels. Consequently, if a farmer's fields suffered because of lack of water recourse in the courts was slow and inefficient. Yet, despite traditions of centralized control over irrigation in both Spain and the indigenous nations in Puebla, the colonial period was marked by a decentralized system of irrigation management.

Decentralization was acceptable to Poblano farmers while resources were abundant. As the Spanish acquired lands in the sixteenth century, the indigenous population was in decline. Therefore, indigenous communities worked fewer lands and had reduced needs for irrigation. There were few problems over water allocation in the sixteenth- and seventeenth-century Poblano countryside. In brief, a decentralized system of water management was adequate for the times and the ratio of population to resources.

The balance between people and their access to water began to unravel at the end of the seventeenth century, however, and as farmers increasingly fought over water, it became clear that the decentralized system of water governance was no longer adequate.

Over the course of the eighteenth century, estate owners began to introduce informal bureaucracies, using their servants to control sluice gates and enforce their power over the water, and to acquire control over even more water rights. Within the restrictions inherent to a decentralized irrigation system, the hacienda and ingenio owners increased their control over water. By the end of the colonial period when they dominated the vast majority of irrigation systems, these large landowners had an incentive to centralize. In fact the San Nicolás ingenio, a sugar plantation with a large number of irrigation rights, called for the creation of a local water bureaucracy in 1808. The ingenio's actions reflected the completion of a process by which power over water had been amassed by a few large landholders who then wished to consolidate their control by centralizing it. Thus, by the end of the colonial period, centralization had begun in Puebla, despite the desires of communities and certainly without their consent or participation.

ENVIRONMENT AND POLITICS

Colonial authorities did not consider hydrology when they delineated jurisdictions whose boundaries determined the limits of political authority at the local level. Streams and rivers, however, linked communities across political boundaries. (See Maps 1 and 2.) For example, the farmers of Huaquechula used water for irrigation from the Huitzilac river which first flowed through the Tochimilco jurisdiction. Before the Conquest and at the beginning of the colonial period, Huaquechula paid Tochimilco tribute in return for unimpeded flow of water. Tochimilco lost the right to collect this tax in 1538 when the Franciscans, who established a monastery in Huaquechula, brokered an agreement which guaranteed Huaquechula water without levies. Yet Huaquechula had never been totally dependent on Tochimilco because the former was able to use water for irrigation from other nearby rivers.[5] This example shows that streams or rivers linked communities and dependence on irrigation forced downstream farmers to come to arrangements with farmers located upstream for access. It also demonstrates the connection between resources and politics. Yet

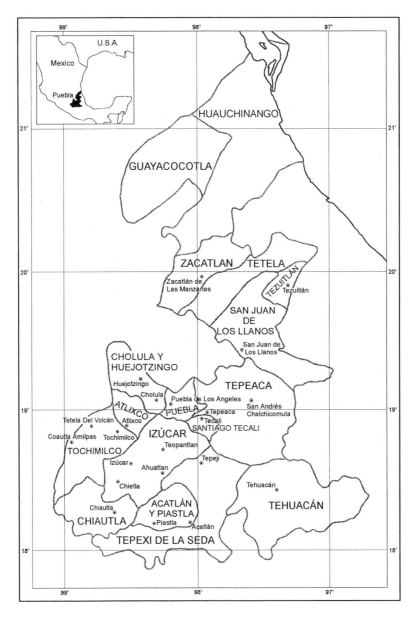

Map 1. Political Jurisdictions in the Intendency of Puebla, Eighteenth Century
The boundaries of Puebla's political jurisdictions compare interestingly to the lo-
cations of river valleys shown in map 2.
(Map by Ryan Ogston)

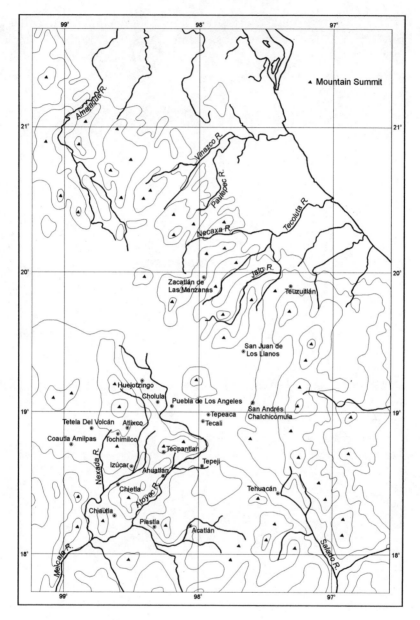

Map 2. River Valleys, Intendency of Puebla, Eighteenth Century
The major rivers of the Puebla region and variations in altitude.
(Map by Ryan Ogston)

the link between water and political power was not as harsh as in some arid regions. Huaquechula benefited from its agreement to pay Tochimilco for guaranteed access to water, but it was not totally dependent on this arrangement.

The relationship between hydrology and political structures can also be seen on a larger scale. The Nexapa river linked the Izúcar region to the Atlixco valley. (See Map 2.) Before water arrived in the former, farmers in Huejotzingo and other jurisdictions used it. As early as 1622, indigenous communities in Izúcar complained that the overuse of resources upstream meant that the Nexapa river was no longer reliably a perennial river.[6] Izúcar region farmers were powerless to stop upstream farmers from the overuse of irrigation because those who had first access to the river were located in another jurisdiction. Political boundaries meant nothing in the network of rivers and streams which joined communities of farmers. Yet, when people fought over water, their efforts were constrained by the rights conferred within a highly localized political system. Even larger towns like Cholula could not always control the farmers within its boundaries, and they had even fewer chances of success when confronted with overuse of irrigation in other political jurisdictions upstream.

The disjunction between political structures and hydrology was only one major problem for Poblano farmers when conflicts arose. The municipalities' lack of authority in water matters when they crossed jurisdictional demarcations was, in theory, countered by the power of the colonial state. In reality, however, the edicts which emanated from Mexico City had little impact when irrigation was scarce and appeals to the Audiencia were slow and ineffective. Without a centralized bureaucracy which covered an irrigation system in its entirety—and thus not limited by political boundaries—Poblano farmers were forced to use multiple informal channels in order to resolve their problems.

This tension between environmental conditions and political jurisdiction also determined the limits of this book. Although I set out to cover the entire modern state of Puebla, as I worked in the archives, I soon discovered that only certain parts of the region were represented in the documentation. Therefore, this book concentrates on central and southern Puebla with no reference to the north where the climate is predominantly humid, and conflicts over irrigation were not recorded.

Because the colonial political structures did not take into account environmental factors such as irrigation zones, farmers developed their own arrangements. But without a mediating force certain farmers—particularly Spanish and later Creole farmers—began to accumulate large quantities of irrigation rights. They became water monopolists within their local irrigation communities. Servants were assigned duties as informal water guards. They were able to change their status within the law from outsiders (without inherent rights) to insiders (with rights). The following examination of conflicts over water during the course of a fairly long period—1680 to 1810—highlights the developing class of water monopolists and explains why representatives of this group called for a centralized water bureaucracy in 1808.

ORGANIZATION

This book is divided into two parts. In the first two chapters, background information about the culture of water in Puebla and the theoretical concepts used in the book are presented. Every society has a relationship to water which essentially is its culture of water. For irrigation dependent societies, the network of canals connecting water sources to fields will be centrally important. Where precipitation is abundant and harvests dependent on only rainfall, the culture of water will be different. Thus, to grasp the context in which the conflicts over water occurred in the eighteenth-century Poblano countryside were taking place, the particular culture of water is an important component. This culture of water will be the focus of chapter two. Its elements include the cultural heritage of both indigenous and Iberian societies; the infrastructure, legal underpinnings, and application of the law; and finally, water allocation methods.

It is not hard to conceive of the connection between control of water and power. People upstream have an inherent advantage over their downstream counterparts. But, although this simple truth underpins the formulation of theories of political power as well as the formation of the state, it is a rather blunt instrument which does not account for many of the complexities of social relations nor for change over time. In a region like Puebla, where there are numerous rivers and streams, it would be difficult to amass power simply by the withdrawal of water. However, when people began to fight over irrigation at the end of the seventeenth century, this upsurge in conflicts affected the balance of power. Centralization/decentralization theories can explain these long-term changes. In chapter three, such theories are explored, as well as their application to Puebla.

The second part of the book is focused on Puebla as a case study. Water was an integral part of the agrarian economy of colonial Puebla. In the sixteenth century, Spaniards began to acquire land and water throughout the region and they developed a new commercialized agriculture. They introduced plants and animals which had to be adapted to the seasonal cycle as well as ecological niches according to altitude. Chapter four documents the development of the Poblano agrarian economy and shows the integral place of water in farming.

Chapter five shows how the large landowners had, by the eighteenth century, altered their legal standing in water matters in a manner which gave them judicial rights to challenge irrigation allocations. Informal structures and methods used by large landowners to wrest irrigation away from indigenous villages as well as other estates are also examined. Finally, the means through which a small group of estates became water monopolists by the end of the colonial period is described. In chapter six, the focus moves to the other side of the struggle for irrigation: resistance. Acts of resistance are classified as passive or active, and charted in terms of how they were used according to the season (wet/dry) and location (upstream/downstream). The many forms of resistance show that rather than acquiescing to the demands of their neighbors, Poblanos fought to retain not only their water but also control over water. Rather than clamoring for a centralized bureaucracy, they opposed it.

Consequences of these struggles for water were felt not only in the fields where plants died or thrived but also in the small agricultural towns of the region. In fact, these communities could be considered a type of barometer for the health or despair of the countryside since most indigenous and many Spanish farmers lived there. The people in these towns were not at all divorced from agriculture; most of them farmed land or were day laborers on *haciendas* and others who were not farmers depended on the prosperity of those who did. Moreover, village or town boundaries did not preclude agriculture; individuals planted wherever they could, often around their homes. Generally, however, the towns were affected by the struggle for water when farmers upstream used so much for irrigation that urban residents were suddenly confronted with dry fountains where they usually collected water for household use and urban plots. The effects were many, ranging from the disturbance of daily routines to sickness and financial difficulties. Town councils lacked the authority to stop such abuses and without the presence of a strong central authority were left with the option of regular complaints. In effect, many of the problems documented in chapter seven for the small rural town were reflections of the larger context of the fight for control of irrigation.

***

In colonial Puebla, Spanish settlers superimposed their forms of land tenure and techniques of cultivation on indigenous farming practices, and at first a thriving agrarian economy resulted. Access to irrigation was fundamental to the success of agriculture in Puebla—both indigenous and Iberian—because the area's climate is semi-arid and dominated by the tropical wet/dry seasonal pattern. Weather of this type entails the use of irrigation over the dry season via perennial streams, and the application of ample waterings just before the rainy period to give crops a head-start. Some form of regulation of hydraulic resources and their allocation between newcomers and indigenous residents was necessary to safeguard harvests and ensure peace among neighbors. The system of governance which regulated the distribution of water rights was cumbersome but sufficient in times of plenty. Conflicts over the issue of water allocation ensued when usage of water surpassed the capacity of the irrigation system in the eighteenth century. The result was strife among farmers whether Indian or Spanish. The discord over water was both a symptom of problems within the agrarian sectors of Puebla and the cause of additional difficulties. By using the relationship of people and water as a focus, the environment becomes an actor in the history of agriculture in the region. This approach allows an understanding of the way that ecological change affected farming societies and in turn influenced the region's sociopolitical structures.

The people of the village of San Rafael who mourned both the death of Rafaela and the slow death of their community as a result of lack of water might find these theories rather puzzling. It is important to remember the people who fought for water did so for a very simple reason: they needed it to survive. The title of this book derives from a 1790 document in which the people of Coxcatlán in Tehuacán jurisdiction present a complaint over inadequate access to water. It represents the feeling of desperation that some eighteenth-century Poblanos had when they fought to gain or preserve access to irrigation at crucial moments of the year and to survive as a community. The case study of Puebla shows how the need for more water stimulated political change on a very local level. It demonstrates the connection between environment and politics. But, clearly, farmers who required water in order to survive were at the center of all these struggles, and therefore their place within this book, like that of all the Rafaelas, is fundamental.

TWO

The Culture of Water

The first Spaniards to arrive in the Poblano *altiplano* found agriculturally based societies with cultural practices developed throughout a long history in the region. By the end of the colonial period, the Iberians had transformed the landscape and had altered the cultural framework of agrarian life. The combination of Indian and Iberian heritages in hydraulic law, irrigation, and agrarian technology and methods of water allocation led to a culture and practices associated with water which were particular to the region and not necessarily replicated in other areas of Mexico.

The Indians and the Iberians shared certain conceptions related to water, and in particular, the belief that water was a communal resource. But this concept had begun to erode in Spain, and then over the course of the three centuries of colonial rule, it gave way increasingly to privatization of access to water. The legal doctrines, bureaucratic methods, and scientific suppositions that governed the division of irrigation slowly implanted a more exclusive conception of water as a resource. The Poblano culture of water forms the context for the rise in conflicts over water during the eighteenth century. This chapter provides important background to understand the information presented in the rest of the book.

INDIAN WATER PRACTICES
The practice of irrigation and its technology, although a strong part of the Iberian heritage brought to Mexico, were by no means novelties to the indigenous populations. Archaeological evidence points to a strong tradition of hydraulic agriculture in preHispanic Mexico.[1] Chroniclers of the sixteenth century as well as early colonial documents such as the *Florentine Codex* and the *Actas del Cabildo de Tlaxcala* (Acts of the Town Council of Tlaxcala) indicate widespread and common use of irrigation in indigenous societies of central Mexico.[2] Archaeologists continue to uncover traces of old hydraulic management systems. But the full extent of such usage will probably never be

known because the Spanish took over many ancient indigenous irrigation systems, and modern constructions have probably covered
many preHispanic canals.[3] Many of the known irrigation systems
that date from the preHispanic period are located in western Puebla.
Although the canals found in the Tehuacán area are probably the
most famous, archaeologists discovered even earlier canals at the
Meseta Poblana and at Amalucan.[4] Clearly, the indigenous population of Puebla used irrigation for agriculture.

Spaniards who described the people and places they observed in
the early years of the colony sometimes mentioned the irrigation systems they encountered. Cortés noted in particular that Cholula and
Izúcar were both very well irrigated.[5] In the late sixteenth-century
Relación Geográfica of Coscatlán (Izúcar jurisdiction), a network of
channels is delineated. The network appears to be part of an elaborate
irrigation system.[6] These canals might correspond to those described
by Cortés in the contact period. Within the relaciones geográficas,
Angel Palerm reports twenty-nine separate villages in the state of
Puebla as having irrigation in preHispanic times.[7] Unfortunately,
these bits and pieces of evidence cannot provide a complete picture
of the hydraulic systems of indigenous peoples before the conquest,
but rather only an indication that such structures did indeed exist
prior to the arrival of the Spaniards.

Apart from physical evidence, the Indians' language, post-conquest
documents, and social practices provide other clues to the importance
of water in their lives. The Nahuatl toponym *Atl* (water) is one of the
most common components in Mexican place names, an indication of
the significance of water for the early Mexicans in defining their surroundings.[8] Atlixco—or water running on the ground—is an obvious
example. Other water-derived toponyms are less obvious. Quecholac,
a town in the Tepeaca jurisdiction, was apparently more properly
called Cachulac, which means "water where a bird is standing."[9] The
Nahua preoccupation with water is also seen in the characterizations
of types of soil or land. The Nahuas had many different categories
of land. For instance, their definition of *Atlalli* was irrigated, humid,
useful land providing abundant production.[10]

The Florentine Codex, an extensive manuscript on preconquest
life assembled by indigenous informants and the missionary Fray
Bernardino de Sahagún, provides descriptions of preHispanic life and

includes information on indigenous methods to work irrigated lands. Through the manipulation of water, the peoples of central Mexico could obtain more than one crop annually, cultivate plants which required constant humidity such as chile and cotton, ensure the ripening of plants where frosts were early, and farm where rains were insufficient. Irrigation works could be permanent or seasonal with canals of differing levels of elaboration or at times, water was distributed manually with ceramic containers, gourds or wooden vessels.[11] Farmers also used *chinampas,* or raised beds, in some parts of Puebla, notably in Huejotzingo, Tepeaca, and Santa María Coronango.[12] In Acatlán, farmers used the silt which accumulated in ditches to improve the quality of soil.[13] The Florentine Codex also reveals the Nahuas' understanding of the connection between forested mountain tops and the source of perennial streams. They believed that the hilltops were the cover or camouflage for a type of receptacle full of water, and so destruction of the *montes* (forested scrub land) would bring about an end to the world.[14] The connection between mountain tops and water was obvious since most streams and rivers flowed from nearby mountain tops or volcanoes where humidity was captured and snowcaps preserved water reserves. Even in eighteenth-century maps, the presence of peaks in water systems was emphasized by the surveyors who painted them. (See Fig. 1.)

Many communities believed that divine intercession could either ensure the continuation of seasonal rains or assist the human community in case of drought. Some hints of religious practices regarding water exist in the scholarly literature. Nahua communities appealed to Tlaloc, through their priests or privately, within the regular pattern of ceremonies or in times of drought.[15] Some of the personal rites may have persisted and fused with Spanish invocations to the Virgin for succor. Colonial Mexicans petitioned the Virgin of Guadalupe in times of flood and the Virgin of Remedios during drought.[16] In the Tehuacán Valley, according to Eva Hunt, the Cuicatec communities made offerings on hilltops associated with rain deities. These locations coincide with the sites of archaeological remains of structures associated with rain or water gods. Among the Cuicatec, devotion to two gods—Tlaloc and Chalchihuitlicue—persisted in the colonial period.[17] Religious practices associated with water are documented in

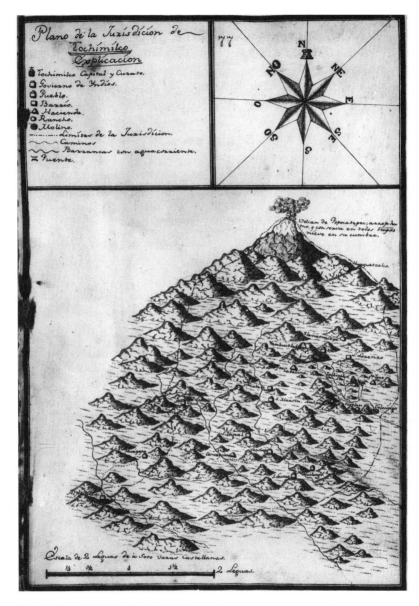

Fig. 1. View of Tochimilco Jurisdiction
Fed by snowcapped volcano Popócatepetl, shown in the background blowing
steam, ravines carry water through Puebla's political jurisdictions.
(Source: Archivo General de la Nación, Padrones, vol. 12, exp. 4, fol. 77, 1792)

the Florentine Codex but unfortunately, much of this information is not specific to the peoples from the region of Puebla.

The indigenous legal and political framework governing access to irrigation appears to be even more elusive. Although archaeological digs can resurrect the remains of waterworks from the past, they do not reveal the social practices or laws associated with these vestiges of material culture. Written documents from the preHispanic scribes do exist but are rare because the Spanish destroyed many of them. Existing preHispanic codices generally ignore the mundane matters of the everyday and concentrate on genealogical topics and conquest-histories.[18] Pedro Carrasco explains this absence of interest in water matters within the codices by pointing to the limited extension of irrigation systems. Because the rivers or streams that supplied the waterworks were not extensive, their management rarely overstepped the borders of a particular territory and inherently restricted possible conflicts between indigenous nations.[19]

On the other hand, in her study of the Cuicatec, Eva Hunt affirms that the various political units of the region fought over water regularly but they controlled the level of hostility through the intermarriage of "royal" lines. (Perhaps accounts of royal marriages in the codices are really about managing water rights.) The zone of conflict, however, would still not have been extensive. With the advent of the Spanish state, this 'marital' solution became less viable but the colonial state offered the alternative of its judicial system and the Indians engaged in extensive lawsuits to protect their resources.[20] Ronald Spores also believes that, at least among the Mixtecs, the rulers of indigenous societies monopolized important and limited resources of which he names water among others.[21] It is difficult to determine from these fragments exactly how indigenous communities undertook the allocation and adjudication of irrigation both within and between communities in the preconquest era. From what little evidence is available, however, control seems to have been centralized in the hands of royalty or nobles.

INDIANS AND WATER IN NEW SPAIN

If the Spanish had adhered to their own laws, indigenous customs regarding water rights would have persisted beyond the period of the conquest. Royal instructions state that the colonial judicial system should respect indigenous legal practices and use the same in lawsuits between indigenous litigants. This principle was very difficult to carry out in practice, however, because few Iberian officials were conversant with both indigenous ways and languages and did not always understand the indigenous methods of conflict resolution.[22] Where Indian conventions meshed with Iberian modes, however, there were some continuities. For instance, indigenous communities in Puebla held water rights as a "patrimony" within the general village holdings and allocated this irrigation to its members according to past use and property.[23] The Indians of Tepejojuma expressed this communal use of water in 1685 as follows: "[W]ithout the interference or encroachment of Spaniards, nor mestizos or mulattoes, the villagers will distribute this water through the *acequias* and *contraacequias* (irrigation ditches) in the manner they wish. The Indian widows as well as all the Indians who live in the village, pay tributes, and have lands, must benefit and have use of this water."[24] Individuals who belonged to the community believed that they, as members of the citizenry, had an inherent right to such resources. Bernardino José, an Indian of the barrio San Bernardino in Izúcar, demanded a share of irrigation for land that he inherited in 1801 because as an Indian of the town he had such a right.[25] *Caciques* or *cacicas* (hereditary leaders) held special rights to irrigation as leaders of the community. They inherited private lands and waters but also controlled communal lands and waters.[26] The sense of collective ownership within indigenous culture did not clash with Spanish law.

Representatives of indigenous communities served their populations by defending collective rights to irrigation in a number of ways. They needed to guard the traditional prerogatives to irrigation by ensuring that documents confirming water rights were neither lost nor stolen, and periodically they had to reestablish their license to resources. In Santíssima Trinidad Tepanco (Atlixco jurisdiction), for example, the village officials regularized water rights which they distributed to the farmers in their midst.[27] Indians rarely took on a struggle for water rights individually although exceptions exist. More commonly, struggles over irrigation were a collective effort. Because Indians owned the resources as a group, they also fought for them as a collectivity pitting themselves against individual Spanish farmers or at times against other indigenous villages. These communal rights to water, which complemented the Iberian concept of water law, survived until the end of the colonial period although they were constantly under attack.

ALLOCATION OF WATER

The formal allocation of water resources took place within a system of measures that was generalized throughout the colony. The largest unit of water was the *buey* corresponding to the water which flowed through the space of one *vara,* or approximately one meter in diameter. (See Fig. 2 and Table 1.) The water allowed according to this measurement was not limited by time. Grants of water or allocations made by judges could, however, restrict the amount to a period such as from sunset to sunrise or on certain days of the week. The most common unit used in Puebla in rural areas was the *surco,* or one forty-eighth of a *buey.* In cities and towns, the *paja,* or one forty-eighth of a *surco* was the most frequently assigned fraction for private use of water.[28] To allocate a certain portion of water, an expert surveyor assessed the depth and width of a stream with a *vara hidromensora,* a water-measuring stick, and thus calculated the volume of the body of water. The method did not take into account the strength and velocity of the current and so generally lacked precision. According to Michael Murphy, *agrimensores* began to calculate the volume of streams with more exactness under the guidance of treatises such as that of Don José Saénz de Escobar,[29] but in Puebla, no evidence of such advances exists in the documentation.

A further weakness of both methods was that neither could allow for future changes in the streams. The volume of water changed according to patterns of rainfall seasonally or more permanently because of ecological degradation and the lowering of the water table. In Puebla, people reported the disappearance or deviation of streams as a result of tremors or earthquakes several times.[30] Human interference could at times result in the silting up of rivers and again as a consequence, available water dwindled.[31] Apart from transformation in the hydrology of the region, no surveyor could foresee alterations in users' consumption patterns. The number of new editions or revisions to the regional *repartimientos de aguas* (detailed plans of regional irrigation allocation) testify to the constant flux in water usage. Because of all these factors, the repartimientos and the grants were very

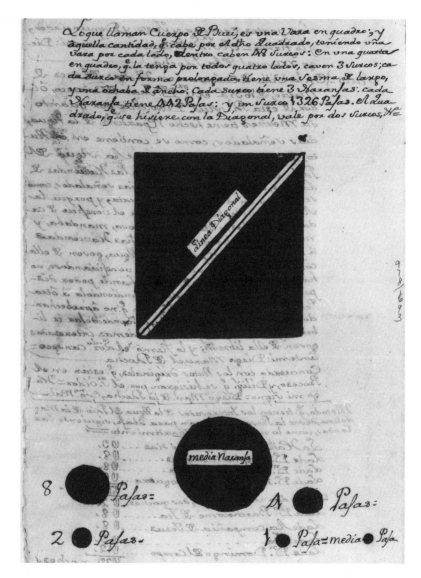

Fig. 2. Water Measurements in New Spain
Colonial Mexicans' system of water measurement included the *buey,* whose measurements are indicated by the square in the middle of the illustration, and other units whose size is indicated by the smaller circles.
(Source: Archivo General de la Nación (Mexico City) Ramo Hospital de Jesús, Legajo 267, exp. 13, fol. 16v, 1635)

Table 1. Water measurement units in New Spain

buey	Water flowing through the space of one square vara (.838 meter or 33 inches)
surco	1/48 of a *buey*
naranja	1/3 of a *surco*
real	1/8 of a *naranja*, also known as *grana*
paja	1/8 of a *real*, also known as *hila*

Sources: "Método de medir tierras y aguas según la costumbre y uso en las Provincias de la Nueva España," Yale University Library, Latin American Collection, Box 21, folder 347; Francisco de Solano, *Cedulario de tierras: Compilación de legislación agraria colonial (1497–1820)* (Mexico City, 1984), 205–08; Michael Murphy, *Irrigation in the Bajío Region of Colonial Mexico* (Boulder, 1986), pp. 163–69.

imperfect instruments with which to regulate use of irrigation and keep the hydraulic peace.

The methods used to allocate water within the agrarian communities of Puebla seem to have developed over time and in response to local conditions. Variations may also have corresponded to differences in Spain and therefore the preferences of various immigrants settling in the area, but there is not enough evidence to make a definite connection. Generally, surveyors allotted water according to the quantities specified in the *mercedes* of farmers and indigenous communities. As long as there were no contradictions or overlapping claims, the system of grants could satisfy all parties involved. The type of allocation was most frequently a unit of water ranging from *surcos* to *naranjas*. (See Table 1.) The recipient of this portion would divert the corresponding amount of water from the stream or river by means of a *caja* or a type of dam made of logs and branches. (See Fig. 3.) Depending on the proximity of the fields to the stream or acequia (main irrigation ditch), the water was diverted directly or via *sanjas* (furrows or ditches to direct water).

In areas of greater consumption, these divisions of irrigation water often had time limitations. Where there were many users in a single irrigation system, water rights were allocated not only by quantity, but also by *tandas* or shifts (e.g., from dawn to dusk, or on weekdays as opposed to feast days).[32] These temporal divisions could become rather complex. In Huejotzingo, for instance, the fourteen *surcos* allowed from the river were allotted by quantity and time in this way:

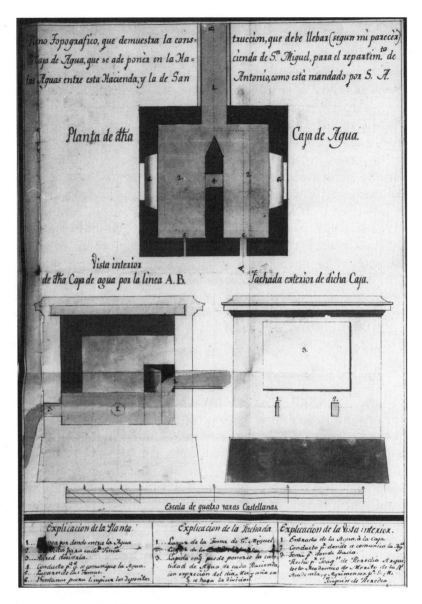

Fig. 3. Topographical Plan of a *Caja*

A *caja* diverted water from a stream or irrigation canal toward the fields of various haciendas. Many irrigators used less elaborate diversions, in many cases simple arrangements of sticks or stones.

(Archivo General de la Nación, Mexico City, Tierras section, vol. 1152, exp. 1, 1796, by Joaquin de Heredía) four *surcos* went by day to the hacienda of Doña Ursula de Arcola and at night to Don Diego de Mosquera; four additional *surcos* went to Licenciado Don Domingo Davila Galindo by day and by night to Joseph Cano de Villegas; three surcos were allocated to Salvador Pérez Forte, and three to Pedro Ramos de Inojosa. At night, these last two owners had to return the water to the *acequia madre* (main irrigation ditch).[33] In such cases, the allocation of water became more complicated and open to abuses.

The more divisions and claims on water, the more difficult it became to administer these allocations, and in areas of heavy agrarian settlement and exploitation, communities often requested a repartimiento de aguas. These documents were more comprehensive studies of the available resources and the methods to judiciously divide the water according to rights, claims, and needs. Surveyors (called hydromensores or agrimensores) performed the studies and produced the final document which became the blueprint for future divisions of water. Not all jurisdictions of Puebla had these repartimientos, but Izúcar, Tochimilco, and Atlixco did. Although various locales seem to have developed allocation methods in a rather haphazard manner in accordance to their needs or history, no system was immune to problems and discord.

SPANISH WATER LAW

The Spanish judicial structure was the product of the intermingling of many cultures, including the Romans, Muslims, and Visigoths. The relative importance of the numerous cultural influences on the Spanish heritage of hydraulic technology is still a matter of controversy. Since 1589, two schools of thought have debated whether the water management systems of Spain owe most of their roots to the Muslim conquerors or to a combination of Roman and Visigothic traditions.[34] Certainly, the Romans were active in the construction of aqueducts to serve urban centers during their occupation of the peninsula and therefore their concern with water access became part of the Spanish legal system. For instance, the concept of *servidumbre* or servitude, which was central to many struggles over water rights in colonial Puebla, was of Roman derivation.[35] Although some of the legal practices derived from the Roman period entered into the Visigothic legal code—the *Siete Partidas*—, the heritage of Roman hydraulic law and practices was strongest in eastern Spain, especially in Valencia.[36] The residents of the southern and western portions of the peninsula generally developed their irrigation systems under the guidance of the Moors who brought with them technology and expertise derived from long experience in arid climates.[37] The common thread in all these systems was, however, the importance of a certain public character to water. In brief, use of irrigation was not subject to monopoly but rather should benefit the community.

The guiding idea of the communality of water resources was applied to the Americas. The King of Spain asserted sovereignty over all territories including rights to the soil and subsoil, the "waters, hilltops, and pastures," and reserved the right to grant these properties for the good of all.[38] In 1642, the Crown asserted the Indians' inalienable rights to "the waters and irrigation; and the lands in which they had made irrigation canals."[39] Later, in the *Recopilación de las Leyes de Indias* of 1680, preHispanic water management systems were upheld: "that the same order which the Indians had for the division and allocation of waters should be kept and practiced among the Spanish."[40] These decrees perhaps had some precedent in the Reconquest because, during the recovery of the peninsula from the Muslim rulers, the Christian monarchs did not try to restructure or alter water management systems previously in use under Arab rule.[41] Furthermore, these laws were an extension of the Iberian legal tradition of prior appropriation doctrine rather than riparian systems, but were also part of a half-hearted attempt by Spanish officials to protect the indigenous population.[42] The doctrine of prior appropriation gave the Indians an inherent right to irrigation because it favored the rights of the people who had used water for the longest period of time.

Spanish water law was based on the doctrine of prior appropriation, and differs fundamentally from riparian legal structure. Prior appropriation makes no connection between land ownership and rights of access to irrigation, whereas within riparian systems, owners of water-side properties have inherent privileges to use the streams or rivers which run beside their fields. Under the system of prior appropriation a landowner such as the Bachiller Don Juan Esteban de Lavera had to apply for permission to use a spring that began on his land.[43] Although the Iberian legal codes seem to indicate a Spanish preference for the prior appropriation system, relationships between land and water varied according to region on the Peninsula. In Valencia and Castellón, land and water were inseparable; irrigation rights were attached to the land. In contrast, water rights could be disassociated from fields in Alicante, Elche, and other southern provinces.[44] Jean Brunhès, a French geographer who conducted an important early study of Spanish water systems, connected abundant water to places where water rights were intrinsic parts of land titles, and in contrast, in areas of limited irrigation, water rights were privatized and alienable from land. Such variations show flexibility in water law and allocation systems depending on local conditions. The two systems also provide contrast in types of allocation; the former uses a proportional distribution and the latter a division by fixed time units which can be exchanged freely.[45]

In general, the doctrine of prior appropriation prevailed in Mexico as it did in Puebla during the colonial period. Poblano landowners sometimes gained rights to water through land grants, but could not count on access to irrigation—legally—unless they had either a grant or a historic right of usage. It would therefore seem obvious to make the connection between relative scarcity of water and the doctrine of prior appropriation. But Theodore Downing shows a flexible system among the modern-day Zapotec of Oaxaca who switch from riparian to prior appropriation depending on seasonal patterns of abundance or paucity of water, and the demands placed on these resources for irrigation.[46] The significance of the use of different systems and their relationship to hydraulic resources is still less than clear but is indicative of the relationship between environment and legal structure. Judicial arrangements also evolved in Mexico over time in response to demographic and economic change and were not so rigid as it may appear by reading judicial doctrines. Indeed, William Taylor suggests a "more spontaneous process" which gained form and organization as more users demanded access to water along a stream.[47] A less rigid view of the legal bases for allocation of water allows an explanation of the erosion of indigenous control of irrigation resources. The judicial doctrines which were the basis of Spanish water law adapted well to the changing situation of Iberian landowners. As they established a presence in the Poblano countryside they were able by various means to acquire legal rights to irrigation.

WATER LAW IN PRACTICE

Antiquity and legitimacy of ownership were the fundamental basis of any claim to irrigation under the doctrine of prior appropriation. Although plaintiffs constantly claimed that they had a dire necessity for water in order to survive, such an argument could not be the central core of any successful defense. Longest tenure of resources without any legal challenge was the most secure claim to irrigation. As such, documents legitimizing or confirming water rights were vital to any protection of rights. Because of the centrality of these manuscripts to any legal action, opponents stole the papers of many indigenous villages or these documents were sometimes "lost." Documents innocently turned over to estate owners or their representatives were often either retained or partially destroyed.[48] Don Antonio Oliban, a neighbor of the village of Teutla, apparently tried various tactics to obtain village documents culminating in the suggestion to one of the "hijos del pueblo" that he would pay for the theft of the village's titles.[49]

When written documents were missing, non-existent or fragmentary, the general practice was to obtain testimony from the oldest residents of the locale in order to establish past usage and rights. For example, Miguel Patricio, an Indian, eighty-five years of age, resident of the village of Santa María Coapa in Tehuacán jurisdiction, testified in 1730 that the village had owned land in Guastla since he reached the age of reason (twenty-five) and that the residents used water which passed through the lands of Tochapa. Villagers never paid nor provided any form of remuneration for using the water nor were they impeded in such usage until the arrival of Don Juan Berdejo.[50] In certain rare instances, the physical evidence of old waterworks could establish the antiquity of usage. In 1760, Licenciado Don Andrés Perez de Velasco, commissioner of the Inquisition, parish priest and ecclesiastical judge, accepted the proof of former ownership of irrigation presented by the village of Tepapayeca in the form of the acequia and conduits previously used to transport water to their lands.[51]

In some unfortunate situations, indigenous groups resorted to rather transparent forgeries which ruined their credibility.[52] When the Indians of San Miguel Teanguisilco, Santa María de los Nieves, and San Simón Tlamicontla in Huejotzingo jurisdiction presented the documents from a grant to uphold their disputed right to water, the judge suspected that they had obtained a fake from the notorious forger Don Joseph de Leon y Mendoza of Atlixco.[53] Their petition was denied. Despite the inherent advantage which the indigenous population possessed under a system of prior appropriation, the Spanish emphasis on documentation weakened Indian control over water rights because paper proof was vulnerable to loss or destruction.

Because the governance of water rights differed in other regions, it seems that these customs were particularly Poblano. In northern New Spain, town councils gained control of water resources and had the authority to divide them among themselves.[54] Officials often applied the criteria of need in the context of water rights conflicts and allocation of irrigation in the north of Mexico, and it could be used to expand or limit irrigation capacities.[55] In the Bajío, officials assumed that indigenous communities had rights to water and rarely required them to produce titles to justify their demands, whereas Spanish officials obligated their Iberian counterparts to back up claims.[56] In the Puebla region, indigenous communities could not defend their resources without documentary evidence of their rights. Although the irrigation rights of Indians were protected by law, the diffuse nature of water management in Puebla did not shield them from encroachments. Next, because they were forced to provide proof of ownership via documentation—unlike counterparts in the Bajío—the Indians were vulnerable to the loss of irrigation rights.

Within the judicial framework, several methods existed to acquire documentary or legal proof of water rights. These procedures were occasionally contested, and rather tortuous claims sometimes stretched the limits and probably the spirit of the law. The most straightforward procedure to gain irrigation rights was through the *merced* (grant). The king, viceroy, or Audiencia bestowed these grants, at times in conjunction with land, but most commonly separately. The grant of water rights was usually followed by a formal *auto de posesión* (act of possession) in which the new owner of the rights to the irrigation symbolically took water or a gourd in his hands, and sometimes threw grass or twigs into the stream or irrigation ditch in front of witnesses.[57] Such events were sometimes the occasion for celebrations. In the sixteenth century, when officials gave the village of San Pedro possession of the local waters, the village officials and the community danced the "baile de Zapotitlán" together.[58] These for-

Table 2. Water rights grants in Puebla, 1680–1810

Decade	Number
1680–1689	5
1690–1699	3
1700–1709	4
1710–1719	8
1720–1729	3
1730–1739	5
1740–1749	5
1750–1759	5
1760–1769	0
1770–1779	0
1780–1789	1
1790–1799	0
1800–1809	0
1800–1810	0

Sources: Archivo General de la Nación, Mexico City, Tierras, Indios, and Mercedes sections, and Biblioteca Nacional, Mexico City, Colección Tenencia de la Tierra en Puebla. Note: This sample does not include the city of Puebla de los Angeles in which many individuals received water rights grants of household use.

malities established formal title to irrigation rights and allowed Indian communities to transfer their ancient usage of water into the Spanish system based up documentary evidence.

Early grants seem to have been awarded with little fuss: cash payment of variable amounts was the only requirement. Over the course of the eighteenth century, officials became more reluctant to grant irrigation rights (see Table 2) and when requested, the grants were often hotly contested. Many grants of water rights included the proviso that "no third parties should be prejudiced" by the allocation of water, very often referring to the local indigenous communities. In order to satisfy this condition, either a local official was required to inspect the site and ensure the authorities that resources warranted such a grant or an announcement of intent was read at the conclusion of mass on a feast day when maximum church attendance was expected. This second safeguard gave people the opportunity to lodge objections to a grant although the ensuing process often followed rather predictable lines.

Officials had to verify whether resources were sufficient for a particular allocation, but at times they were also besieged by the objections of third parties. Neighbors were frequently able to block or delay the distribution of water grants.[59] In 1742, the village of Santa Isabel in Tecali attempted to gain the rights to a very weak spring coming from the barranca Acachichimitla. The *cacica* Doña Francisca de Amaro, however, managed to delay the village's petition by protesting that this watercourse ran through her lands. Her argument was rather feeble but there is no indication that the villagers were able to overcome her opposition and no documentary record of a *merced.*[60]

Lodging an objection did not always guarantee results. In 1694, when Joseph de Arévalo requested additional water in order to transform his land into a sugar *trapiche,* the Indians of Agueguezingo opposed his plan stating that the water belonged to their community. The question of control over this particular water was not a novelty because the Indians had already filed a lawsuit over the very same stream in the *Juzgado de Indios* (General Court of Indians). Their protests were overruled, however, because Arévalo presented twelve Spanish and four Ladino witnesses to contradict the community's contention; the greater weight given to Spanish witnesses meant that the court valued their testimony more than that of the Indians.[61] In both examples, the significance of status and authority within rural society seems to have tipped the balance.

When there was relative parity between the parties petitioning or challenging, the result was very often a compromise. When the villages of Epatlán, Necoxtla, San Miguel, and San Mateo allied themselves with the Racionero Melchor Marquez de Amarillo, Pedro García Palomino, and the monastery of Santo Domingo to protest Hernan Pérez de Neyra's 1734 petition for the *remanientes* (leftover waters) of the Epatlán river, the communities had more potent allies than in the cases of Santa Isabel and Agueguezingo. The Audiencia eventually issued the grant but with the condition that some water was to be reserved for the communities' fields.[62] The concession was perhaps sufficient for the moment but made no provision for fluctuating community populations nor water levels. The settlement was probably a means of weaning the communities away from their more powerful allies. The system of third party objections was evidently inadequate to ensure the safeguarding of water rights in many instances, but even so, the number of mercedes granted in the eighteenth century dropped quite dramatically by mid-century.

Control over water could also be achieved through the process of denunciation. Similar to the better known process through which vacant land was denounced, the evaluation of unused water was a viable means to acquire rights to water. In simple acts of denunciation, the land or water, or both in conjunction, were reported as *baldíos* or unoccupied, and after an operation of inspection and verification, they could be awarded to the denouncer.[63] The process left ample room for abuse and dishonest acquisition of resources. For example, in 1781, the villagers of Huilango and Huaquechula somehow discovered that officials of the community of San Martín Sacatempa had misplaced their titles and so could not defend their claim to their water rights. Consequently, with a facade of respectability and uprightness, the residents of Huilango and Huaquechula denounced the water which Sacatempa traditionally claimed and they were able to take it over legally and formally.[64] Don Pedro de Chaves Osorio also denounced an old hacienda near Teutlan, but upon obtaining it appropriated the springs which originated on the hacienda land and thus deprived his neighbors—both Spanish and indigenous—of their previous use of this water.[65] Such stratagems certainly deformed the spirit and intent of the law, but were common. The denunciation of *remanientes* (water left over from irrigation) from other farmers' irrigation was much less controversial as a rule. Neighbors could thus gain title to the overflow and excess from the water rights of those who had formal title to water.[66]

Composición, in ideal terms, could be considered the inverse side to denunciation. In theory, the process of composition consisted of the regularization of occupied lands or waters—to which rights were questionable—through a cash payment. The Spanish Crown introduced the practice in 1591 and continued it as a revenue-enhancing scheme during most of the colonial period. Although composition is generally viewed as a means for Iberian landholders to gain legitimate control of resources, Poblano indigenous groups also used it. In 1717, the villages surrounding San Andrés Calpan presented their titles and asked for composition of their lands and waters. The quantity of irrigation used by these communities ranged from one and one-half to two *surcos*—not large amounts by any means but important enough to pay for secure ownership.[67] Most of the composiciones located for this work were found in the Colección Tenencia de la Tierra en Puebla in the Mexican National Library. Indian petitions for composition of water found in this collection numbered 25, compared to 23 petitions by Spaniards or *hacendados*. Some jurisdictions were absent from this sample, but in Izúcar the relative number of Indian composition petitions was very high—13 compared to 6 Spanish requests. It is possible that this group of compositions, in addition to the five for Atlixco jurisdiction, skews the picture and makes the indigenous propensity to use composition in Puebla seems much more common than it was in the region as a whole. Yet, it is important to note that Poblano indigenous communities were not at all reluctant to employ a judicial strategy which might give them ammunition in the battle to preserve irrigation rights. Sometimes, the larger agrarian communities, such as Atlixco, Cholula, and San Juan de los Llanos, asked to compose their holdings collectively in order to save money and prevent conflicts during the process.[68] Composition could be used to guarantee legitimate claims to water as well as those which were illegitimate, and served as a means to solidify control of irrigation which was not always legally acquired.

While streams were bountiful, it was a fairly common practice for relative newcomers to rent partial access to water from the region's long-term residents who held the most extensive claims to irrigation. The rental of water seems to have had preHispanic roots.[69] Indigenous communities were required to procure approval for such contracts from the Juzgado de Indios before leasing their water. The community of Tecamachalco, for instance, decided in 1693 to rent a spring of brackish salty water in perpetuity for thirty-five pesos annually.[70] Generally, the agreements to rent irrigation were based on a cash payment, but other arrangements existed. Doña Luisa Lestrada paid the community of Huaquechula eight *cargas* of wheat annually for the rental of their land and water, whereas the village of Chietla received one cow, four *arrobas* of honey, and two loaves of sugar from the ingenio of Xaltepeque.[71] Other communities had contracts which specified that the tenant incurred the obligation to clean the acequia every year—an onerous, time-consuming, and labor-intensive job.[72] These arrangements were rarely satisfactory and, especially over the course of the eighteenth century, became the object of complaints and suspicion. Rental arrangements were dangerous because they allowed a usufruct which could be transformed into rights of servidumbre (a kind of squatter's right). In 1738, Doña Elena Velásquez de la Cadena and the man who was in turn leasing land from her tried to claim waters within the patrimony of the village of Coronango (Cholula jurisdiction). In this instance, however, the community was able to thwart the plan by showing that the plaintiffs had paid ten pesos for the use of water every year and therefore could not demand ownership.[73] In the late eighteenth century, tenants repeatedly refused to pay their rent and claimed possession of resources. Without a clear contract and regular enforcement, the continual use of water over several years could be transformed into squatter's rights.

Although the *merced* was the most straightforward method to acquire water rights, other forms of appropriation emerged in response to the decreasing level of grants in the eighteenth century. Such forms as denunciation, composition, and rental or sales of irrigation became more frequent because they were more effective. These methods deformed the original conception of water law because they allowed deterioration of the principle of prior appropriation and the fundamental rights of indigenous communities to control water as they had before the conquest. Although the authority of the Audiencia and other officials was not absent in this process, their authority did not prevent abuses of the system. The superimposed claims and counterclaims to irrigation rights made the allocation of water rather less than clearly defined. The authority of the Audiencia or other officials was, in some sense, distant because it could not be brought to bear rapidly enough to reinforce control. Without a bureaucracy specialized in water matters and with the power to enforce allocations, the farmers of Puebla were left to try to limit the level of strife within the irrigation usage systems without support.

With the increasing limitations of the *merced* system, many farmers developed a more informal strategy in which they offered rewards in return for access to water. A common strategy was to offer a tangible construction. For example, in San Andrés Chalchicomula, an hacendado provided a masonry aqueduct in return for a small grant of the water,[74] and the villagers of Huilango acquired a claim to a stream in return for assistance in the building of the Tochimilco monastery.[75]

The losses of water rights in return for the assumption of debts, however, were more insidious. In one instance, Don Pedro Pinto bankrolled the Indians of Chalma in their legal battle with Doña Teresa Pérez Delgado—a rival hacendada—only to reap a double benefit when Doña Teresa gave up and the Indians were forced to give him a fraction of their water supply to redeem their debt to him.[76] Not all such incidents were the result of such Machiavellian scheming, but several indigenous groups sold or rented water rights to pay for village debts.[77] Such *quid pro quo* arrangements occasionally still relied on Audiencia approval, but also represented a process in which acquisition of water rights did not pass through the jurisdiction of the authorities and thus created a back door avenue to such licenses.

The actual enforcement of water-related laws was not always straightforward because the lines of authority were often confused by overlapping jurisdictions and the creation of unofficial authorities. In Puebla, the alcalde's function in the allocation of water and adjudication of disputes was limited. Judges and agrimensores (surveyors), as representatives of the Audiencia, had more authority and were often sent to the location of the problem to investigate and settle problems. After the innovations of the eighteenth-century Bourbon administrative reforms began to trickle down to the local level, the appointed *subdelegado* began to exercise considerable authority in such decisions and the power of these officials began to be the subject of many complaints.

The hierarchy differed from northern practices where municipal officials usually settled conflicts and the influence of the Audiencia seems to have been slight.[78] Northern communities developed local institutions to regulate and ensure the smooth running of their water management systems.[79] The bureaucracy common to the north represented a centralized irrigation system that did not exist in Puebla. No such corps of guardians existed in the Poblano countryside, despite a sometimes high level of strife. Large landowners used their servants or employees to protect their water rights. Some of these workers were actually called *guarda aguas* although they had no official capacity and their identity was created outside bureaucratic sanction.[80] Poblano landowners exerted unofficial authority to enforce their control of water in a way that sometimes contradicted the decisions of the Audiencia. The authority of the Audiencia was therefore diffuse and ineffective. In 1808, the owners of the Ingenio San Nicolás in Izúcar—a property with the benefits of extensive rights to irrigation accumulated over the colonial period—called for the creation of a group of *guardianes de agua*.[81] The fact that this proposal, which reflected a desire to centralize control over irrigation, was made by the owners of a property which possessed enormous irrigation rights was not coincidental, but rather the culmination of the process of accumulation occurring throughout the eighteenth century.

In order to resolve differences Poblanos appealed first to local officials, but if this recourse proved unsatisfactory, they resorted to other means. While many informal channels existed, and indeed Poblanos were inventive in their use of intimidation and coercion, many petitioned higher judicial authorities. Such cases ended up at the level of the *Audiencia*. Indians had the added option of using the Juzgado de Indios and in some Audiencia cases, *procuradores de indios* (lawyers subsidized by the General Court of Indians) at times represented indigenous communities rather than independent lawyers. By the eighteenth century, a standard procedure had developed to deal with challenges over water rights. The documentary claims of proof of ownership had to be determined through mercedes in the first instance, if available, and then through composiciones or repartimientos de aguas. If no paper record existed or the paper record was unclear, the Audiencia proceeded to an investigation that included the testimony of many witnesses, and usually a visual inspection. Cases could last several years and in a few instances were part of the legacy left for new owners or heirs.

WATER SYSTEMS

In Puebla the irrigation infrastructure was not extremely elaborate. The canalization of water was accomplished through a series of ditches (*sanjas* or acequias) with wooden or masonry conduits. Tepeaca had a stone aqueduct that carried water from the sierra de Tlaxcala seven leagues away.[82] San Andrés Chalchicomula used wood conduits which transported water from one league of distance.[83] Stone conduits in the village of Tochimilco still lead to a fountain in the main square. (See Figs. 4 and 5.) Many hacendados and indigenous communities conveyed water from faraway springs or streams

Fig. 4. Central Fountain in Tochimilco
The shield of Ocopetlaycan crowns the central fountain in Tochimilco. Some schol-
ars believe Ocopetlaycan to have been Tochimilco's pre-conquest name.
(Photo by Sonya Lipsett-Rivera)

to their lands.[84] In Tehuacán the Spanish introduced a technique
called "filtration galleries," consisting of tunnels cut into the slope of
a gentle hill which reach deep aquifers.[85] Water systems that supplied
towns were typically also employed for agricultural purposes in the
smaller municipalities of Puebla.

Some convents and monasteries had elaborate canalization and reservoir facilities. The Huejotzingo monastery's walls double as water
conduits. (See Fig. 6.) Even the most rudimentary of canalization systems required considerable maintenance. Wood and stone conduits
had to be cleaned and constantly repaired. In both types, users

Fig. 5. Colonial Aqueduct in Tochimilco
This stone aqueduct—dating from the sixteenth century—brought water from
the streams descending the Pocócatepetl volcano to the central fountain.
(Photo by Sonya Lipsett-Rivera)

along the way constantly broke or pierced the structures to steal
water. Wooden conduits were vulnerable not only to rot but also
to the ravages of livestock. Although ditches were not as fragile as
wooden conduits, they required regular attention. The waterways
silted up, accumulated stones and twigs, and were subject to cave-ins.
Yearly cleanups as well as repairs to dams and openings were essential.[86] The work required to properly maintain a water system was
often a bone of contention. Individuals attempted to evade this duty
because it was long and arduous. The Chietla community marshaled
thirty men to work on the annual cleanup for fifteen to twenty days.[87]

Fig. 6. Aqueduct of the Huejotzingo Convent
The walls of this convent doubled as aqueducts, directing water both into the con-
vent and to its orchards.
(Photo by Sonya-Lipsett Rivera)

Some individuals or communities gained access to water in return for agreeing to perform *limpia* tasks, but later tried to evade the responsibility.[88] Local governments often ignored wooden and stone conduits until they were unusable. By 1789, the fountain which supplied the town of Tehuacán was so broken down and covered with moss that barely a trickle entered the city center.[89] Improperly maintained water systems caused the overflow of water before it reached its destination, and silted up canals caused flooding in both towns and fields.[90] Poorly maintained canals meant that users took advantage of the spillage to take more than their share of water.[91] Such floods could destroy plantings and make roads unusable.

***

The culture of water in Puebla was composed of many elements: technology, customs, religion, law, and daily routines. This body of customs and actions was neither solely Iberian nor Indian in quality or character, but derived from a synthesis of the two traditions. Although it is impossible to clearly differentiate practices, Spanish legal procedures dominated. Through the judicial structure, it was possible to acquire water rights directly through grants and indirectly through composition, denunciation, rentals, and servidumbre. Over the course of the eighteenth century, the Audiencia accorded fewer grants of irrigation rights; consequently, farmers resorted more and more to circuitous routes to water rights. This trend was possible under the loose control of the Audiencia and allowed a fundamental shift in water control patterns away from the indigenous communities and into the hands of Spanish landowners. It was within this setting that relations over water rights became increasingly conflictive and even violent.

THREE

The Problem of Water

Like other commodities, the more scarce water is, the more valuable it becomes. When irrigation was inadequate, understanding why people fought over it is easy. Placing the numerous conflicts over water rights within an analytical framework that takes into account long-term change is more difficult. Beyond the annual shortages occurring at key stages of the seasonal cycle, the rise in conflicts over water in late colonial Puebla signaled a transformation in the balance of resources to consumers and altered the relations of power in the countryside. Puebla had conventions—*repartimientos de agua* and *mercedes*—to deal with water allocation. Consequently, the rise in hostilities marked a breakdown in the governance of irrigation. In the late eighteenth century, the decentralized system began to deteriorate. Long-term variations in the Poblano countryside can be understood only within a theoretical framework that illustrates the connection between water and power. This chapter opens with discussion of theoretical models that link water and political structures, and continues with a discussion of the ways in which changes in Puebla fit centralization theory.

WITTFOGEL AND HYDRAULIC SOCIETIES
By controlling the headwaters of major rivers, certain ancient civilizations, such as Egypt of the Pharaohs and the Chinese empire, based their political power at least partially on control over irrigation. Karl Wittfogel used the connection between water and power to assert that the institutions derived from control over water fostered the creation of the state. Wittfogel argues that the central authority of such "hydraulic societies" withheld irrigation to force peasants to accept its domination. A bureaucracy emerged which oversaw irrigation, all aspects of the economic system, and other aspects of life, at the behest of a despotic elite. Wittfogel's analytical framework was applied to China and other civilizations where people channeled large river sys-

tems through massive irrigation works covering or affecting large territories.[1]

Although the simplicity of Wittfogel's theory is appealing, it is too streamlined to be useful in the examination of societies that do not conform to his rigid definition of "hydraulic societies."[2] Some scholars have nonetheless applied Wittfogel's model to the Mexican Basin civilizations, but their interpretations are controversial and much criticized.[3] Because Mexico has no major rivers on the scale of the Yangtze, Nile, or Tigris, power based on the control of water can have encompassed only relatively small areas. Therefore, it is difficult to imagine how the formation of empires such as the Aztecs, Toltecs, or even the Spanish colonial state could depend on such a mechanism.[4] While irrigation existed within all three imperial systems, it was extremely localized, likely the concern of local elites. The highest levels of organization of the hydraulic model in Mexico were regional elites and the *señorío*.[5] In a region such as Puebla, many streams descended the sides of volcanoes and mountains. Users upstream could block one but not all such bodies of water. Take, for example, the case of Tochimilco and Huaquechula. Tochimilco controlled the headwaters of the Huitzilac river; Huaquechula paid Tochimilco a tribute to let it run freely. Because Huaquechula also had access to another river, the village's agreement with Tochimilco was not grounded on despotism but rather the desire to have access to even more water.[6] In brief, certain despotic governments' power was based on control over large irrigation systems. The assumption that such governments can be found wherever irrigation systems exist ignores local characteristics such as the extent of irrigation systems.

CENTRALIZATION THEORY

While the Wittfogelian model of "hydraulic" states is not appropriate to Mexico, the connection between water and power or between irrigation works and political structures is valid. The relationship between irrigation and political power was much less direct, much more elusive in Mexico. The monopoly of water or water-related positions of influence did not form the basis of a despotic state in Mexico, but it was a factor in local elites' domination or authority.[7]

Anthropologists Robert and Eva Hunt shift the debate over water and power away from the concept of hydraulic/despotic states to the process of centralization. The Hunts studied the Cuicatec region of Mexico located just south of the Tehuacán valley in the state of Oaxaca. They focused on the Valley of La Cañada—an arid zone crossed by a river—for their study of a twentieth-century irrigation system. Eva Hunt researched the history of the Cuicatec people before and after the Spanish conquest.[8] The Hunts' long-term perspective of one irrigation society combined with a broadbased review of studies of irrigation-dependent peoples on other continents throughout other time periods allowed them to formulate an alternate theoretical model more appropriate for societies lacking all-powerful and extensive bureaucracies such as that of the Chinese empire.

The Hunts argue that centralization is a process by which a society dependent upon irrigation accepted the creation of a central political power responsible for water matters. In essence, it implies the organization of a specific bureaucracy—usually water guards or judges—who allocated, adjudicated, supervised repairs, and defended the irrigation network. It implies a loss of autonomy and independent decision-making as well as a financial commitment in terms of fees, taxes, or tributes. Therefore, the process of centralization leads to a new political structure: a centralized bureaucracy of water. In the Hunts' view, even though such water bureaucrats may seem localized and independent, in a truly centralized system, they are part of a larger, often national, system. Centralization can, however, be found in exclusive authority over irrigation matters or as a general political authority in which control over water was but one aspect.[9]

The centralization process was stimulated by conflict; that is, the rising level of strife in a given society made desirable the creation of a central authority that could impose order. Unlike Wittfogel, the Hunts imply an implicit consent, and even on occasion a request for a centralized political structure. They cite the example of the town of San Juan. After the Mexican Revolution, both large and small landowners appealed to the federal government to install a branch of the Junta de Aguas (Federal Water Commission) in their district to resolve the continual fighting over water rights.[10] As seen in this example, when the level of conflict was too great, a community requested the imposition of a water bureaucracy; thus, the centralization process was complete when a cadre of officials controlled the irrigation network.

The catalyst for the centralization process was a water shortage that led to almost continual battles for access to irrigation. When consumption outstripped supply, people fought over water. But, why did such imbalances occur? Conflict over water usually resulted from population pressure. Increasing numbers forced communities to compete both externally and internally for insufficient resources. The Hunts state that, "When there is no pressure on the land or over water resources because of low population density, there is no water conflict either between communities or between neighbors in a community, nor is there pressure to unify the polity to insure peace."[11] The tension over access to water and the resulting friction typically leads to greater centralization of authority, and thus the resolution of problems with the creation of a bureaucracy.[12]

Susan Lees extends the Hunts' argument to suggest that confrontations over irrigation arise from a disequilibrium in the balance between population, land, and water.[13] Daniel Powell also notes that short-term degradation of the environment can have the same effect.[14] The expansion of cultivated fields should be underlined because farmers then needed more irrigation. Only a finite amount of water existed in any irrigation system, and at some point, the extension of planting surpassed system capacity.[15] When irrigation was insufficient, farmers began to fight over water. Lees adds that population growth need not be limited to the countryside. Larger cities implied a greater demand for food. Increased markets and consumer needs could set off the same cycle of demand, increased planting, and clashes over access to irrigation.[16]

Based on the processes described above, a type of equation can be formulated to explain the trigger for the cycle of conflicts over water. When the equilibrium between population, land, and water was disturbed, the result was an increase in the level of hostilities over irrigation which in turn stimulated the centralization process.[17] Pressure on land as a result of rural or urban population growth strained the capacity of irrigation systems and led to conflicts over water. Application of the equation of population, land, and water to Puebla is described later in this chapter.

DECENTRALIZATION

The centralization process began because of conflict over water rights. People fought to increase or maintain access to water because as population grew, the extension of cultivated fields caused irrigation shortages. However, if population pressure and the demand for food stimulated the centralization process, can the inverse also be true? What happened when population dropped dramatically? What effect did lower population and the consequent reduction of market demand for food have upon the governance of irrigation? Donald Worster makes a case for decentralization in his explanation of the water-works created by the Mormons in Utah.[18] In the case of Mexico, the demographic collapse of the Indian population after the Spanish conquest was extremely dramatic. The indigenous population of central Mexico dropped from 25.2 million in 1518 to 1.075 million in 1605.[19] In Puebla, the indigenous population in 1570 was 94,475. By 1600, it had declined to 52,466, and by 1650, it hit a low of 25,903.[20] As a result, many indigenous communities left land fallow and some even ceased to exist.

Before the conquest, local elites in the *señoríos* controlled water rights and formed a type of bureaucracy which defended irrigation systems. The Hunts argue that Mesoamerican city-states conform to their model of a centralized irrigation society.[21] In city-states such as Tepeaca or Tochimilco that were part of the Aztec empire, power over water was localized and under the control of regional elites.[22] The management of irrigation did not cross the boundaries of señoríos, and was not part of the Aztec imperial system. Nevertheless, Indian communities had a local, central authority to oversee their irrigation networks.

Under Spanish rule, however, Indian elites lost their power monopoly over water systems. The Spanish colonial state and its officials did not compensate for the undermining of the preconquest system. No local bureaucracy was created to govern the administration of irrigation systems in the place of Indian officials. Within indigenous communities, Indian leaders continued to allocate water to their members but they no longer had exclusive authority to impose settlements. They could not force their decisions on the owners of *haciendas* or *ingenios*. As discussed in chapters five and six, even members of indigenous communities undercut their authority by appealing their decisions to external judicial arenas of the Spanish colonial state. In colonial Puebla, authority over water matters was diffuse, ineffective, and sporadic. Instead of entrusting control to local officials, the Audiencia periodically adjudicated conflicts, but not very quickly nor effectively. Clearly, political change as well as decreased pressure for water favored the creation of a decentralized system. For most Poblano farmers, but especially the Spanish, the decentralized nature of water governance was adequate until the balance between land, population, and water shifted and the level of conflicts rose.

Decentralized water systems occurred in areas where irrigation was *comparatively* abundant. Within colonial Mexico, water rights governance differed in places with arid climates. Unlike Puebla, the relationship of population, land, and water in the arid regions of the north was more easily disrupted because water was scarcer. Therefore, from the onset of their occupation of territories in the north, the Spanish imposed centralized control over water. Cabildo officers (mayordomos and so forth), reminiscent of the Iberian model of irrigation management and allocation controlled water rights.[23] Beyond a rudimentary sense of community ownership, no such administrative structure existed in colonial Puebla. Indeed, problems of irrigation rights were dealt with in the usual judicial channels. If centralization is denoted by bureaucratic structures, then Puebla was singularly lacking in such trappings.

The contrast between water governance in Puebla and northern Mexico can be explained by regional ecological differences: northern Mexico is arid and Puebla is only semi-arid. The ratio of people to resources could be higher in Puebla before the process of centralization was prompted because ecological conditions were more benign. With a greater abundance of water, Poblano farmers in the early colonial period required less strict control over irrigation. In contrast, in arid regions, even a small population put pressure on available resources. Variations in the presence of bureaucracies can be explained by the ratio of population to the quantity of available resources. The model links population pressure to the tensions which give rise to the creation of a bureaucracy. Lack of population pressure had the inverse effect—decentralization—in an environment such as Puebla's with greater resources and a more benign climate.

THE BALANCE OF POPULATION,
LAND, AND WATER

The centralization theory links ecological conditions to political structures. When population grew, more people in farming communities needed land. As a result, the area of cultivated fields expanded, and farmers required greater access to irrigation. When users' requirements surpassed the quantity of available irrigation, consumers began to fight over water. Therefore, demographic change that affected land use led to increased hostilities over irrigation; increased hostilities provoked the centralization process, which in turn led to a consolidation of political authority.

How does Puebla fit into this model? In the sixteenth and seventeenth centuries, water management systems in Puebla were decentralized. Political authority was not vested in a local bureaucracy and adjudication of water conflicts was slow and ineffective. Yet, the first two centuries of colonialism in Puebla correspond to establishment of large Spanish landowners in the area and the creation of a flourishing agrarian economy. In this period, the balance between population, land, and water favored a decentralized system. But by the eighteenth century, changes in demography, land use, and ecological conditions disturbed the equilibrium, and as a result, the level of strife over irrigation grew.

In the sixteenth and early seventeenth centuries, confrontations over water use were not numerous. As the Spanish took over land, they often settled near preconquest irrigation canals and began to use them for their estates. They repaired and extended the existing networks, and at times built new constructions of masonry arches or hollowed logs. The relatively problem-free usage occurred when the pressure on land and water was inconsequential. Even before the conquest, a series of devastating wars between city-states had reduced the indigenous population. The subsequent battles of the Spanish conquest did further damage, and the introduction of European diseases led to the outbreak of epidemics and a high mortality rate among the indigenous population. Abusive labor patterns as well as the displacement of Indians through the policy of congregation and coerced migration to other regions also meant a drastic reduction in population and the forced abandonment of land and waterworks. The demographic collapse of the Indians altered the balance of land, population, and water; it reduced the pressure on available resources and favored a decentralization of political control over water. Where local indigenous elites had regulated irrigation, they were replaced by a distant authority in Mexico City.

While the Spanish acquired land grants and consolidated them into estates in the early colonial period, the indigenous population was in crisis. Despite their weakness, Indian elites attempted to maintain control over valuable land, but it is not clear whether they made similar efforts to retain authority over irrigation. Some Indian towns abandoned irrigation systems because with a reduced population base, maintenance was simply too labor intensive. As the Spanish presence increased in the Poblano countryside, they sponsored *repartimientos de agua* to clarify individual rights of all irrigation users, which seems to have prevented major conflicts. In this period, Indian communities sold irrigation rights and rented them in other situations. Generally, however, through lack of use and sufficient numbers indigenous people gradually lost rights to their former irrigation networks and control over water.[24] Yet, with a reduced population and many plots lying fallow, despite some complaints and lawsuits, the situation was relatively problem-free and peaceful in the sixteenth and seventeenth centuries.[25]

POPULATION, LAND, AND WATER UNBALANCED

If the centralization process was to begin, the balance of land, population, and water could not remain as it had in the early colonial period. Coexistence within the irrigation system lasted for nearly two centuries in Puebla. Beginning in the late seventeenth century, conflicts over water rights in rural Puebla rose sharply.[26] (See Fig. 7.) The increase in hostilities over irrigation can be explained by examining alterations within the balance of population, land, and water. When these factors were no longer in equilibrium, the inevitable result was a breakdown of the social relations underlying irrigation allocation over the past two centuries. The collapse of the equation was caused by increased demographic pressure which led to changes in land tenure and usage. It accentuated the centuries-old process of ecological change which affected the availability of water. It is this chain of interlinked processes which explains the beginning of the centralization process.

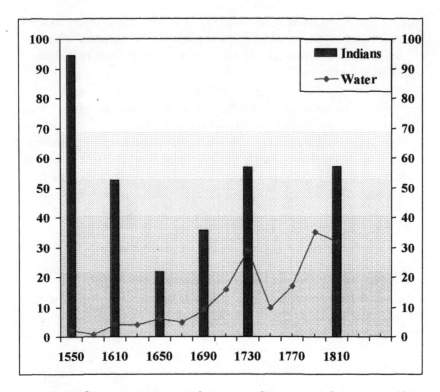

Fig. 7. Conflicts over Water in Relation to Indigenous Population in Puebla, 1550–1810
(Archivo General de la Nación, Mexico, Ramos of Tierras, Indios, and Mercedes, Biblioteca Nacional, Colleción Tenencia de la Tierra en Puebla; for population data, Gunter Völlmer, "La evolución cuantitativa de la población indígena de Puebla [1570–1810]" *Historia Mexicana* 23 [1973–74]:43–51)

By the late seventeenth century, the indigenous population in Puebla had stabilized and began to increase.[27] Demographic growth occurred not only in rural society but also in the cities. As indigenous communities grew they were able to work more land than previously. All villages held some land in common which was divided among members; other land was held privately and divided among individuals. After two centuries of colonial rule, the land area of many villages was sharply reduced, but in theory, they had minimum rights to certain lands. By law, Indian communities owned the *fundo legal*, defined as 600 *varas* of inalienable land measured from the town center. With the growing population, community lands were no longer sufficient and some younger men were left landless. In Tochimilco, Spaniard Salvador Martínez stated in 1742 that the indigenous population had grown so dramatically that the community no longer had enough land to maintain itself.[28] Arij Ouweneel and Catrien Bijleveld note that in the late eighteenth century, indigenous communities in Puebla had reduced access to agricultural land in relation to their numbers.[29] Herbert Nickel estimates that around 1650 the effect of a growing Indian and colonywide population began to have an impact on the use of land and water.[30] Many Indians left their home communities to migrate to cities or the Bajío.[31] At the same time, Spanish land-owners sought to increase their holdings and even expanded into pre-viously undesirable areas. In Tecali—a region previously disdained by Iberian farmers—there was a surge in rentals to Spanish farmers in the eighteenth century.[32]

The urban population also affected land use. Cities were an impor-tant market for the agricultural goods produced in Puebla—wheat, corn, sugar, fruit, and vegetables. Therefore, urban expansion meant an increased demand for these goods. At the same time the indige-nous communities required more land, both Indian and Spanish farmers had an incentive to plant more to take advantage of rising demand for agricultural products in the cities.[33] Population growth in Puebla in the late seventeenth and early eighteenth centuries upset the balance of population, land, and water.

Meanwhile, colonywide population growth, among other factors, stimulated the economy in the eighteenth century. More capital was available for investment in many economic sectors. Concurrently, the rising demand for agrarian products made investment in land an at-tractive proposition.[34] Because Puebla was traditionally considered the colony's breadbasket,[35] it is not surprising that investment was channeled to the region. In practical terms, economic demand as well as increased investment translated into a consolidation or expan-sion of landholdings and a greater emphasis on cash crops such as wheat and sugar.[36] In Puebla, such crops were not the sole domain of Spanish farmers; as discussed in chapter four, Indians did plant both wheat and sugar. Contemporary observers noted the expan-sion of cropland and increased orientation toward wheat and sugar.[37] Don Juan Crisostomo Zubia, owner of the Ingenio San Juan Bautista

Atotonilco, complained in 1783 that the indigenous community of Epatlán was planting more fields.[38] Joseph Saénz de Escobar, a lawyer and agricultural surveyor, noted in 1749 that higher wheat prices precipitated the extension of its cultivation.[39] Clearly, the increased demand for cash crops magnified the pressure on land that had already begun as a result of population growth.

As farmers began to plant fields that had previously been abandoned, their requirements for irrigation grew. The rising prices and demand for wheat and sugar meant that more irrigable fields were used for these crops. Spanish farmers needed more water but so did Indians where they still controlled substantial land area. Along with his complaint about Epatlán's expanded land use, Don Crisostomo Zubia also grumbled that indigenous farmers used their lagoon as a reservoir for water and diverted more irrigation to their fields than previously.[40]

Many Indian farmers, however, were increasingly relegated to *temporal* and marginal lands.[41] Some communities had already lost most of their lands and survived by cultivating orchards within garden plots in town or collecting wood.[42] Domingo Vicente, a mestizo of ninety-nine years of age from Tochimilco, explained in 1742 that the town and its barrios had during his lifetime expanded dramatically, not only in terms of the indigenous population, but also Spaniards and castas. Even given all the water allotted to the town, when farmers irrigated community lands with the springs of Chichimalac and the Arco, shortages occurred, and there was very little water in the public fountain.[43]

As the population grew and farmers expanded their fields, the limitations of Poblano irrigation systems began to affect farmers. Demand for more water simply could not be accommodated since there were no new sources or rivers to be tapped. The Poblano farmers' dilemma contrasts with the experiences of farmers in the Bajío who responded to the same market demands by building new aqueducts to take advantage of previously unused water sources.[44] Such a strategy was not possible in Puebla where the long history of intensive and commercialized agriculture meant that most rivers and streams were already in use. In Puebla, the pressure caused by expanded land use and intensified cultivation of irrigation dependent crops could not be alleviated by building links to canal networks.

In addition to the limitations of the irrigation systems, eighteenth-century Poblano farmers complained that less water was available because the volume of water carried by streams and rivers had declined.[45] Ecological change of this type is difficult to chart over time without systematic reports of meteorological and hydrological data. One way to piece together ecological change is to examine testimonies of elders and stream measurements over time. The authorities often asked the oldest residents such as the previously cited Domingo Vicente to testify in the claims of plaintiffs; their testimonies provide a picture of decreasing resources. In these early eighteenth-century reports, residents described depleted streams in the Axalpa, Huejotzingo, Tehuacán, Chietla, Cholula, and Izúcar jurisdictions.[46] Ouweneel believes that annual rainfall after 1770 declined in Puebla.[47] Reduced precipitation in the late eighteenth century, however, must only have aggravated the problems caused by reduced stream volume evident at the beginning of the century. In addition to reduced rainfall, ecological change resulted in a lower water table. Less water flowed in rivers and streams; the already burdened irrigation systems failed the region's farmers. The unbalancing of the population, land, and water equation was complete; tensions were accentuated and water shortages led to conflict. The explanation for the decline in available water can be found in two centuries of agricultural practices.

The conditions which the Hunts and Lees propose as the catalysts for the centralization process existed in eighteenth-century Puebla. Moreover, ecological damage to the land over the course of two centuries of colonial rule made the water shortages even worse.

CHANGES IN THE LAND

When the Spanish began farming in Puebla, they implemented techniques and technologies familiar to them as well as plants and animals from Europe. These innovations had an impact on the land. The Spanish also intensified deforestation, both directly for construction and use in ingenios and indirectly by creating groups of landless Indian charcoal producers. In addition to these alterations, the Spanish failed to maintain certain important agricultural practices such as terracing that the indigenous population traditionally used to prevent excessive runoff. All such transformations accelerated ecological degradation and led to a lower water table in the region. The reduction in available water affected the irrigation networks upon which farmers depended and aggravated the already disjointed balance between population, land, and water.

As the Spanish established haciendas and ingenios, they introduced the plow. The Indians used a digging stick, known as the *coa*,[48] that allowed them to cultivate corn in rocky uneven fields and on slopes. They simply made small holes with the *coa* and planted the seeds. In contrast, because wheat and sugar required well-broken ground and an even surface, the plow was indispensable.[49] The plow, however, broke up the soil much more than a digging stick, and thus promoted the loss of topsoil through runoff.[50,51]

Juan Carlos Garavaglia notes that in the rainy season, the intensity of precipitation meant heavy runoff, and with it, particularly severe erosion.[52] Without interlocking vegetation characteristic of the *coa* planted field, the heavy rainstorms typical of Puebla caused more damage in terms of runoff and erosion in a plowed field. Ursula Ewald presents evidence that the Jesuits (and probably other Spanish farmers) accelerated erosion by using flood irrigation in plowed fields on a gradient. It should be noted that a large proportion of the arable land suitable for wheat was on hillsides. (See Fig. 8.) The use of irrigation actually promoted the loss of topsoil. In several cases, fertile land subjected to such techniques became unusable in as short a period as twenty-eight years. Ewald describes the transformation of land in the Jesuit hacienda Jesús del Monte that belonged to the Colegio San Pedro y San Pablo. Over a short period of time, fields that had produced 3,000 *fanegas* of wheat were denuded of topsoil. Instead of farming these lands, the Jesuits transformed them into a recreation center and also used them to produce charcoal.[53]

In addition to planting with the *coa*, the indigenous population employed other techniques that promoted topsoil retention. Examples included planting squash or beans around corn, and building terraces that blocked runoff with walls or rows of maguey cactus.[54] Because many plots were located on hillsides, the use of terracing was a logical solution to the problems of runoff. The Spanish often did not recognize the benefits of indigenous agricultural techniques, and failed to maintain or promote them. As their population collapsed, indigenous villages frequently could not maintain the terraces and freely

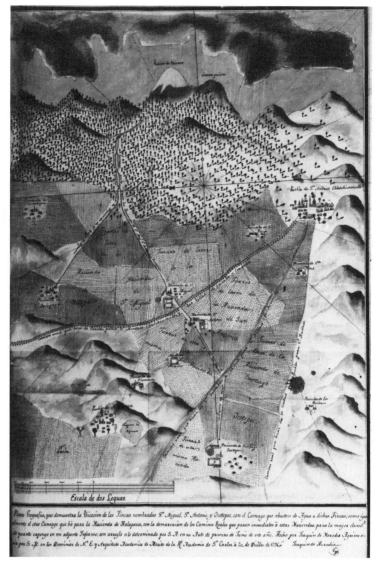

Fig. 8. View of San Miguel, San Antonio, and Ocotepec Haciendas
The farms and the town of San Andrés Chalchicomula lie in relation to the snow-capped Orizaba volcano. The fields lie down the sides of the volcano and none is completely level. Contrast this arrangement to that presented in figure 10, where San Andrés Chalchicomula is depicted lying below the haciendas of the region. (Archivo General de la Nación, Mexico City, Tierras section, vol. 1152, exp. 1, fol. 170, 1796, by Joaquin de Heredía)

grazing livestock (another European introduction) also caused the destruction or deterioration of terraces.[55]

Irrigation, as practiced by the Spanish, was not particularly good for the environment. Because the Spanish tended to plant crops such as wheat and sugar that were heavily dependent on artificial watering, use of irrigation was intensified and applied to larger areas. The Spanish also counted on irrigation to fertilize the soil for the most part. The irrigation waters carried silt from upstream plots and left these deposits on the fields as the soil absorbed the water. Of course, the silt was topsoil from higher altitudes which indicates how irrigation redistributed the soil. Because the Spanish generally created larger fields which eliminated terraces or the walls of maguey cactus serving as barriers to runoff, they tended to use flood irrigation. Ewald describes the process of erosion caused by irrigation in the Jesuit hacienda of Chicomozelo in Puebla. After twenty-eight years of wheat cultivation and flood irrigation, fertile topsoil was washed away and only *tepetate* (hardpan) remained. The same process of ecological degradation occurred on the Jesuit haciendas of La Mendocina and San Juan Bautista Ojo de Agua.[56]

In contrast, indigenous farmers were not as lavish in irrigation use; they sometimes carried buckets of water to individual plants and they planted in smaller units.[57] Spanish techniques accelerated the dispersal of topsoil, particularly since many fields were located on gradients. Next, the continual use of irrigation led to salinization everywhere, although the problem of salt buildup was especially severe in the Tehuacán Valley. Salinization led to heavy mineral deposits that prevented farming. As a result, certain plots in Chilac and Altepexi in the Tehuacán region could no longer be cultivated.[58] Lands which had once been fertile became unusable after a few decades of such practices. While soil fertility declined, farmers needed more land and water to try to counteract the effects of a deteriorating ecology.

The Europeans also imported animals such as cattle, sheep, goats, horses, pigs, and mules. A 1543 report claimed that so much livestock grazed freely in Puebla that measures to control these beasts were necessary. Carlos Paredes reports that a 1579 document reveals that cattle in Puebla increased from 15,000 to 30,000 in a nine-year period.[59] Haciendas and *ingenios* kept large herds and the Indians also raised many animals. With the exceptions of Tepeaca and San Juan de los Llanos, animals subsisted via grazing rather than consuming fodder grown by farmers. Animals climbed hillsides and destroyed plants which kept soil in place.[60] Their destruction of the ground cover caused a more rapid runoff of precipitation and with this, erosion and a drop in the water table over time.[61]

Contemporary observers recognized that the livestock introduced by the Spanish could be harmful. The great landowners of Atlixco banned small livestock such as sheep and goats, and limited the grazing of the larger animals.[62] However, despite these attempts to limit ecological damage, animal grazing changed the land. Jack Licate estimates that in the area of Tecamachalco-Quecholac, livestock grazing along steep slopes in general, but sheep and goats in particular, led to the replacement of edible plants by the palmetto.[63] Ewald also notes the harmful effects of the introduction of livestock on the Jesuit estates of Puebla. She says that constant grazing fostered erosion and destroyed the soil.[64]

Unfortunately, no exhaustive study of this problem exists for the Puebla region. But scholars who examine neighboring areas come to similar conclusions.[65] Spores states that damage by livestock in the Mixteca Alta eventually led to "overgrazing, forest stripping, erosion and ultimately the reduced carrying capacity of Mixteca lands."[66] Charles Gibson reports a decrease in moisture in Chalco after the introduction of livestock into the local economy and describes the colonial period as a period "of progressive desiccation."[67] Melville documents falling water levels in areas of the Mezquital Valley in Hidalgo after the conversion of Indian agriculture to pastoralism centered on sheep.[68] Grazing animals ate grasses to ground level and the denuded areas allowed water to flow over rapidly rather than being absorbed. As a result, the groundwater was not replenished, and topsoil was dissipated by the runoff.[69] The damage caused by the grazing habits of livestock was part of the process by which the Poblano ecology was slowly changed.

Deforestation also accompanied Iberian settlement in Puebla. The construction projects of the Iberians, cane processing on the large sugar estates, as well as daily household requirements led to the razing of forest reserves, especially in the *montes* (scrubland) which Indian communities had preserved.[70] In the Atlixco valley, farmers cut down trees to make room for pasture.[71] By the end of the sixteenth century, wood cutters from the Puebla de los Angeles and Tepeaca regions began to cross into Tlaxcala to find new supplies of lumber.[72]

As many indigenous communities lost their lands, they turned to the business of harvesting wood for charcoal. María de la Luz Ayala states that by the eighteenth century, land scarcity forced many indigenous villages in New Spain to turn to wood harvesting to survive.[73] The villages of San Miguel and Santa Cruz in Tochimilco jurisdiction derived most of their livelihood from wood by the eighteenth century.[74] The residents of San Miguel Teanguisilco, Santa María de los Nieves, Santiago Xaltepeltlalpan, and San Simón Tlamicontla in Huejotzingo jurisdiction lost most of their land and sold wood at five weekly markets.[75] These villages also often complained of reduced streams and water shortages.[76]

The shift from farmers to charcoal producers meant that rural residents began to clash over who owned or controlled the woods. Don Pedro Pinto complained in 1754 that the Indians of Tepapayeca had taken over the woods on his *monte*.[77] In the region of Tepeaca, an employee of the Hacienda San Martín del Monte discovered some of the Indians from the village of Santa María Acaxete making charcoal on the estate's land. The intruders admitted to using estate land for such purposes for at least six months.[78] The chronicler Antonio Diego Bermúdez de Castro described the cerro de Amalucan, just outside Puebla de los Angeles, as "much consumed and denuded" by 1746.[79] With the destruction of forest reserves, especially on mountain sides, the ecology of Puebla was dealt another blow and the inevitable result was increased erosion and reduced water reserves. In his study of New England, Cronon finds that deforestation in the early colonial period led to lower water tables and erratic, and often less plentiful streams.[80] Wherever a massive harvest of trees occurred, the harmful effects on the habitat accelerated the processes of erosion and loss of topsoil.

The agricultural techniques adopted by the Spanish caused the loss of the fertile layer of humus and led to the reduced carrying capacity of the land.[81] William Sanders, Jeffrey Parsons, and Robert Santley connect the disappearance of streams to environmental destruction in central Mexico.[82] Hunt suggests that certain irrigation systems fell into disuse because there was less water and that colonial agriculture caused the desiccation which occurred under Spanish rule.[83] The Atlixco valley, the preeminent fertile region of Puebla, began to suffer from the effects of ecological change by the seventeenth century. Gara-vaglia notes that despite the expansion of cultivated fields, the Atlixco valley rarely surpassed 100,000 *fanegas* of wheat per year. He attributes the output stagnation to environmental deterioration.[84] Paredes does not believe that the farming techniques of the Spanish caused soil exhaustion or erosion in the valley of Atlixco. But his study concentrates on the sixteenth century when such effects were not yet a factor.[85]

Poblano farmers noted the altered environment when in 1766 they complained that farmers in Michoacán had an ecological edge over them.[86] Garavaglia and Juan Carlos Grosso even remark on the advantages of "newer" areas of exploitation within Puebla by comparing the relative prosperity of Cholula, San Martín Texmelucan, and Huejotzingo to the first colonized area of Atlixco.[87] Ecological changes as well as the decline in available water could only aggravate the already intense rivalry for irrigation resources. The resulting phenomenon—conflicts over water rights—was the obvious outcome of the convergence of these forces and changes in the Poblano countryside.

Reports of particularly severe examples of erosion in many areas of present-day Puebla abound, and the presence of tepetates where once a thick layer of topsoil allowed agriculture to flourish are testimony to the changes in the land. Because tepetates are caused by erosion, their presence is evidence of previous ecological degradation. Hans Aeppli and Ernest Schönhals studied the soils of the Puebla-Tlaxcala basin, and found tepetates in many areas of Puebla. To the north of Puebla de los Angeles, for example, tepetates account for three-quarters of the surface of certain hills.[88] Luis Henao points to especially serious erosion problems near San Juan Bautista Ajalpan, San Gabriel Chilac, and Coxcatlán in Tehuacán jurisdiction; the vegetation in these areas is now characterized by an abundance of cacti.[89]

Quite clearly, although Spanish agriculture in Puebla was extremely successful, its toll on the environment was not so laudable. Excessive use of the plow, flood irrigation, and the failure to maintain terracing contributed to the loss of topsoil. Livestock grazing patterns as well as deforestation also promoted erosion. By the eighteenth century, the effects of these changes—a lower water table and reduced agricultural productivity—were obvious to contemporary observers. Because of reduced irrigation, conflicts over water increased in eighteenth-century Puebla and the centralization process began. Human activities changed the physical environment, which in turn affected social relations and political structures.

RISE IN CONFLICTS

These connected processes—rising population, increased land use, and decreased water availability—explain why farmers in Puebla began to fight over irrigation. The surge in conflicts marked the beginning of alterations in the Poblano countryside that included the consolidation of control over water, the weakening of many Indian communities, and finally the beginning of the centralization process. The Spanish settlers' cultural baggage in the early colonial period included customs and laws pertaining to water. However, in Puebla certain parts of the Hispanic culture of water were omitted. In fact, because Spanish irrigation systems were centrally governed with water guards,[90] it seems odd that the men who established themselves in the Atlixco Valley and elsewhere did not establish these institutional structures. Glick notes the absence of Spanish cultural imports in San Antonio but he attributes it to changing mentalities in Spain. He believes that the Spanish were beginning to "patrimonialize" water rights, and increasingly emphasized private over collective rights.[91] Patrimonialization meant that communal structures were not as important or necessary.

Such a trend toward private over communal rights can also be noted in the history of Puebla. It is entirely possible that the patrimonialization that Thomas Glick notes for Texas also affected Puebla. Attributing the forms of water governance particular to Puebla solely to a process of patrimonialization is problematic. Indeed, in the sixteenth century, the Spanish had no incentive to impose a system in which communal rights to water superseded private rights. Under the prevailing legal doctrine of prior appropriation, at the time of their establishment in Puebla, the Spanish had no inherent water rights. As newcomers, they had no stake in the system. Because of the legal doctrine of prior appropriation, the Spanish could not easily take control over irrigation. It was only over time that the Spanish acquired rights by virtue of their use of irrigation. A decentralized system was the best forum for such a slow takeover of water rights. The relative abundance of irrigation made this system acceptable and it worked for nearly two centuries. The movement in Puebla away from communal control of water coincided with the increased competition for water and thus local conditions, rather than Spanish imports, led to a patrimonialization or privatization of water rights.

In the eighteenth century, as the system of governance which had regulated water rights disintegrated, tensions over irrigation stimulated a new centralizing tendency. As the environment failed, the more successful, powerful landowners consolidated their holdings and expanded. Yet, they did so within the limitations of the seasonal cycle and the confines of altitude and location. Although the centralization process was not completed in the colonial period, the owners of haciendas and ingenios began to operate as if they had the right to impose a local authority. Many used bands of servants to defend water rights and to wrest away the access left to their indigenous and less powerful mestizo neighbors. Shortly before the end of Spanish rule, the owners of the Hacienda San Nicolás—a water monopolist in Izúcar—called for the creation of a guardian corps to regulate water usage.[92] The situation in Puebla had changed so much that a new rationale emerged. The great landowners controlled irrigation, and the time had come to centralize control over allocation. The system had in some sense been centralized; it lacked only a formal bureaucratic apparatus for complete legitimation.

***

The people of the Poblano countryside who lived these changes were not blind to them. They complained of a deteriorating environment, a rising level of hostilities, and ups and downs in population. Their individual stories tell these tales, but it is only by placing these accounts within a larger framework of long-term change that the separate events and stories make sense. The model employed here explains that the centralization process was initiated because of increasing conflicts over water rights. It is clear that by the eighteenth century, population, land, and water in Puebla were no longer in equilibrium. Demographic growth meant more extensive agriculture focusing on wheat and sugar. Increased cultivation meant a greater demand for irrigation within a limited hydraulic system plagued by a reduction in volume of streams and rivers; consequently, all farmers' needs for

irrigation could not be met. These factors set into motion the centralization process in eighteenth-century Puebla. Subsequent chapters
show why water was so valuable to the agrarian economy, as well as
the effects of the centralization process in Puebla and how conflicts
over water led to the creation of at least an informal bureaucracy.

FOUR

Water in the Poblano Agrarian Economy

The success of the Poblano agrarian economy was based on farming adapted to ecological niches and dependent on irrigation. Access to water allowed Poblano farmers—Spanish and Indian—to manipulate the natural cycle of wet and dry seasons and produce commercially valuable crops such as wheat and sugar. The agrarian economy could not function without adequate supplies of water at specific times; therefore, the prosperity of Poblano agriculture depended on irrigation. By understanding why access to water was so vital it is possible to appreciate why people were willing to fight over it. This chapter is focused on the Spanish entrance into the Poblano countryside via the acquisition of land and irrigation rights, and the creation of an economy based on this new form of agriculture. Major crops of the period—wheat, sugar, corn, fruit, and livestock—and how they were introduced into the natural conditions of Puebla are also discussed. Farmers in the different regions of Puebla specialized in certain crops and these activities formed the basis of a regional and international commerce. Water was important to individual farmers for their economic survival, and individual farmers and estates were tied into larger networks of trade and manufacturing.

A NEW AGRARIAN ECONOMY

In the early sixteenth century the Spanish initiated the redefinition of the countryside and agriculture with grants of labor or *encomiendas*. These grants provided a means for the Spanish conquerors to establish themselves in the Puebla region by demanding labor, taking over land, and introducing Spanish agricultural techniques and crops. Cortés awarded *encomiendas* in Huejotzingo, Tepeaca, Tehuacán, Tecali, and Izúcar.[1] When *encomenderos* were successful they demonstrated the potential of the Poblano countryside for prosperous agriculture to other Spaniards. Diego de Ordaz, the most productive *encomendero* in the region, was one such example. He introduced cattle farming and the cultivation of wheat on his land in the Atlixco Valley early in the colonial period. His success made other Spaniards eager to own land in the area.[2] By 1570, Atlixco farms produced 80,000 *fanegas* of wheat and, by the end of the century, regional output was 100,000 fanegas (55,000 hectoliters).[3] The Atlixco Valley was known for wheat production, and in the sixteenth and seventeenth centuries valley farmers sold grain at one peso above the accepted price because of its superior quality.[4] These wheat farms of the Atlixco Valley represented the beginning of a new commercialized farming in Puebla.

The Spanish presence in the region was further defined and given focus in 1531 when they founded the regional capital, Puebla de los Angeles. The new city integrated the region as an economic unit and became a base from which Spaniards sought land in the surrounding countryside. The creation of the capital was part of a utopian plan to form a New World society of Spanish yeoman farmers who would not rely excessively on Indian workers.[5] The comparatively small land grants awarded at the foundation of the city reflected the new policy. By allotting plots of land suitable to be farmed individually, the Crown hoped to establish a society of Spanish peasants in the Poblano *altiplano*.

Land granted by the Crown in the area immediately surrounding the new city, however, failed and thus did not prove to be very suitable for the new agriculture. In addition to a tendency to flood, the land was not suitable for wheat. Corn was the only feasible crop.[6] These setbacks encouraged city dwellers to look farther afield to acquire land. The Crown and the Audiencia also granted lands in the Atlixco Valley—an area noted for its fertility and which had a sparse indigenous population. Even before the conquest the Indians had abandoned land in the Atlixco region because of constant warfare between Tlaxcala and various city-states. The preHispanic warfare as well as depredations of the Spanish conquest meant that indigenous numbers were reduced at the time of Spanish settlement. Further demographic losses occurred because of epidemics and labor drafts of Indians sent to work in other cities or the north of the colony. Therefore, the Crown could easily grant land and indigenous leaders found the loss of their lands hard to resist.[7]

In the Atlixco Valley the Crown first granted land along the banks of the Nexapa river to its juncture with the Cantarranas river. But soon Spanish farmers occupied lands on both sides of the Cantarranas river as well.[8] The areas of greatest penetration by Spaniards in the Atlixco Valley were near rivers and streams around the towns of Atlixco, Huaquechula, and Tochmilco.[9] Because most recipients of the original land grants—one to two *caballerías*—considered the size of their grants too small vis-a-vis their status, they sold them to other, more well-heeled Spaniards. Instead of a society of Spanish yeoman farmers, large estates emerged from the multitude of small land grants.[10] By 1643, the original grants of land which had numbered over two hundred no longer existed. Spanish entrepreneurs had consolidated the small plots of land into eighty-four units of which forty-four percent were irrigated and a large proportion of the remainder had potential for irrigation.[11] These larger farms represented the beginnings of the estate system in Puebla.

From the Atlixco region, the Spanish spread into neighboring areas such as Izúcar, Cholula, and Huejotzingo, and from Puebla de los Angeles, they acquired lands in Tepeaca and Tehuacán. By the late sixteenth century, Spaniards owned much of the land previously controlled by the Tepeaca Indians. As the Indian nobles lost control over commoners' labor, they sold much of the land they held. By the mid-seventeenth century, 300 haciendas and ranchos were in place in the immediate area of Tepeaca, and by the end of the colonial period, 400 haciendas and ranchos as well as three mills had been established. Large estates dominated the agrarian sector, while small farms only accounted for a modest proportion of the wheat and corn crops.[12] By the mid-seventeenth century, the Spanish had taken over the land of many indigenous communities in Tehuacán. The towns of Altepexi, Ajalpan, Chilac, Zinacatepec, Miahuatlán, and Coxcatlán existed in the midst of large estates, which had absorbed most of the villages' land and water. Land appropriated by the Spanish was often the best situated for irrigation, and they took over the irrigation systems developed by the Indians before the conquest.[13] Although water rights were not implicit in land grants, the process of acquiring land in the Poblano countryside was marked by a parallel process of getting access to irrigation. Many of the early land grants were located near rivers and networks of irrigation canals built originally by the Indians.[14]

The land grants allowed the Spanish a foothold in what had been land controlled by the *señoríos;* they expanded their properties by purchase from other Spaniards or Indians and they acquired much irrigable land. As the Spanish carved out large estates from formerly indigenous lands, not only was land appropriated, but these estates gradually built up water rights and sometimes took over usage of canal systems constructed and developed by the indigenous peoples.[15] As the Spanish acquired much of the most valuable irrigable land, in many cases Indian farmers were left with *temporal* (unirrigated) fields or marginal lands of poor soil quality. The Indians were forced to modify their agricultural practices to match their limited access to land.

MARKETS

Products of the Poblano countryside were funneled into regional, colonywide, and international commerce. Poblano farmers sold their wheat in Cuba, Florida, Caracas, and Maracaíbo.[16] Only wheat was truly an international export, but other products—such as corn—were sold throughout the colony. The sugar sector was small and the Puebla region was its primary market. Animal products such as wool, pork fat, and hides were transformed into manufactured goods in Puebla de los Angeles and other smaller towns. The fruit orchards of indigenous communities were marketed locally, in cities, and in other regions. The production of farmers and estates passed through a network of markets at the local, regional, and international levels. Puebla de los Angeles served as an important hub for this commerce but also for the transformation of agricultural products into manufactured goods.[17]

Most of the products of the Poblano countryside passed through Puebla de los Angeles, with notable exceptions. For instance, farmers in Tehuacán and San Andrés Chalchicomula directed their commercial activities partially toward the South. Particularly in years of scarcity, they sold wheat and corn to the *tierra caliente* in Oaxaca, Chiapas, and even Guatemala. In San Andrés Chalchicomula, farmers sold surplus production of corn, wheat, and vegetables in both Puebla de los Angeles and on the coast in Veracruz.[18] The trade that some Poblano farmers enjoyed with regions in the tierra caliente was facilitated by their location on the *camino real* (the royal road). But at the heart of this cross-colony commerce was the supply of products from temperate regions—especially wheat—which could not be produced in the lower, warmer climes. At the same time, regions such as Izúcar, Chietla, Chiautla, and Acatlán, in the tierra caliente of Puebla, sold not only sugar, but crops such as pomegranates, cumin, garbanzos, anise, saffron, dates, and melons to consumers in the colder regions where such produce was not locally available.[19]

In the eighteenth century Poblano farmers began to lose certain markets because of increased competition. Farmers from the Bajío and Michoacán began to supply wheat to Mexico City as well as the mining regions to the north. At the same time, wheat produced in the United States displaced Poblano wheat in Caribbean markets except during the war years. Poblano farmers continued to sell wheat in New Spain, especially to Veracruz and the Spanish navy, but the wheat sector was no longer as prosperous. Some scholars have explained the decline of Poblano agriculture in the eighteenth century to increased competition as well as inefficient farming.[20] The environment must also be considered because the agrarian economy was very dependent on water.[21] In the following sections, the importance of water is demonstrated through a discussion of how farming was adapted to ecological niches and the cycle of seasons.

ECOLOGICAL NICHES
As the Spanish acquired land in Puebla they began to change agrarian patterns to suit their needs by introducing new plants and animals. They built on the previous indigenous agrarian system, but such reorientation of agriculture multiplied the uses for irrigation and intensified it. Spanish farmers, however, were limited by ecological conditions. Over time certain Poblano regions became characterized by particular specialties adapted to the locale. Because it determined temperature, altitude played a key role in determining the ecological conditions and therefore the adaptability of plants to the environment. Sugar could be grown only in the lower and therefore warmer regions of the *tierra caliente,* such as in Izúcar and southern Tehuacán where it was both warm and irrigation existed. Wheat flourished in the higher altitudes where the climate was more temperate, or at 1,400 meters or higher.[22] Elevation also determined the growing season because at higher altitudes the frosts came earlier. At higher elevations where farmers had access to irrigation, they planted wheat.

In other areas where neither of the two most desirable and profitable crops could be produced, farmers raised livestock, and grew corn and other cereals such as barley. All these agrarian activities implied access to water. Only corn could be successfully grown on temporal (unirrigated) land, although yields were better and harvests more secure with irrigation. From the early sixteenth century wheat was predominant in the Atlixco Valley. Pockets of wheat production existed in Tepeaca, Tecali, and Tehuacán.[23] In the tierra caliente to the south, sugar estates flourished around Izúcar and Coatzingo and in the south of the Tehuacán valley. In the highlands of Tepeaca, San Juan de los Llanos, and El Seco, pastoralism dominated the agrarian economy.[24] Farmers in these regions grew corn and other cereals for human consumption and sale in various markets, but also to feed livestock.

Plants imported into the Mexican environment had to be adapted to prevailing conditions. They had to be inserted into the schedule of rains and ecological niches suitable for their needs. Poblano farmers used irrigation to defeat the constraints of the wet/dry seasons, and they planted at higher or lower altitudes depending on the crop. The two most important cash crops—wheat and sugar—displaced traditional indigenous agriculture, although Indians continued to grow corn and they adopted European fruits and livestock as alternatives. Large estates dominated the wheat and sugar sectors, but Indians also grew these crops in smaller quantities.

Each agricultural activity in the Poblano countryside was characterized by a particular calendar and limitations. It is impossible to understand the complexities of Poblano agriculture without a more detailed examination of the plants and animals and how they fit into the local environment.

WHEAT

The Puebla region gained importance because of the abundance and quality of the wheat produced on its estates. Poblano basin farmers were the first in New Spain to develop a form of commercial agriculture,[25] which serviced both local markets and more far-flung destinations. Residents in Mexico City, Veracruz, Campeche, and Oaxaca, but also in Cuba, Florida, Caracas, and Maracaíbo consumed Poblano wheat.[26] Poblano wheat also fed the mining districts of the *tierraden-tro* to the north and northwest of Mexico City, as well as the miners of Zacatecas.[27] Puebla wheat yields were so abundant that during the 1692 famine Poblano farmers sent surpluses to other jurisdictions.[28] The chronicler Bermúdez de Castro commented that millers ground 270 *cargas* of flour daily in the fifteen mills of Puebla de los Angeles for use in the ten bakeries of the city and to be shipped to various locations.[29] Bakers processed this flour into *bizcocho* (hard biscuits) which Spanish sailors ate during long voyages to Spain or the Philippines.[30] Because of the abundance and quality of their product, Poblano wheat farmers dominated the trade. Their grain was sold internationally, made into bizcocho or unprocessed, as well as in the region and the colony.

Mills also provided local markets with flour. For example, although there was only one area within Tecali—Acathahtuac—where wheat could be produced, an enterprising Spaniard established a mill there to provide flour for the city of Tepeaca.[31] Tepeaca also had three mills to process local wheat. The city consumed at least one-third of the wheat produced by the estates in the surrounding countryside.[32] Many communities had mills even if not all were located in wheat-producing regions. For example, Tehuacán, Izúcar, and Huejotzingo all had three mills; Atlixco had four; Cholula, five; and Chietla, one. But Acatlán, Tepeji, and Chiautla had no mills,[33] and the mill in San Juan de los Llanos was dedicated to making oil from turnips rather than grinding wheat.[34]

Spanish farmers adjusted their planting schedules for wheat according to the local climate and seasonal rains; in brief, they could not grow wheat in the same way as they had in the Iberian peninsula. In Spain, Castilian and Andalusian farmers grew wheat during the rainy season which fell over the course of autumn and winter. In Aragón and Murcia, wheat farmers used irrigation to supplement precipitation.[35] In Mexico, planting during the rainy season—the summer—meant the risk of fungal parasites such as the *chahuistle* and *la roya*[36] but, despite the risk, summer planting was a common practice in Puebla. Wheat in Mexico was often planted during the winter, and therefore could not be cultivated without irrigation. In Puebla, however, and especially in the Atlixco Valley, irrigation often made two annual crops of wheat possible;[37] and watering from perennial streams extended the growing season before the rains arrived or during the dry season.

The wheat production cycle lasted between four and five months. Workers typically prepared the fields in June by plowing so that the earth absorbed the sun and the rain. During this process called the *barbecho,* farmers also tried to make the fields as level as possible. Planting occurred in July or August depending on local conditions. Both procedures took place in the summer rainy season. The harvest occurred in November or December when the rains stopped. The end of the rains was important because the wheat had to dry for ten days before it could be harvested. Starting the harvest a little early was less hazardous than bringing it in wet.

Once the harvest was completed, workers began to prepare the fields for the next wheat crop. The *barbecho* started again almost immediately. Cattle and other livestock might be allowed to feed on the stalks left over after the harvest but for a very limited time. The next planting occurred in late December or early January during the dry winter months. For this crop, irrigation was vital and replaced precipitation as the source of moisture for the growing plants. During this period, the fields were irrigated nearly every week. This crop was harvested in May or June, but preferably before the start of the rains. Because the wheat could easily get wet during this critical period if the rains started early, farmers tried to finish the later harvest very quickly. After the harvest, workers threshed the wheat to separate the grain from the chaff. Threshing could be carried out immediately or in small batches as the need arose. Some farmers used mules which walked about on the wheat while others sold the wheat as is and let customers perform the threshing themselves.[38] Wheat could only be produced within the constraints of the cycle of wet and dry seasons. Farmers were able to manipulate nature with the application of irrigation, but if their timing was faulty, their crops could be ruined by early rains. When irrigation was vital, particularly at the seedling stage, any interference with the flow of water could be devastating.

Different varieties of wheat existed, and some were more valuable than others. Iberian farmers introduced the varieties called *candeal, largo, arisnegros,* and *pelones rubios.* The candeal fetched the highest price, but each variety was valued differently. Each variety could be obtained in three qualities: "good, reasonable and *pachacate* (poor)."[39] Because of the climactic differences, Mexican farmers generally planted "soft" wheat rather than the "hard" wheat most common in Spain.[40] In the sixteenth century, the Spanish introduced the *trigo blanquillo o pelón* variety, which was very popular among farmers, and became the principal type of wheat planted in the Atlixco Valley. It had such high yields that prices for all types of wheat were driven downward.[41] Farmers liked it because it matured more rapidly—in approximately four months—than many other varieties.

The Spanish dominated the wheat sector of Puebla from the mid-sixteenth century, but Indians also planted it. The Indians of Tochimilco, in particular, began planting wheat in the sixteenth century and bought corn from other villages at lower altitudes.[42] They continued to do so despite numerous decrees which *forbade* them such practices.[43] By the eighteenth century, many indigenous farmers planted wheat. In many of the smaller villages around Tochimilco such as Huilango, San Lucas, Santiago, and San Martín, farmers also grew wheat alongside corn.[44] The villages of Chalma, San Bartolomé Quespala, Santa María Magdalena, and San Martín were reported to grow wheat.[45] Spanish-owned estates were still dominant in the wheat business, but their cultivation of this grain was not exclusive.

As wheat became an increasingly important part of Poblano agriculture, irrigation became vital. Wheat could not be grown over the dry winter months without access to water. Therefore, at critical moments during the year—planting and growth over the winter—farmers used irrigation. If streams and rivers were lower than usual or too many farmers used too much water, inevitably those who planted downstream suffered. Because wheat was such a profitable crop, many farmers planted it and competed for water.

SUGAR

Sugar, the other major cash crop, also appeared early in Mexican history but occupied a different ecological niche than wheat. The Spanish introduced sugar first to the Canary Islands and then, from that vantage point, it was part of Columbus's transfer of plants in his 1493 voyage to the Caribbean.[46] In Mexico, several Spanish entrepreneurs established sugar plantations in the sixteenth century. The earliest experiments with the suitability of sugar for the Mexican climate and environment took place in San Andrés Tuxtla near Veracruz, but the first large-scale plantings were carried out at the Hacienda Atlacomulco in Morelos.[47] The Cuernavaca and Cuautla regions became the most important centers of sugar production during the colonial period, but smaller centers developed south of the Atlixco Valley around Izúcar and in Tehuacán, and to the west in Michoacán.[48] Poblano sugar estates made their cane into *piloncillo,* a hard brown sugar, or *aguardiente* (cane brandy). The authorities prohibited the production of aguardiente throughout most of the colonial period, but it was manufactured clandestinely. In Puebla, seventy-five percent of the sugar crop was funneled into the manufacture of aguardiente and the rest served for local consumption.[49]

Sugarcane requires temperatures above twenty-one degrees Celsius, and preferably between twenty-seven and thirty-eight degrees Celsius. The conditions to grow sugarcane do not exist throughout Mexico. Constant water is also a necessity; if rainfall is inadequate, or a marked dry season prevails such as in Puebla, irrigation is used to fill the precipitation deficit. At present, in Tehuacán ten thousand cubic meters of water are necessary to irrigate a hectare of sugar.[50]

Unlike wheat, sugar could not be inserted into the natural cycle of wet and dry seasons. The complete growth cycle was so long that it could not be accommodated to local conditions. In the sixteenth and seventeenth centuries, sugar required between eighteen and twenty-two months to reach maturity. By the eighteenth century, optimization of growing techniques shortened this period to between twelve and fifteen months.[51] In addition to the lengthy maturation, producers had to constantly water the plants. The entire process was extremely labor intensive and demanding. Workers began by burning a new plot intended for sugarcane and then plowing it. Mixing plant materials into the soil, ensuring that the soil absorbed water well, and proper leveling of the fields were important to prevent plant rot on the one hand, and uprooting young plants due to rushing water on the other. Once the plowing and leveling were finished, workers marked *surcos,* or furrows that crisscrossed the field in regular lines through which the irrigation water would flow. Finally, the workers planted the cane by placing pieces of mature cane in the soil. In New Spain, the most common variety was the *criolla* or creole.[52]

Once the planting was complete, the workers proceeded to the first irrigation. In the next growth period, they watered the field every three days until the plants sprouted shoots or buds. Workers then weeded around the plants and irrigated only every eight days until the plants had leaves. At that stage, they could terminate the weeding and water the crop only every fifteen days, although they continued to cut off dead leaves and fertilize the soil around the plants. If signs of disease were noted, the only treatment was to flood the fields.[53]

Clearly, sugar agriculture was impossible without ample water and regular, unimpeded access to irrigation. In addition to the requirements of the growing plants, large estates staggered harvests to keep the sugar mills working. Therefore, at any time of year on such estates, plowing in one field coincided with planting in another and harvesting in still another. Sugar plantation owners had a resident labor force, but depended to some extent on seasonal workers from nearby villages. In these cases, planting new crops was sometimes delayed while estate laborers waited for the seasonal workers to finish working in their own fields.[54] Water also played an important role in cane processing. Many sugar *ingenios* used streams to power the mills which crushed the cane to siphon off the sugar-carrying juice. In Puebla, a distinction was made between the two forms: ingenios used water power, while in *trapiches* animals powered the machinery. The final step consisted of boiling down the juice to extract the sugar crystals—a process which required an abundant supply of fuel.[55]

The timing of irrigation in sugar agriculture cannot be as clearly elucidated as in the cases of wheat and corn because plantings did not follow a set calendar and were staggered throughout the year. Although the most frequent waterings were required at the initial stages, irrigation continued throughout the growing cycle until the harvest. Heavy water usage meant that to be successful, the owners of large sugar estates needed to guarantee year-round access to water. They could not operate without a large irrigation grant, nor could they withstand competition for water from other farmers. The consequences for people living downstream from a sugar estate were that they often went without water.

In the sixteenth century, investment in a sugar estate was an attractive proposition for a number of reasons. In contrast to wheat or corn, the government did not control the sugar sector through price controls. Because sugar was a luxury item, it was highly profitable. As a result, in the sixteenth century estate owners replaced other crops with sugar where conditions permitted. In Puebla, sugar tended to be successful in areas like Izúcar where people had previously grown cotton. In 1599, the Spanish Crown reversed itself and implemented a very restrictive policy toward sugar production. The authorities forbade the practice of using *indios de repartimiento* and prohibited the development of new ingenios and trapiches. In 1631, Spanish authorities disallowed the export of Mexican sugar to Peru. Yet, during this period of supposed restriction, the viceregal government granted fifty-five new licenses for sugar estates. In the eighteenth century, the Bourbons changed these policies and opened up the sugar market. The Mexican sugar industry flourished between 1750 and 1821 as abundant labor, high prices, and ample investment capital buoyed the sector.[56] It was only in the eighteenth century that a global mass market for sugar was established.[57] The return on investment was sufficient to make sugar ingenios an attractive investment to many institutions and individuals in Puebla and in Mexico.

Because of the startup costs and, after 1599, the licensing procedure, indigenous involvement in sugar production was rare. But there were exceptions. The Indians of Tepejojuma complained about their *alcalde mayor* because he wished to prevent them from growing sugarcane. The alcalde mayor stated that the community had not renewed its license. If this indigenous community had obtained permission in the past, it seems evident that the cultivation of cane was not a new custom. Indigenous farmers even stated that they sold their product (whether processed or not is not specified) in the *tianguis* of Tepejojuma. The inhabitants argued that without access to this source of revenue, they could not pay all the fees and taxes levied against the community.[58] In Chiautla de la Sal, Indians owned four trapiches which produced *panela* (a type of brown sugar).[59]

Sugar was a much smaller part of the Poblano agrarian economy than wheat because ecological conditions were right for it in only a few areas. Nevertheless, sugar was a very profitable crop with an important market in Puebla de los Angeles and the region in general. Unlike wheat, sugar could not be inserted into the cycle of wet and dry seasons. Therefore, irrigation was even more important for its cultivation. Farmers who grew sugar needed constant and plentiful access to water and there were few moments in the life cycle of a sugar plant when it did not need regular watering. Consequently, sugar production very often meant competition for water and its producers often left neighbors downstream with reduced access.

CORN

Wheat and sugar frequently displaced corn and other plants that were traditional in the indigenous agrarian economy. But maize continued to be the foundation of indigenous farming; in fact, Spanish *hacendados* used the grain to feed workers and livestock, and the stalks as fuel.[60] Small producers grew maize for their own consumption but, according to Garavaglia and Grosso, in Tepeaca smallholder production represented twenty percent of the crop sold in the local market.[61]

Corn could be grown over the rainy season. In this case, farmers planted it in temporal fields, or on land lacking access to irrigation. For irrigated corn, plowing began some time between December and February, and planting took place between February and May, according to local conditions. In these cases, farmers irrigated the seeds because the rainy season had yet to begin. The young plants required a large amount of water, and if left unirrigated, delayed rains could be disastrous. The harvest for irrigated corn took place between December and January.[62] Corn could be stored in the fields. It was common practice to bend over the stalk so that the ear hung down thus assisting the process of maturation and protecting the ear if there was unexpected rain. Ouweneel believes that after 1770, the annual rains were not as plentiful as previously in Puebla. Such a shortage would have been devastating for the indigenous population since by then most of their lands were temporal.[63] When farmers planted unirrigated corn, they gambled on the arrival of the rains. If precipitation was late, farmers usually lost seedlings, and if possible, had to scramble to plant more corn.

In contrast to sugar and wheat, corn could be grown within the annual period of rains. Crops were more likely to be successful, however, if they were planted before the rains. Therefore, irrigation was necessary for the seeds to germinate. Such an early start ensured that the corn ripened before early frosts. In addition, corn—like wheat and sugar—could be grown during the winter only with irrigation. However, because of irrigation requirements at specific times during the cycle of seasons, corn farmers periodically competed for water with other farmers. Corn remained an important element of the Poblano agrarian economy in that it was a staple of daily life for urban and rural dwellers, and in the Tepeaca region, corn was also used to fatten pigs for slaughter.

FRUIT

Fruit was a small part of the Poblano agrarian economy but an important one for certain Indian villages. As indigenous communities lost communal lands, some turned to fruit orchards as a means to earn their living. Many such groups adopted fruits and vegetables introduced by the Spaniards,[64] which they sold in local markets, and in some cases, Puebla de los Angeles. For example, residents of San Antonio Alpanoca in Tochimilco jurisdiction produced mainly fruit because they did not have enough land for other crops.[65] These orchards, which seem to have replaced more extensive lands in some cases, also required a certain amount of irrigation although the actual quantity is rather unclear. Some communities complained that their fruit trees deteriorated, particularly in droughts, and they were thus left without income. The Indians of Agueguetzingo (Chietla jurisdiction) protested in 1705 that Don Nicolás Torres was diverting their water and that their orchards were not producing. Again in 1736, they stated that Manuel de Cardenas, the owner of a trapiche, had appropriated so much water from the canal that their fruit trees were suffering and the Indians would be hard pressed to pay their tributes.[66] As indigenous communities lost most of their communal lands, they had to resort to farming activities feasible with a small land base. Fruit became the central farming activity of communities without adequate land area, and fruit orchards required irrigation in order to survive.

LIVESTOCK

Livestock were another Spanish introduction which became an important part of the agrarian landscape. Horses and oxen were an important complement to wheat and sugar cultivation because they were used for transport and plowing. But, in some areas, animals and animal products were the major crop. Poblanos used cattle for hides as well as meat; they ate ham, pork, and *chicharrón,* but also transformed pigs into lard and soap. Sheep furnished meat and wool for textile workshops.

In Atlixco, where wheat was supreme, there was little tolerance for livestock. Although farmers needed horses and oxen, the intensive nature of wheat agriculture meant that pasture was scarce. Therefore, the Atlixco cabildo forbade the grazing of small livestock such as sheep and goats, and estate owners sent their large livestock to pasture in other regions, such as the tierra caliente and Chalco.[67] In the Tepeaca region, livestock were central to the agrarian economy, and therefore, practices differed substantially from those common in Atlixco. In San Andrés Chalchicomula, pigs fed on corn and in San Juan de los Llanos, farmers grew barley for their livestock.[68] Around Tepeaca and El Seco, herds of goats and sheep became a mainstay, and cattle were also important in Tepeaca and San Andrés Chalchicomula.[69]

Indians in Tepeaca and Tecali adopted European animals in parallel with the loss of their land. Livestock, and sheep in particular, became one way to own property. Also, with small herds, animals could be pastured on the margins of the cultivated fields. In 1773 *cacique* Don Onofre Ximenez represented himself as the person responsible for provisioning all butchers in the Tepeaca region with pork.[70] Indian communities were forced to find alternate crops such as fruit, or concentrate on pastoralism when inadequate cropland forced them to abandon traditional farming in whole or in part.

Animal products fed tanneries, textile workshops, and soap manufacturers. Livestock then constituted an important element of the agrarian economy and connected the countryside to regional networks of trade and industry.

Pigs were an extremely important part of the Poblano economy. In *tocinerías* located in Puebla de los Angeles pigs were transformed into hams, soap, tallow, and lard sold both within and outside the region. The value of pork byproducts was almost as important as that of wheat.[71] In San Andrés Chalchicomula farmers used irrigation to raise abundant corn crops; a portion of their crops was sold in Puebla de los Angeles, and the remainder was used to fatten pigs for sale in the regional capital.[72] Many of the tocinerías in Puebla de los Angeles bought pigs from Apam and San Juan de los Llanos, fattened the animals on location on a corn diet, and then butchered them. In 1775 Puebla de los Angeles accounted for forty-five tocinerías, and in 1804, thirty-six. In 1747 tocineros butchered 80,000 pigs.[73]

Numerous tanneries, located along the banks of the San Francisco River in Puebla de los Angeles, produced leather of different qualities which was also used in the saddlery trade.[74] Tanners also exported leather to other parts of the colony and to Spain.[75] In 1775 tanneries numbered twenty, but the industry was in decline. By 1802 only eight continued to process leather.[76] Leather work was also present in Tepeaca.[77]

By 1566 Poblano sheep farmers produced 90,000 *fanegas* of wool per annum. In the sixteenth century, Puebla was an important production center for wool broadcloth with forty workshops in the 1570s. However, this industry did not continue to thrive, and by the end of the eighteenth century only ten workshops still produced wool cloth.[78] Workshops in Tepeaca absorbed a large part of the wool and produced rough fabrics used by Indians for work clothes. At the end of the eighteenth century, weaving remained one of Tepeaca's principal industries.[79] It was also an important activity in Huamantla, Santa Ana Chiautempan, San Juan de los Llanos, and Cholula.[80]

Livestock competed for water during the dry season because they needed to drink. In addition, they caused problems on occasion by breaking irrigation canals or fouling towns' potable water sources. The animals also sometimes became pawns in the struggle for power in the countryside. In Tecali, for example, Don Bartolomé Pelaez, the mayordomo of an unnamed hacienda confiscated the livestock of the Indians of Aguetepeque when they took them to drink at the barranca Tesaguapan. Because the stream was the village's only source of water, depriving the residents of their animals as well as the possibility of watering remaining animals, the mayordomo was able to exert considerable pressure on village residents.[81] In other situations, such as that of Santiago Teutlan (Izúcar jurisdiction), the denial of irrigation led to water shortages for cattle as well as human consumption.[82] As livestock became important to the agrarian economy, animals competed with humans and crops for water, and suffered during natural and artificial droughts.

The animals introduced into New Spain by the Spanish became an integral part of the Poblano countryside. They complemented wheat and sugar cultivation, and they were the basis of the small industries in Puebla de los Angeles and other smaller centers like Tepeaca. Livestock became an important part of the agrarian economy, but one which was also dependent upon the perennial streams and rivers during the dry season. As such, large and small herds competed with crops and town residents for access to the water used for irrigation.

**

Because of the cycle of wet and dry seasons, many crops could not be produced without regular and unimpeded access to irrigation. The prosperity of Poblano agriculture was the outcome of an environment that suited the commercial agriculture of the Spanish. The fertile valleys located at reasonable altitudes protected from excessive cold were ideal for wheat cultivation. In the lowlands, warmth combined with abundant streams made sugarcane production feasible. These natural conditions—altitude, water, and soil—were a recipe for success.

The Spanish who settled in Puebla also benefited from the traditional practices of the indigenous population. The history of intensive agriculture based on irrigation meant that Spanish-style agriculture could begin without much investment. Field preparation work, particularly on mountainsides, and the irrigation canal network were already in place. As the Spanish expanded their holdings and the land under cultivation, they extended irrigation ditches and canals. Their efforts resulted in the first commercial agriculture of New Spain. The manipulation of the natural cycle along with a generous environment allowed for a booming economy, but one which depended on irrigation.

FIVE

The Ebb and Flow of Conflicts in the Countryside

Although the eighteenth-century Puebla countryside was still composed of decentralized irrigation societies, the process of centralization had begun. Large landowners began to move toward a more centralized system although the bureaucracy and path to centralization did not involve communal consent. The estate owners used their servants as an informal bureaucracy to allocate water, and in the first decades of the nineteenth century, the *ingenio* owners of Izúcar imposed the first formal water bureaucracy on the region's irrigators. The men who called for the creation of a centralized irrigation society had amassed impressive water rights during the colonial period and had become water monopolists on a local level. The call for a water bureaucracy did not arise from a communal response to conflicts over water nor from a central government concerned over problems in the countryside, but rather from the *hacendados* and ingenio owners who had profited from the accumulation of irrigation rights over the course of the colonial period. The surge in conflicts signaled the forced transfer of water rights from communities to large landowners and the creation of a system based on monopolization and centralized control.

The large landowners were able to legally amass water rights to irrigation essentially because of their long-term presence and water use. By the eighteenth century, these landowners were largely Creoles (of Spanish heritage but born in Mexico) who were part of the elite that controlled wealth and power in the Poblano countryside. As such, although they were natives of Mexico, they belonged to the Spanish elite in racial and social terms. The doctrine of prior appropriation allowed them to transform themselves from outsiders (without rights) to insiders (with rights). But, the process by which water monopolists were created was not entirely peaceful. The social relations and comparative power of various contenders reinforced the authority of large landowners. Legal rights were important but the ability to impose judicial decisions was just as vital in a decentralized system without an effective bureaucratic apparatus. As certain owners acquired more irrigation rights, other estates lost their competitive edge and indigenous villages suffered the effects of an artificial drought. Indian communities increasingly fought each other for irrigation. By the end of the colonial period, power over water was consolidated into the hands of a few large landowners who moved to formalize their control with a new bureaucracy. This chapter is focused on power relations in the Poblano countryside and explains the creation of a water monopolist class who moved toward the development of a centralized water system at the end of the colonial period.

OUTSIDERS BECOME INSIDERS

The legal doctrine of prior appropriation in Spanish water legislation was based on one fundamental tenet—ancient and peaceful possession. In effect, the emphasis on previous use gave indigenous communities an advantage they lacked in many other aspects of their contact with the Spanish. Who could deny that the indigenous communities had existed in the area for the longest time? Unless the Indians themselves revealed past conflicts over water resources with other neighboring communities, who could deny that they enjoyed peaceful possession of the streams that they used?[1] Many indigenous groups were also able to secure documentation from the colonial authorities which further guaranteed their control of water resources. In the sixteenth century, officials granted *mercedes* and in the seventeenth and eighteenth centuries many communities purchased *composiciones*. Yet, by the end of the colonial period, the control of water resources by Poblano Indians was elusive at best. Some communities or individuals fared better than others, but during the eighteenth century, Poblano indigenous communities' irrigation rights became a highly valued prize. The position of strength given to the indigenous peoples by the legal definition of water rights was insufficient to secure their rights against the backdrop of demographic growth and economic boom of the eighteenth century.

In the early eighteenth century, large landowners began to expand their control over local water resources. As the equilibrium between population, land, and water changed, all farmers required more irrigation. However, because the Spanish slowly acquired rights over the first two centuries of colonialism, they could therefore claim "ancient and peaceful possession." During the period of contact, a smaller indigenous population reduced the pressure on land and water resources, which allowed the Spanish to take over certain water rights without causing undue harm to the indigenous residents. In the sixteenth and seventeenth centuries, the presence of the Spanish landowners was not a major threat in terms of irrigation because the low population density meant that the existing streams and rivers were more than adequate.

The long-term presence of Spaniards as landowners created precedent. When irrigation became scarcer and more valuable, the descendants and new owners of estates could claim rights to water under the doctrine of prior appropriation. Through purchase, grants, rental, composition, and outright appropriation, the outsiders—the Spanish newcomers—became insiders by the eighteenth century. The descendants and successors of the first Spaniards who established estates in Puebla created a very valuable legacy: the right to water.

How did the process of transformation from outsiders to insiders work? Once Spanish proprietors proved that they too had "ancient and peaceful possession," challenges to Indian ownership became possible within the legal framework. These contests usually came after a period of gradual encroachment on irrigation rights culminating in a confrontation—sometimes after several dry years aggravated the situation.[2] Even if total victory could not be claimed on either side, these suits caused irreparable damage to the indigenous semi-monopoly on water rights both because it meant that the Indians could no longer claim an entirely "peaceful possession" and because judicial decisions often meant a compromise that chipped away at their rights. The Audiencia did not always rule entirely in favor of one party or the other, but frequently divided the irrigation between the two instead. As a result, the more often water rights were challenged, the more likely that the irrigation allocations would be reduced over time.[3] Second, continual usage of hydraulic resources without clear agreement or contract created a *servidumbre*—a type of squatter's right. Farmers could assert these rights if they failed to pay rental fees over a long period of time, or if they were able to use irrigation without rights to the same, but also without being challenged for a long time. Once individuals could establish a long-term pattern of usage without challenge, they acquired inherent water rights that could then be regularized. Third, with a history of past legal or illegal usage, the Spanish took advantage of the opportunity to compose water rights. Within the Iberian bureaucracy, the avenues to circumvent strict legalities seem to have been plentiful and certainly mostly profited the Iberians. In essence, the abundance of water in the early colonial period provided conditions under which new owners could acquire water rights that led to serious challenges to the Indians' access to irrigation in the last century of Spanish colonization. These confrontations were feasible for the Iberians—in legal terms—because they had long-term access to the streams and rivers used by the indigenous communities.

The weakness of the Indians' water rights became apparent when demographic, economic, and ecological pressures were brought to bear on the problem in the eighteenth century. The resurgence of the indigenous population by the end of the seventeenth century as well as the expansion of Iberian settlers accelerated the growth of cities and markets. These changes were part of the long-term process of transformation which altered the need for water described in chapter three. This transformation affected rural societies by increasing the competition for water resources and leading to a consolidation of control over irrigation. Many factors influenced the outcome of each conflict: political influence, control of land and other resources, and access to the means of force. Obviously, within rural Poblano society Iberians had many advantages. The legal system gave their word more weight than that of Indians. In addition, many landowners had more money and political influence than the indigenous communities.[4] As water became more scarce at the beginning of the eighteenth century, the fact that large landowners were no longer outsiders in terms of water law gave them an advantage. They were in a better position to take over irrigation rights and then, once control over water was monopolized, they could move to a centralized system that guaranteed a peaceful allocation of irrigation as well as prioritizing their water requirements.

SPANISH LANDOWNERS' STRATEGIES

Large landowners gained rights to irrigation within the framework of Spanish law but their ability to impose their control went beyond legalities. Because these hacendados and ingenio owners tended to be Creoles or Spaniards, they often held positions of power within colonial society or had easier access to the men who did. Apart from their comparative political clout, estate owners were able to enforce their version of water allocation because, through their servants, they could police access to water. The power of large landowners was occasionally limited when indigenous communities used their strength in numbers to riot as described in chapter six. But, quite clearly, large landowners could intimidate and browbeat neighboring indigenous communities in ways that were ineffective with other Spanish landowners and in response to which the Indians could not easily reciprocate.

Large landowners could effectively cancel legal water rights held by Indian villages because of their power of coercion and domination of local resources. Campaigns of intimidation created villages with little ability to resist as seen in the examples of the village of San Juan Evangelista Coscatlán and the barrios of San Gerónimo Ajochitlan. In 1769, they abandoned a justified, well-founded, and *successful* lawsuit in order to placate Captain Joseph Francisco de Meza y Veristain. The villagers held the rights to all waters of the Tochiatla irrigation ditch which the Captain used to irrigate his hacienda. The Indians seem to have backed down from their demands partly because of intimidation but also because de Meza y Veristain had taken control of some of their lands. The people of the village dropped the suit in July when the seasonal rains were at their peak.[5] Perhaps the villagers' situation seemed less desperate than in the winter when it was dry.

Several years later in 1790, residents of the same village were still under siege from Don Antonio Lucas de Apezechea, owner of the *trapiche* Calipa. Lucas de Apezechea inspired such fear that one witness declared that "in the day, against our conscience and better judgment, we do not show our faces and defend our water with the blood of our veins."[6] These examples reveal the level of intimidation which estate owners could bring to bear on Indians who lived nearby. Unfortunately, the historical archives tend to report the consequences of strongarm tactics, or capitulation in the battle to preserve irrigation rights, rather than the tactics themselves.

Albeit powerful, large landowners could not change the allocation of water overnight. Villages resisted encroachment of their irrigation but, over time, Indian communities lost their water rights little by little. As part of the process of attrition, the intimidation of large landowners weakened the communities' resistance. Moreover, as they lost resources, the community itself was weakened and therefore, resistance to the will of estate owners became more difficult. Without protection from such abuses of power, villages gradually lost access to water.

In 1730 Pedro Fernández Ronder, a witness from the community of San Miguel Aguacanuliace (Atlixco jurisdiction) testified about the appropriation of community water resources by Felipe Melendes, owner of the Hacienda San Bernardo, who "with a powerful hand" diverted the water the community residents used to irrigate their fields. Melendes paid them nothing and as a result of the lack of water, their lands were barren. There was no basis for Melendes' claim to own these waters but when the villagers protested, he "molested and abused them in word and in deed." The villagers made this statement as part of a complaint lodged in May, perhaps before the start of the seasonal rains. Registering complaints was also part of an ongoing process of attrition; the village complained about usurpations of water again in 1759, 1779, 1799, and 1801.[7]

In San Francisco Chietla, the tenant of a trapiche beat a village boy severely when the latter attempted to take water in November of 1736—at the beginning of the dry season.[8] The level of intimidation existed on a continuum that ranged from warnings to actual blows in a situation in which official intervention was rare and ineffective. The authorities seem to have recognized the need for drastic action in one case when they declared that a death penalty by strangling would be imposed on anyone—Indian or Spanish—guilty of interfering with the irrigation canals of Tochimilco.[9] In this case, however, it was the Indians who were usually guilty of water theft because they were upstream from the majority of the haciendas. Without an effective water bureaucracy, the most powerful in the Poblano countryside could bully others into accepting water losses. These usurpations of irrigation access were possible because the system was decentralized and no effective intervention by bureaucrats checked abuses nor protected the rights of indigenous communities.

The process of attrition in village resistance over time could result in total abnegation. Without a sufficient land base, Indians depended on haciendas and ingenios for seasonal work and their reliance on income from estates weakened their capacity to resist encroachments on their own water supplies. In 1733 lawsuit, the residents of San Gerónimo Coyula lost all their water but a single *surco* by day to the Castillos, owners of the Haciendas Coyula and Ayacocotla in the Atlixco Valley. In return, these estates were obliged to contribute 100 pesos annually to the village for water usage. The Castillos never respected the agreement. Most of the villagers were kept in a state of terror because they worked on the Castillos' haciendas. As a result of their dependence, the village residents did not feel capable of resisting the Castillos' mistreatment; as the years passed they received no money and had access to smaller and smaller amounts of water. By October 1805, the Castillos not only had appropriated all the water, but, even though they knew the villages had rights to a surco of water, "demanded arbitrary fees every time the Indians pleaded with great obsequiousness and submission for a little bit of irrigation for their little gardens."[10] In brief, lacking sufficient land to avoid dependence on estates and ingenios for income, the Indians were forced to give up water rights, and the subsequent lack of irrigation further weakened their local economy.

Confrontations and physical violence were not uncommon in the continual jousting over control over water rights but the owners of haciendas and ingenios were represented by their intermediaries, the estate servants. These employees served on the front lines absorbing the wrath of neighbors and dishing out punishment to those who challenged the dictums of their masters.[11] For instance, in 1731, Captain Don Juan Felix Prieto constructed an enormous dam on his property which, although it must have served his needs, flooded the fields of indigenous and Iberian residents of Cholula and the barrio of Santiago Thomaspa. It caused extensive damage both to surrounding properties and the main road. Via fines and warnings the Audiencia censured Prieto's casual destruction of the property of others as well as the suspension of respective productive capacities. Prieto ignored all claims against him, however, and ordered his servants to resist any attempts to modify the dam. His instructions led to violent confrontations which escalated over a period of about ten years until Doctor Domingo de Apreza y Moctezuma, fearing that the hostilities would lead to a fatality, tried to mediate.[12] Servants became an informal corps of water guards but rather than represent a communal agreement to share water as in the Hunts' model of centralization, they served only one user in the irrigation system. Rather than represent centralization, they were the product of a decentralized system in which no clear authority imposed order. Indisputably, legal doctrine and the actual decisions of the colonial judiciary did not favor Prieto but he was able to ignore these censures because he could potentially coerce affected parties. Moreover, in a decentralized system, Prieto's access to the means of force essentially gave him a monopoly over strongarm tactics.

Another intimidation tactic was confiscating the property of Indians or others attempting to use the water to which they believed they had rights. Because servants functioned as guardians of the regulating doors which gave access or cut off irrigation, they were present on the front line of conflicts over water. By preventing access to the resources available in or around streams and to the water itself, indigenous groups were weakened until they finally accepted the new *dominio* over water rights. Control over the access to water could be used as a weapon; it could weaken rival users and over time force them to accept relations of submission.

An example of progressive intimidation lies in the relationship between Don Crisostomo Zubia and the residents of Epatlán. In 1783, Zubia complained that the villagers of Epatlán were planting wheat and, consequently, they used too much irrigation.[13] The following year Zubia convinced the residents to rent him the remaining waters from a lagoon that they controlled. The people of Epatlán used the lagoon to irrigate their fields, but mainly to fish for *mojarras*. These fish provided an important source of cash—especially in the Lenten season—since the people of Epatlán sold them in Puebla de los Angeles. By 1795, Zubia's construction of new dams and outlets as well as his practice of extracting greater quantities of water from the lagoon had caused ecological changes. There was less water in the lagoon, and the remaining water was very dirty, and full of silt and livestock cadavers. When animals tried to drink from the lagoon, they got stuck in the bogs of the depleted body of water; when they could not get out, they died and were left there to putrefy. Water for irrigation was sparse since the lagoon had descended to the level of only half a *vara*. Yet, when the lease expired in 1795 and the people of

Epatlán tried to reassert their control over the lagoon, Zubia exerted his hold over the water by ordering his servants to confiscate any fish caught there. The servants also mistreated and abused the fishermen. The use of force turned Zubia's illegal control over the lagoon into a weapon. Such an action was only possible in a decentralized system in which no central authority enforced the law. Although the people of Epatlán had legal rights, they had no official recourse nor rival means of force. By 1797, the villagers decided that, because of the inconveniences associated with the possession of their lagoon and their continued conflict with Zubia through the intermediary of his servants, they preferred to sell the lagoon to Zubia with the proviso that they should continue to enjoy fishing rights.[14]

Of course, not all bodies of water provided sustenance through fish but most were used at least minimally by livestock for drinking water. People who raised livestock and depended on animals partially or totally for their livelihood needed access to streams so that their animals could drink, particularly in the dry season. Bartolomé Pelaez exploited the need to water animals when he asserted control over the waters of the barranca Tesaguapan in Santa María Aguatepeque, Tecali, in January, 1739. Pelaez's mayordomo impounded the villagers' livestock whenever his servants found animals drinking at the ravine. To add insult to injury, Pelaez then required a fee of four *reales* per donkey to return them to their rightful owners. The servants beat persons caught cutting *mesotes* (plants that grew in the barranca) or collecting water, and took their *tilmas* (cloaks) or their axes. During the dry season other water sources disappeared, so access to the waters in the ravine was particularly important.[15] By seizing resources necessary to the economic life of the villagers when they tried to use the water, the Iberian landlords could, through their servants, deplete the reserves of resistance possessed by all indigenous collectivities. Although not directly linked to the appropriation of water rights, these tactics weakened the resolve of the Indians by preventing access to important resources.

Without the intermediary of their servants, large landowners could not have enforced new irrigation arrangements. The servants took the place of water bureaucrats but they did not represent all members of the irrigation society. Instead, they worked for one master. Their actions and the inability of many Indian villages to resist the strongarm tactics of estate servants reveals the Audiencia's ineffectiveness as guardian of social order in irrigation matters. In effect, large landowners were creating a type of informal water bureaucracy without benefiting users as a group. Although the estate servants do not conform to the Hunts' model of a centralized irrigation society, perhaps their role in eighteenth-century Puebla reveals an informal mechanism which predated centralization. If so, Puebla did not follow the path to centralization as elaborated by the Hunts because only one sector of society supported the use of servants as water guards. In contrast, centralization in Puebla was imposed by one sector of the society; it was not the result of a common desire for a centralized bureaucracy that could end the rising level of conflict over water.

POWERS OF THE SPANISH LANDOWNERS

Apart from the use of servants as a force to impose control over water, some large landowners had positions of authority in colonial society or established alliances with officials. Their direct or indirect political power allowed landowners to impose new irrigation allocations and to imprison or harass the opposition. Landowners' authority, combined with other advantages such as the use of servants and legal rights gained through the doctrine of prior appropriation, reinforced their ability to assert control over water. Authority was manifested in different functions: as *alcalde mayor,* as official in the Acordada, in alliances with *subdelegados,* and finally, as clerics. Each role within colonial society implied deference and submission by others which strengthened the position of landowners who wished to expand their irrigation.

As clerics in a small town, the monks who owned the Hacienda San Luis Evangelista in Huejotzingo enjoyed considerable authority. The Dominican monks obtained several Royal Provisions confirming their rights to a stream near the hacienda. As a result of their authority and legal control of water, the monks achieved a relationship of cringing dependence on the part of the indigenous community. In October 1743, the mestizo cacique Juan de Guevara related how Brother Don Antonio gave him either 100 or 200 pesos to close the gates of the stream and prevent the waters from reaching the Santa

Ana community's fields. Village residents pleaded with the Brother, and presented him with numerous gifts of fruit, flowers, and chickens. After this display of submission, Brother Don Antonio allowed the gates to be reopened.[16] The monks both held authority over water and exercised political clout. They used these powers as tools to impose relations of extreme dependence and submission on local indigenous communities. Their control over water reinforced the hierarchies of power in the region.

Iberians were also officials at times and often enjoyed considerable influence with local bureaucrats. The *alcalde mayor* of Huejotzingo, Ignacio Ruiz, for instance, went to great pains to explain that the residents of the town "spontaneously" and "as a gift," but certainly without any intimidation on his part, donated the water he was using to irrigate his gardens. He further stated that the town never lacked water in all the years he had lived there[17]—a statement that is directly contradicted in other documents.[18]

Via a combination of tactics, Don Miguel Raboso used his position as alcalde mayor to usurp three surcos of water from the community of Santo Domingo Izúcar. When the residents objected, Raboso defended his appropriation through his servants.[19]

In addition to complicity with officials, some landholders held authority themselves and thus could influence the outcome of conflicts. Don Juan Zubia, as the proprietor of the Hacienda Raboso, held extensive irrigation rights, but he was also the local official of the Acordada (police). His position allowed him to use prisoners for work on the hacienda; a right which he abused and for which he was eventually denounced. Zubia used prisoners extensively to create and maintain his irrigation canal system.[20] With the fruits of generations of water rights acquisitions, Zubia, in essence, took his official position one step further: descendants of those from whom the irrigation was wrested were forced to preserve and repair the canals.

The collusion of Iberian landholders and officials was often suspected, especially when "troublemakers" who were actually protesting changes in irrigation allocations, were imprisoned.[21] For example, the *subdelegado* Cristoval de Paz Xinzon imprisoned Antonio Flores of the town of Teutla in Chiautla de la Sal from November 16, 1797, to December 16, 1797. He released the prisoner only after receiving several orders from the Audiencia to do so, which happened to occur once the planting for the dry season was well underway. Antonio Flores, along with other members of the community, protested the usurpation of the town's only source of water by Doña María Gertrudis Díaz de Olivares, owner of the Hacienda de Huachinautla. Her late husband had previously injured the community by allowing his livestock to destroy their fields and pastures. The hacendado had also managed to obtain the community's titles to land and water and only returned them to the village heavily damaged. His widow continued this intimidation campaign by having stones placed in the irrigation conduits so that the water did not reach the village's fields. A few years later, the lawyer representing Teutla residents revealed that the subdelegado Paz Xinzon owed money to the Olivares family; his impartiality was very much in doubt.[22]

Positions of power and authority, informal structures such as armies of servants, or economic dependence and the intimidation these could exert upon the indigenous members of communities in the Poblano countryside were formidable weapons. Yet, not all Iberians were in a position to browbeat or coerce their neighbors. Indeed, as will be discussed later, many Spanish landholders were themselves the victims of intimidation from both other Iberians and indigenous communities working together. Power within the countryside was not a simple ethnic attribute but the result of the interplay of many factors and the accumulation of advantages over the course of many years. Can we say that those Iberians who were local tyrants were necessarily also water monopolists and therefore derived their power from access to irrigation? Did their despotism come from their control of water? Certainly, it is clear that once they controlled access to water they could use it as a weapon. But they gained this control through diverse methods. Most large haciendas or ingenios accumulated rights to irrigation over the course of many years, and sometimes generations, by purchase, usurpation, and other means. That they undertook and successfully achieved these impressive buildups of water rights is perhaps the most indicative of their power but, once they had significant access to irrigation, they also became important economic agents in the community. They could then afford armies of servants, hold sway over local officials, and perhaps even official positions for themselves. Can we say that control over water was power, or was it simply one more attribute of a successful and powerful hacendado or the skillful accumulation of power in a situation of decentralization?

SPANIARD AGAINST SPANIARD

As competition for water intensified in the eighteenth century, Spanish landowners also fought each other for the control of irrigation. Conflicts between Spaniards were not as common as between Spanish landowners and Indian villages, nor were they usually as violent. The strategies used to acquire water rights when two Spanish landowners confronted each other differed from when they sought to wrest away water from Indians. Intimidation, the use of servants, and outright violence were uncommon. Instead Spaniards relied upon legal remedies more than informal weapons such as strongarm tactics.

Because these feuds over irrigation essentially were part of the consolidation of economic power in the Poblano countryside, the battles transferred from the Indians who had the earliest claims to water rights to those Iberians who had properties with rights acquired during the two previous centuries of colonial rule. Not surprisingly, these battles between Spaniards occurred generally within the jurisdictions first settled by the Spanish, which therefore had a greater density of Iberian population. Peter Gerhard's population figures for 1681 show that occurrences of Spanish versus Spanish conflicts over water rights were higher in regions such as Atlixco in which Spaniards accounted for six percent of the total population than Tecali with an Iberian community accounting for only 0.3% of the people. (See Table 3.) Of course, there are exceptions to this generalization: in Chiautla de la Sal, where the Spanish formed only one percent of the population, intra-Iberian divisiveness was much more significant than in Tehuacán, where Spaniards represented three percent of the population. (See Table 3.) With the growing competition for irrigation, the Iberian agrarian community fought amongst themselves and provoked a process of water rights consolidation under the control of major estates.

The accumulation of water rights for a particular hacienda developed gradually, often over several generations or periods of ownership. Part of the process of accumulating water rights involved the gradual encroachment and appropriation of indigenous water

Table 3. Proportion of Spanish population relative to intra-Iberian conflicts in Poblano jurisdictions, 1681

Jurisdiction	Spanish	Indians	Castas	% Spanish	Conflicts
Izúcar	640	9,980	3,130	4	8
Tepeaca	1350	26,400	1,990	4	2
Cholula	760	18,280	1,280	3	7
Chietla	120	1,380	1,160	4	1
Chiautla de la Sal	30	2,110	150	1	1
Atlixco	1,040	13,570	1,340	6	6
Huejotzingo	720	10,580	1,400	5	7
Tecali	20	5,450	20	0.3	0
Tehuacán	470	12,800	1,290	3	0
Tepeji de la Seda	40	7,720	100	0.5	0

Sources: For demographic data, Peter Gerhard, "Un censo de la diócesis de Puebla en 1681," *Historia Mexicana* 30:4(1981):530–60, and for number of intra-Iberian conflicts, Archivo General de la Nación, Mexico City, Tierras and Mercedes sections.
Note: Jurisdictions not represented for lack of demographic information include Tochimilco, San Juan de los Llanos, San Andrés Chalchicomula, and Tepejojuma.

rights—which has already been described in part—but in the eighteenth century, the process of gaining irrigation rights became one of consolidation. Rather than focusing solely on irrigation controlled by Indian communities, many Spaniards turned their attention to the resources acquired by their Iberian neighbors. Part of this consolidation process occurred rather naturally and peacefully through the purchase of properties or inheritance but, as demand for irrigation grew in the eighteenth century, the pressures brought to bear upon Iberian competitors increased and the acquisition of irrigation rights from Spanish neighbors began to resemble hostile takeovers.

The Iberian landowners who were enmeshed in the struggle for control of irrigation were no less dependent on the results of struggles over water for their economic survival than the indigenous communities. Yet, the character of the battle between Iberians seems to have been attenuated by an understanding that the strongarm tactics used against Indians were simply not acceptable or perhaps ineffective against a fellow Spaniard. In only one instance were actual blows exchanged between Spaniards,[23] although attacks against property were not unknown. Instead of the power plays common with the Indians, (intimidation, confiscation of property) Spaniards simply appropriated water or took more water than was allowed. Then they stood back to see how quickly the courts settled the matter. In January 1723, for instance, Don Pascual García reported that Atlixco hacienda owners who had not participated in the last *repartimiento* and therefore had no irrigation rights, had nevertheless built dams and were taking water illegally.[24] The strategy of action and then legal delay was perhaps the preferred tactic, but another method involved an actual attack on the productive capacity of neighbors. In essence, the landowner would either retain water or divert it away from neighbors' properties. The diversion of irrigation from downstream farms was sometimes carried out simply to harm neighbors who were also competitors. Gerónimo de Fuentes, for example, blocked four surcos destined for downstream users.[25] In some cases, the water was not used in the fields of the culprit but simply diverted away from the fields of the person or persons downstream. Rather than fulfilling a farming-related need, the action served solely to harm the person deprived of water. Many of the battles between Iberian-owned estates were part of a long-term struggle, one which transcended generations and ownership, and probably were the product of location and inherently conflicting needs. The same names appear repeatedly in the documentation as new owners or sons of former plaintiffs battled over identical resources and issues.

As the agrarian economy expanded in the early eighteenth century, Spaniards established new farms which frequently had no attached nor inherent rights to irrigation. By this period, officials began to refuse to grant new *mercedes* for irrigation rights and therefore the acquisition of water rights could not be accomplished by grants, the simplest route. The other legal method was to purchase or rent water rights, usually from Indian villages but indigenous communities increasingly needed all their irrigation capacity and had become more suspicious of involvement with Iberian landowners. Spanish farmers complained of either purchasing or renting estates for which they discovered only after the completion of the deal, that water was either unavailable or rights were tied up because of longstanding legal problems.[26] Some of these unfortunates turned to the law to try to establish certain rights, but many simply encroached on the rights of their

Table 4. Monthly averages of water usurpation complaints, 1680–1810

January	7
February	11
March	10
April	9
May	9
June	4
July	4
August	5
September	9
October	8
November	7
December	7

Source: Archivo General de la Nación, Mexico City, Tierras section.

neighbors. Several built illegal dams and diverted water—to which they had no rights—to their lands.[27] Don Felix de Sandoval y Roxas, owner of the Hacienda Huezoquapa in Atlixco, built a new dam in April 1754. His neighbors, owners of the Haciendas Coyula and Acocotla, complained and renewed their objections in October when Sandoval had not yet dismantled the dam. Sandoval planned to plant chiles over the winter and definitely needed a lot of irrigation. But, by February, the Audiencia ruled that he had no rights to the permanent dam and had to return to the previous practice on the hacienda, which was to irrigate by buckets over the winter. The Audiencia's ruling came too late to do much good for his neighbors, but it meant that Sandoval's future irrigation costs would be higher. One witness estimated that the Audiencia's ruling would triple the price of the chiles or other crops.[28] Other Spanish farmers expanded the flow of irrigation beyond the amount allowed.[29] These complaints were for the most part lodged over the dry season. (See Table 4.) While such strategies satisfied their water requirements over the short term, the long-term result was to involve these newcomers in legal battles over control of water. The results of such judicial contests cannot be generalized but often gave the usurpers certain de facto water rights.

The struggle to dominate irrigation resources also had an offensive nature. Spanish agriculturalists used legal weapons to prevent their neighbors from expanding their farming capacity or exerting their de jure water rights. Tactics were extremely diverse and cannot be easily generalized except in terms of the motivations behind these challenges. Groups or individuals sometimes tried to block or successfully impeded the licensing of new arrangements for nearby farmers. While in the midst of a court battle over usurpation of water, the Monastery of Carmelites—owners of the Hacienda la Sabana—officially lodged an objection to the licensing of a mill on the property of Don Manuel del Callejo, owner of the Hacienda Tlacoscala.[30] Did the monks really object to the creation of a mill adjacent to their property? Or was their complaint simply another means to pressure a competitor for resources? Other examples show a more direct connection with water resources. Some challenges involved the creation or destruction of dams or reservoirs. Through judicial intervention, opponents attempted to force the destruction of reservoirs in the dry season,[31] hindered or destroyed illegal or legal *tomas* after the rains ended,[32] or challenged water allocation arrangements.[33] These tactics had diverse results, but the actual verdicts were not always meaningful. Instead, these actions distracted opponents and weakened their defenses.

In other instances, however, judicial doctrines were used to good advantage such as in the denunciation of unused water.[34] Don Pedro José Anchoa's challenge falls within this category. In 1789, he claimed that his neighbor, Don José Bartolomé del Portal, had lost irrigation rights because of inadequate usage. Quoting the legal code, the *Recopilación,* with great precision—XVI of Title XXXI of the third Partida—Anchoa informed the court that neither Portal nor anyone at the hacienda had used the waters granted to them for thirty years, and consequently, they had forfeited these privileges.[35] Anchoa's knowledge of the law paid off; the Audiencia awarded him the irrigation rights. In another instance, Juan José de Malpica shot down the claims to "ancient and peaceful possession" of a rival hacienda owner by delving into the past and finding evidence of a past lawsuit.[36] The law could be used in many ways as a preventive or as an offensive weapon and was easily manipulated for utilization against Iberian farmer counterparts.

Legal stratagems, while effective in many cases, were replaced with more direct methods under certain circumstances. As a result of frustration with the judicial system, many Spanish farmers, such as Don

Juan Francisco Aldas and Don Juan Felix Prieto among others, destroyed the dams which blocked their access to irrigation.[37] When individuals interfered with irrigation works, such an act could lead to violence because it constituted a major attack on the productive capacity of any estate. The Pinto family rose to prominence in Izúcar jurisdiction while developing an enviable resource base. But, in January 1754, the monks residing at the monasteries of Chicuasengo and Quatepec blocked Don Pedro Pinto's tomas.[38] As a result, he and his tenant were not able to complete their initial watering of seedlings. Frustrated by the monks' defiance, Pinto and his tenant attacked three of the monks and broke the conduits of the monastery's irrigation system.[39] Recourse to violence was not as common between Iberians, but certainly effective since Pinto's actions seem to have intimidated not just the monks but other farmers in the region. In the same year, Fray Sánchez de Leon, the parish priest of Tepapachecan, complained of Pinto and his tenants: "[T]hey only want problems, or that no one else may sow; well, there are so many threats that I cannot find anyone who wants to work my lands."[40] Other farmers diverted streams away from properties downstream or blocked and retained water in reservoirs.[41] By changing the course of streams, or diverting the return of water to another place, upstream farmers could literally eliminate the source of water for those downstream.[42] The farmers upstream used the diverted water, and the net result for those downstream was crop failure and financial ruin.

Problems over access to irrigation were sometimes resolved in an apparently permanent fashion, but much evidence points to the long-term nature of conflicts. The finite nature of available irrigation and the built-in competitiveness of farms requiring water resources meant that durable solutions were rare. As mentioned previously, suits over the same issue presented by new landowners or a new generation of landowners were common. In Huejotzingo, from 1741 to 1787, various landowners engaged in three separate lawsuits over the Amichaque stream. The Dominican order as owners of the Hacienda San Juan Evangelista and other farmers fought for control of the stream, first with the Canon of the Cathedral of Puebla, then with the Bachiller Doctor Don Juan Pérez Fernández de Salgo, followed by Doña María Saens de la Corte along with the first plaintiff, and finally, with Don Manuel Rodríguez Mantilla.[43] Farmers with greater financial resources could often withstand these long-term battles over water rights. Those who survived these contests sometimes turned their properties into water monopolies.

The fact that high levels of strife over water had spread to the Spanish community supports the hypothesis that the upsurge in conflicts over water corresponds with setting the process of centralization into motion. But centralized irrigation systems were only established in Puebla when a few large landowners had consolidated their control over irrigation.

INDIANS AGAINST INDIANS

Indigenous communities in colonial Puebla usually displayed a unified front to the external world but strife over water rights also existed among various communities. Indian village residents usually worked as a group and defended their resources as a collectivity against Iberian interlopers or other villages. The organization of the village polity was such that officials, governors, or the caciques assumed a leadership role to defend water rights against others.[44] Indigenous communities clashed with each other especially as resources became less available and the rights of Spanish landowners began to be entrenched in law.

The increased competition for water and the alienation of many of their traditional rights to irrigation led some Indian communities to compete among themselves for the remaining spoils. In 1666, the villages of Putla, Ayutla, and Geloasco initially challenged Don Martin Calvo Viñuelas, then owner of the Ingenio San Nicolás, over the rights to use the Atotonilco River for irrigation. The officials of these three communities argued that they owned two-thirds of the river. At that time, they received a Royal Provision which they used to uphold their rights again in 1705. In 1708, Putla and Geloasco composed some land and three surcos from the Epatlán river. But, by 1785, the villages had, for some unexplained reason, compromised and settled for only half of the Atotonilco even though the communities complained that they suffered from water shortages and that Don Martin Calvo allowed them less access than they required.[45] The documents do not shed much light upon the activities which fostered their concession in the period from 1705 to 1785.

Around 1785, the last Calvo died but the village of Geloasco also succumbed to a devastating epidemic. The population of Geloasco was so reduced that the remaining residents dispersed between the villages of Putla and Ayutla.[46] With the disappearance of two of the opponents in the fight over irrigation, the remaining two villages chose to concentrate their energies not on the guardian of the Calvo estate, but to try to wrest the remaining water rights from each other. What followed was an extremely rancorous fight between Ayutla and Putla which lasted until at least the nineteenth century, and occupied innumerable lawyers, notaries, and paper merchants.[47] After this point, the two enemies never targeted the Ingenio San Nicolás, even though the property was under guardianship. The ingenio became one of the region's water monopolists. Perhaps the communities of Ayutla and Putla believed that they stood a better chance of winning back some irrigation by taking on an opponent closer to their status and power within society. Moreover, their decision to fight each other confirms that the Calvos and the Ingenio San Nicolás had become insiders in terms of legal water rights; that is, their rights were clearly enough established as to be challenged only with great difficulty.

Putla residents argued in 1791 that because they had taken over the Geloasco lands, they should receive the irrigation associated with the same and the former village. Ayutla rebutted in 1792 that it should receive the irrigation because its population was larger. In 1794, Ayutla added that Putla residents only planted corn, and therefore had no need for so much water. The Audiencia waffled back and forth, and there were many accusations of skullduggery by lawyers and leaders of both sides. The leaders of these communities became so absorbed in the battle that in 1789 the wives of Putla farmers wrote to the Audiencia that their crops suffered, not because of inadequate water, but because their husbands were constantly in Mexico City dealing with the lawsuit instead of home tending the fields.[48] The wives' complaint should not be used to dismiss the problems suffered by Ayutla and Putla, as Ouweneel mistakenly does, because clearly the Calvos had deprived these two villages of a large part of their water rights. Rather, the women's petition shows how absorbing and difficult fighting a long legal battle could be, and how highly the farmers of Ayutla and Putla valued their irrigation rights.

Records pertaining to this case are so voluminous that it is impossible to provide an exhaustive account here. However, despite the massive documentation, some questions regarding the case remain unresolved. The Ingenio San Nicolás somehow lost its position of usurper and newcomer in a short period of time, and the two communities' aggression was redirected at each other. As stated earlier, the change in strategy can be partially explained by the fact that confronting another indigenous community was an easier road to take. Nonetheless, the reorientation of the two villages and the creation of such vehement enmities between Ayutla and Putla seem rather sudden and fortuitous. One cannot help wondering if an actor or actors behind the scenes existed, perhaps encouraging one side or another, or advancing lawyers' fees as occurred in the case of the Indians of Chalma and Don Pedro Pinto. The depth of animosity and the vindictiveness of this longstanding legal battle, however, belies any notion of harmonious relationships between the different indigenous communities when their interests were at stake.

Much older antecedents may have sparked the battles between Indian villages. Francisco del Paso y Troncoso provides information in his *Papeles de la Nueva España* regarding the enmities existing between Indian groups before the conquest, but it is difficult to find any data to link these wars with irrigation matters.[49] Yet, in the eighteenth century, the pressure on resources focused the aggression between indigenous villages on water rights. Indian communities clashed with each other over such matters as the amount of irrigation each was allowed, the position or aperture of sluice gates, and whether the other group even had rights to a stream or river. In essence, the legal conflicts between Indian villages were not very different from those between other entities.[50]

Lawsuits over irrigation matters between Indian villages did not differ very much from those involving Spaniards in terms of legal definitions and rights. Approaches toward lawsuits and wresting control of water rights sometimes differed from conflicts involving Spaniards due to an intimate knowledge of neighbors. The residents of Santiago Teutlan initially gained access to the water rights of their neighbors in Huaquechula because of a loan used for a lawsuit, but then also somehow persuaded a governor of Huaquechula to give them some of the village's water rights titles.[51] Other communities appropriated water from adjoining villages. The Barrio San Martín

turned the use of the *remanientes* of Santa María Tlalteca into usurpation through servidumbre. Even though their actions harmed communities downstream, Huilango and Huaquechula purposefully did
not clean out a piece of earth which happened to fall into a stream
because it diverted the flow to their fields.[52]

Indian communities fought each other for control of irrigation and
used both legal and illegal tactics to secure access to water. As their
water rights were taken over by the Spanish estates, indigenous communities tried to preserve sufficient amounts of irrigation to make
cultivation of their croplands viable in the dry season and secure
early harvests by irrigating before the rains began. They did so by
resisting encroachments on their water supply as described in chapter
six, but also by trying to wrest access to water from neighboring villages. Indian villages struggled to maintain and expand access to
water using methods very similar to those of Spanish estates: outright
appropriation as well as recourse to the courts. Although Indian officials such as governors had authority to distribute water internally
within communities, their powers did not go beyond village boundaries. Without an effective force or bureaucracy which could impose
allocation across jurisdictional lines, Indian villages could not always
peacefully decide water allocation matters.

CONFLICT INSIDE INDIGENOUS COMMUNITIES

The inner life of indigenous communities is fairly opaque, hidden
from contemporary scholars because it was not always recorded and
probably concealed from outsiders except when the prevailing order
broke down. When residents appealed to external authorities because
they could no longer deal with individuals, most often officials who
had betrayed the common trust, the breakdown of communal har-
mony was recorded. Elected or hereditary officials had the weighty
task of marshalling the resistance to outside encroachments on resources, but they also frequently enjoyed considerable latitude in controlling communal resources. In some instances, they used their official license to sell water rights to outsiders without the community's
consent.[53] Indian officials did have authority to dispose of communal
resources and certainly they often sold land, but in these cases, the
other residents argued that the water rights were sold for personal

gain rather than community needs, and that the sales were detrimental to the welfare of the village as a whole.

At times Iberian landowners perceived the tensions inside indigenous communities, and they attempted, sometimes successfully, to exploit the internal problems of Indian communities by recruiting village residents to betray the rest, particularly by stealing titles which documented irrigation rights. Antonio Flores, of the village of Teutla in Chiautla, stated that Don Antonio Olivan, owner of Hacienda de Huachinautla, tried to obtain the village's titles by suggesting that he would pay one of the Indians to steal them. The hacendado later obtained the titles and returned them incomplete and damaged.[54] When the residents of San Miguel Acomuluican in Atlixco jurisdiction tried to sue Don Antonio del Vado y Cosio, all their titles were reported missing from the archive.[55] San Francisco Huilango faced the same problem when residents tried to compose their waters in 1709. First, they had to sue Don Francisco Santiago and Doña María Margarita for the return of the land and water titles of the village.[56] But, apart from this outside interference, individuals in these communities at times betrayed the group and abused their positions in order to gain irrigation rights.

Huejotzingo had a repartimiento of nine *surcos* of which one and a half went to the hacienda of Don Juan Davila Galindo, three and a half were allotted to the public fountain in the main square, and the remaining four were channeled to the hacienda of Don Francisco de Avila. Village residents had access to this water, however, before it reached the hacienda, and they used it for their homes and gardens. Despite access to the nine surcos, Huejotzingo residents occasionally experienced water shortages because farmers in the surrounding region frequently broke the pipes which carried the water to the town. The periodic water shortage did not stop Don Juan de Guevara, during his term as governor, from selling four of the nine *surcos* available to the town to Don Andrés Arze on December 22, 1712, for the sum of four hundred pesos.[57] The official who succeeded Guevara argued that the sale of the water should be canceled because the real value of the water rights was closer to 6,000 pesos than 400, that the city was short of water in the first place, and finally, that Guevara had posed as a cacique and thus was illegitimate as governor when he undertook to sell the water rights.[58] Intimidation of witnesses characterized this case. Guevara and his family members were responsible for intimidation that was reinforced by the presence of Don Arze, the beneficiary of the water sale. The people of Huejotzingo were so terrified of Arze that many would not testify in his presence.[59] Guevara, although ostensibly the leader of a faction in Huejotzingo, evidently strengthened his influence by his association with the ominous Arze. Huejotzingo residents' appeal to external authorities reveals the breakdown of a unified front against external threats. It shows how certain individuals in indigenous communities placed their own welfare above that of the community, and that Spanish landowners could exploit this weakness.

Other Indian officials seemed capable of exerting their authority without any assistance from the outside. Even when no longer in office, Antonio Joseph took liberties with the aqueducts and crops of Santa Cruz Tlacotepeque in Tepeaca jurisdiction. Joseph was the leader of a group of former officials and governors who were implicated in various frauds while in office, and who had used their influence to take over a large portion of the community's cropland. For instance, in 1773 Joseph destroyed the village's communal crops and redirected the irrigation water used to water them. In November of the same year, village governor Don Pablo de Roxas confronted Joseph and lodged a complaint regarding his behavior. In response, Joseph robbed the water Roxas used for his fields; subsequently, Roxas' bean plants died. When reproached, Joseph only insulted Roxas further with "denigrating words," and he and his group further rejected the community by refusing to participate in communal activities, flaunting their wealth, and constantly disparaging community members. Joseph struck fear in the hearts of even the leaders of Santa Cruz Tlacotepeque although he, like Guevara in Huejotzingo, was considered a "fake cacique."[60] In both cases, Don Juan de Guevara and Antonio Joseph were apparently leaders of factions within their respective communities, factions which no longer worried about the village's welfare and no longer respected the values of communal life.

Although aggressive individualism seems to contradict the rather idealistic image sometimes presented of the indigenous community, certainly by the eighteenth century the communal indigenous identity was not always paramount.[61] Not all individuals acted in as rapacious a manner as Guevara and Joseph, but many placed their interests before those of local communities. In 1723, the Convent of Santo Domingo of Puebla which held lands locally in Justepeque (probably in Santa Clara Huichitepec) wanted to build irrigation canals. Residents of the local village, Justepeque, were in favor because they had experienced problems with flooding. However, the *cacicas* of Tecali were reluctant to agree to such an endeavor because the canal would pass through their land. The Tecali leaders finally provided permission for building the canal, but only in return for a fee of 170 pesos annually.[62] In 1742, the cacica of Santa Isabel Tecali opposed the composition of the waters of the village which, in theory, she was supposed to protect. Her reasoning was that the water in question passed through her land, and she worried that such a legalization could entail the creation of a servidumbre. The villagers argued that she should not be able to block their access to water because the community needed it for survival.[63] The cacica, not so surprisingly, protected the integrity of her rights to irrigation, but what is perhaps more extraordinary is that she perceived her own community as a potential competitor.

Within indigenous towns, there were also rivalries over water which did not involve the rest of the community. For instance, Thomasa Colexqua, a widow in the town of San Andrés Cholula, restricted the flow of water to the land of Don Manuel Roxas, an *indio principal,* because of what he called "caprichos" and ignorance.[64] Bernardino José, an Indian residing in the San Bernardino barrio in Izúcar, blocked the course of water to the land of his cousin Don Antonio Chimboro.[65] Although individuals in the community clashed over the allocation of irrigation in both of these cases, other people did not seem to be affected, nor did they seem to be very serious. Indeed, the most extraordinary feature of these cases is that they were recorded and that at least one party involved decided to appeal to an outside authority.

Another example suggests that some indigenous groups did pressure individuals to contribute to the needs of the community. In 1716, local officials in a barrio of Chietla imprisoned the Indian Diego Melchor because he mistreated another Indian, Nicolás de Castillo, in word and deed. But a contributing factor to Castillo's imprisonment was that he did not contribute money to the community in return for his "derrames" or the overflow of water that he received. His refusal to contribute to the community made him more vulnerable to arrest.[66] The barrio of Chietla was experience water shortages, thereby providing an added stimulus to taking action against Melchor. Because the internal life of Indian villages was not often recorded or understood by outsiders, it is difficult to know where to place these few examples on the spectrum of daily life experiences. It is probable, however, that these instances were representative of the type of everyday tug-a-war between two individuals or communal versus individual needs.

During the eighteenth century, indigenous communities were under considerable pressure. Having lost much of their land in the sixteenth and seventeenth centuries, they found themselves not only short of cropland for their members but also cut off from irrigation, the resource which could make the remaining plots more productive. Indians not only fought other communities to try to retain or expand water rights, but they also struggled among themselves. The betrayal of community by members of indigenous villages signaled a change in values associated with water. No longer a resource to be shared equitably, water became increasingly privatized. In other words, the notion that water was a resource of and for the community was being replaced by the belief that water was private property.

THE EVOLUTION OF WATER MONOPOLISTS

By accumulating extensive irrigation rights from various sources through purchase, usurpation, and legal maneuvers, a handful of estates came to dominate the countryside, not only by virtue of the extent of their landholdings but also because of the magnitude of the resource base defined broadly to include irrigation. Whoever owned these properties had the irrigation to plant profitable crops with the security that over the dry season, they would be able to water their fields. Their resources guaranteed them a measure of wealth and influence which protected them from encroachments. As the owners gradually acquired water rights, they became potent forces within the countryside.

The Ingenio San Nicolás is a good example, not only because of its dominance of the Izúcar region, but also because the owners first broached the idea of a water bureaucracy in the early nineteenth century. In 1644, Don Juan González de Peñafiel assigned the ingenio three surcos in his repartimiento of the Izúcar region. Don Martín Calvo bought the ingenio from Don Felix Pérez Delgado in 1699 and he also took over some land owned by the village of Santiago Azala.[67] In the early eighteenth century, Don Martín Calvo Viñuelas, then owner of the Ingenio San Nicolás, bought the Hacienda Santa María Magdalena. As such he combined the nine surcos of his acquisition with the eight surcos of the ingenio and seven additional surcos acquired by previous owners of San Nicolás, for a total of twenty-four surcos.[68] Later, the ingenio benefited from more water rights taken from the villages of Ayutla, Putla, and Geloasco. In 1666 the three villages owned two-thirds of the Atotonilco River, but by 1785 had lost half that amount along with some land to Calvo and his heirs.[69]

Apart from the major acquisition of water rights from indigenous villages, the various owners of the Ingenio San Nicolás also clashed with Spaniards over the use of water.[70] By the late eighteenth century, farmers in the surrounding region complained collectively on two occasions that the ingenio owners dominated the region, especially in the allocation and consumption of water.[71] Spanish and Indian farmers of the region both complained about the dominance of the ingenio in the sugar industry of the Izúcar countryside as well as the monopolization of water.

Whoever owned or inherited estates such as San Nicolás was the beneficiary of a gradual buildup of water rights over the course of the eighteenth century. As the balance between population, land, and water favored an upsurge in conflicts over water rights, the owners of these properties were able to use their influence, political offices, and access to servants to enforce their dominion of water. They expanded the resource base during their respective lifetimes so that each successive generation or owner had more irrigation rights. They became powerful within the countryside and they dominated the use of irrigation. The push toward a water bureaucracy came from one of these water monopolists once the water rights were consolidated in the hands of a few estates. Centralization came only when the dominant landowners could control its outcome and guarantee that it advanced their interests.

***

By the end of the colonial period, certain estates in the Poblano countryside monopolized irrigation rights. The creation of such water monopolies was not accomplished overnight. Spanish water rights dated back to the original establishment of estates in the sixteenth century when the Crown and Audiencia granted water rights to individuals, and the newcomers acquired rights from indigenous communities by purchase, rental, and denunciation. In the context of water law, the Spanish changed their status through historical continuity from outsiders without water rights to insiders who had rights.

When the equilibrium of population, land, and water was unbalanced and conflicts over irrigation multiplied, the Spanish estate owners were able to assert their legal water rights. The Spaniards used their power as dominant resource holders, officials, clerics, and allies of local authorities to impose expanded water rights. In addition, the hacendados' servants enforced their decisions and prohibited access to vital resources. As such, the Spanish operated both within and outside the law, but essentially they were able to enforce a new allocation of irrigation rights. Through their servants, they were moving toward a centralized system that was not grounded on communal consent.

The struggle for water did not occur solely between Indians and Spaniards. In fact, Spanish estates clashed over irrigation as did Indian communities. These antagonists were connected by hydrology, that is, they shared streams, rivers, or irrigation ditches. There was no effective authority that crossed the jurisdictional lines that bodies of water so easily traversed. Therefore, all these groups skirmished without recourse to a judicial body which could quickly and effectively adjudicate and allocate water. Without such a bureaucracy, they fought within the existing court system and used a variety of illegal tactics.

These conflicts occurred within a decentralized system. But the result of these struggles over the course of the eighteenth century was the creation of a group of water monopolists. At the end of the colonial period, these same large landowners had effective authority over water but no formal bureaucracy. In 1808, the owners of the Ingenio San Nicolás in Izúcar proposed the creation of a water bureaucracy—in effect, a centralized system.[72] Over the next few years, the large landowners of Izúcar named a water rights guardian.[73] They did so after they had accumulated massive amounts of water to the detriment of the indigenous communities and other Spanish estates. Their model of centralization, however, was not based on communal consent but rather upon the imposition of a bureaucracy by a small group to protect the resources they had acquired from all other farmers.

SIX

The Undertow of Resistance

As water became a prized commodity in eighteenth-century Puebla, farmers attempted to secure adequate resources for successful crops. The need for larger quantities of irrigation, however, often meant taking more water than allowed, and essentially stealing it from downstream consumers. Such radical reductions in the flow of streams, rivers, and irrigation ditches represented a fundamental threat to farmers, whether Indian or Spanish. The defense of water resources played a vital role in the survival of towns and individual farmers; their opposition to encroachment on water resources was paramount. Because those affected by the usurpation of water could not depend on rapid or effective intervention by the Audiencia, they often took action themselves. In fact, instead of demanding the creation of a centralized water bureaucracy, as the centralization model suggests, those most affected by the upsurge in water rights conflicts took matters into their own hands whenever possible.

Resistance aimed at the preservation of irrigation was characterized by specific parameters and timetables. Popular resistance resulting from attempts to preserve control over land has been extensively documented, and its parameters and timetables are different. In the case of irrigation related resistance, factors such as altitude and seasonal patterns of rainfall affected the intensity and immediacy of any attempts to fight back encroachments on water resources. These determinants explain the use of different forms of resistance at different times and geographical locations. Circumstances such as season and location dictated the choice of either passive or active strategies of resistance. Indian and Spanish farmers who practiced resistance were able to survive and delay the consolidation of water resources in the hands of a few monopolists. This chapter examines the factors of time and place in acts of resistance to water usurpation and relates them to patterns of active and passive resistance.

RESISTANCE IN COLONIAL SOCIETIES

Scholars often attribute resistance and revolt in agrarian societies to the stresses of survival in circumstances of unequal power relations. Peasant societies, according to these theorists, resort to violence and insurgency when traditional forms of subsistence are endangered.[1] In Puebla, most conflicts over water during the colonial period were clustered in the eighteenth century. The pressures on the rural economy during this period were caused by demographic growth, and a deteriorating resource base, but were aggravated by the intensification of commercial agriculture and its consequent expansion of irrigation requirements. These trends multiplied the challenges faced by all farmers, although the threat to the continued survival of indigenous communities was especially acute.

Rebellions and other forms of resistance used by both Indian and Spanish farmers to protect their water rights in the eighteenth century were a reaction to the takeover of irrigation and the consolidation of water rights described in the previous chapter. The actual causes for acts of resistance, however, cannot be explained in general terms such as the exploitative relations between Indians and Spaniards. Rather, specific acts of resistance were a reaction to specific usurpations of water. William Taylor argues that rebellions cannot be explained solely by assigning the blame to the system of production; specific causes are also necessary to spark resistance movements.[2] The actual motivations for acts of resistance were not as a rule opposition to the colonial state, but rather protest against a particular act which endangered the community's survival. For example, many indigenous communities rioted when inspectors came to measure their lands. Experience with previous land surveys indicated that such acts preceded the loss of cropland and consequently, constituted an attack on farming capacity and the community's survival as a viable entity.[3] While the pressures of the intensified struggle for water provide a general context for resistance, the individual acts of rebellion surfaced in reaction to a precise incident or problem such as the construction of a new dam or the diversion of irrigation away from fields. Indian and Spanish farmers attacked and destroyed dams, and indigenous communities rioted in reaction to such deprivations of water.

Not all resistance was so dramatic or violent. In fact many acts of resistance were much more subtle, or what James Scott calls "everyday" forms of resistance. In his study of Asian peasant societies, Scott lists different forms of passive resistance including "foot-dragging, dissimulation, false compliance, pilfering, feigned ignorance, slander, arson, sabotage, and so forth."[4] Acts of resistance ranged from the violent and sometimes bloody rebellion to ephemeral and ambiguous actions which forced others to accommodation on a daily basis.[5] Periodically the times dictated an "active" resistance while everyday, "passive" resistance secured resources over the long term. The strategies of resistance in Puebla resemble those described for other farming societies, but were unique in their timing and methods since the objective was to retain control over water, a resource which, unlike land, had seasonal fluctuations. Farmers' long-term goal was to preserve access to water. They did so throughout the year but access was most critical during the dry season.

TIME AND PLACE

Resistance over water rights followed certain patterns which were determined by the configurations of the environment and were particular to different ecological niches. In a region such as Puebla, characterized by a semi-arid climate with defined seasonal rains, access to water was especially critical only during specific times. Poblano farmers used irrigation from perennial streams before the rainy season to give plants a head start, and thus avoid, as much as possible, the risk of frost damage at harvest time. Irrigation was also applied over the dry season, particularly for wheat and sugar; in fact, both of these commercial crops required copious amounts of water. The implication of these seasonal practices was that unlike the fight over land—which was occurring concurrently—the control of hydraulic resources was most important at particular periods of the year rather than all year round. Irrigation during these peak times was highly concentrated and extremely critical. Although farmers remained vigilant in their control over water resources at other times, it was during these decisive moments that the struggle to control irrigation was most intense and vehement. Thus, the fiercest tactics took place during the dry season, while other strategies were employed in the rainy season. Therefore, to understand the logic of the various types of resistance used by Poblanos, the agricultural timetable is the best guide to develop a chronology of resistance.

Apart from seasonal variations, the position of farmers on the stream, river, or network of ditches used for irrigation also had an impact on their capacity to retain control of irrigation. It is common-sensical that users upstream were at an advantage to usurp resources. Downstream farmers were therefore more vulnerable to the theft—whether temporary or permanent—of their resources.[6] Location of farms along waterways then was an important factor in determining appropriation strategies as well as resistance. Why then did individuals not simply choose to plant further upstream? In addition to pragmatic concerns such as occupation and ownership of land, moving upstream in the Poblano landscape often also signified moving up the slope of a mountain or volcano. Altitude altered the viability of certain plants, and the soil in the highlands was not always as rich. Thus, farmers generally were limited in terms of crop location, and simply adapted to the situation by modifying forms of resistance to their inherent geographical limitations. Wherever possible, farmers downstream used active forms of resistance because they were otherwise powerless.

Poblano farmers adapted to the conditions of their environment by planting according to the seasons and depending on precipitation or irrigation. They also adapted to the altitude of their cropland, planting wheat in the higher elevations and sugar in the lowlands. When their patterns of cultivation were disrupted by the actions of farmers upstream who took more water than allowed, they reacted vigorously, particularly if they were planting or caring for young plants. Their actions were influenced by the season and downstream location.

TOCHIMILCO AND SAN ANDRÉS CHALCHICOMULA

The comparative advantages derived from location can best be appreciated by examining the contrasting experiences of two communities. When Tochimilco and San Andrés Chalchicomula confronted local farmers outside their communities, the disparity in their capacity to prevent the appropriation of resources shows the importance of geography to their respective resistance potential. Tochimilco residents—mostly Indians—were accused of illegally diverting the stream which ran through their community seven times, whereas no instances of such diversions were ever recorded for San Andrés Chalchicomula—a town of Spaniards and Indians.

Tochimilco is located on the southern flank of the Popocatepétl volcano at 2,070 meters above sea level, ten leagues from Puebla de los Angeles, and twenty leagues southwest from Mexico City.[7] At the end of the colonial period, its principal economic activities were centered on the cultivation of wheat. Residents also harvested fruit (sold in the markets of Puebla de los Angeles and Mexico City), corn, bean, barley, chiles, peas, and cochineal.[8] The town was located at a higher elevation than most of the Iberian haciendas which clustered around the streams descending the side of the volcano. There were a few estates above Tochimilco but they do not seem to have presented any problems to the village. Water for agricultural use flowed through the village before it reached the estates downstream. (See Fig. 9.) At one time, the Indians of Tochimilco possessed 1,400 *varas* in communal lands. By 1770, however, village officials had sold half the land to pay for tributes.[9] The residents farmed the remaining land, and also cultivated large walled-in garden plots within town boundaries.[10]

Spanish farmers had been quite successful in acquiring land below the village in the sixteenth and seventeenth centuries, but they could not change the hydraulics and so were left vulnerable because of the fundamental disadvantage of their location downstream. The Spanish landowners tried to correct this imbalance by using the legal system. Through judicial channels they sponsored the elaboration of a *repartimiento de aguas* which prohibited the Indians from planting wheat.[11] The Spanish estate owners implemented the ban on indigenous wheat cultivation quite obviously to reduce the amount of water taken from the waterway as it passed through the village.

Legal control and rights were, however, not sufficient to protect the farmers downstream because it was very simple to break pipes and redirect water within the confines of the community. Evidently, the Indians of Tochimilco were not intimidated by the legal interdictions and took the water they needed. The Spanish farmers tried to enforce the prohibition and protect their resources in 1648, 1650, 1698, 1700, 1716, 1742, and 1802.[12] The sheer repetition of such attempts shows the structural disadvantage of the Spanish farmers in this situation. Although the Indians of Tochimilco had lost most of their land

Fig. 9. Colonial Map of Tochimilco
This figure shows the relative position of the village and the greater part of hacienda lands below.
(Archivo General de la Nación, Mexico City, Tierras section, vol. 635, exp. 1,
cuadro 4, fol. 48, 1743, by Lorenzo Xavier Santa María Olmos)

to outsiders, they derived their power in matters of irrigation not from the law, nor from political alliances or positions, but simply from the topography and hydraulics of the region. The Indians could withstand in practice what they could not resist in the legal system.

The village of San Andrés Chalchicomula was not so fortunate. Although the surrounding croplands were not part of the more prosperous wheat producing areas, several haciendas were located upstream from the town. The haciendas in the region concentrated on the production of corn, with wheat and beans as secondary crops. In the weekly market village residents sold cotton, wool, and goatskins.[13] Livestock was also a very important part of their livelihood. Unlike the people of Tochimilco, the residents of San Andrés Chalchicomula were quite susceptible to the usurpation of their resources despite legal protection and rights. The village held the title to a spring only a league distant. The residents spent considerable sums on materials and provided the labor to construct an aqueduct to carry the water from the spring to the town square.[14] Despite these efforts, the townspeople suffered from a chronic water shortage about which they complained to the Audiencia in 1708, 1723, 1745, 1753, and 1763.[15] They were easily hurt by the overuse of water by upstream farmers because the spring was their only source of water during the dry season. Several estates were located upstream from the town. (See Fig. 10.)

The example of the town of San Andrés Chalchicomula serves to emphasize the importance of upstream versus downstream location in the relations between water users.[16] The residents of San Andrés Chalchicomula shared the frustrations of the Spanish landowners on the lee of Tochimilco; legal rights could not, in practice, override location upstream, especially since the Audiencia was not effective in imposing the rule of law in water matters.

In a decentralized irrigation system, where no effective force adjudicates and allocates water, farmers downstream are vulnerable. Puebla's hydraulic system was composed of rivers and streams which flowed down the sides of mountains and volcanoes and then through the valleys. As such, few farmers did not have an upstream neighbor. Sometimes the farmers upstream were Indians, as in the case of Tochimilco, and in other cases they were Spanish, as in the example of San Andrés Chalchicomula.[17] Location upstream in the hydraulic network provided some measure of protection, but did not guarantee

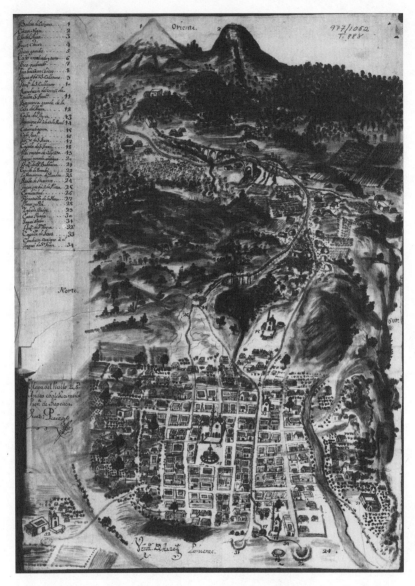

Fig. 10. Colonial Map of San Andrés Chalchicomula, and San Cayetano, San Baltazar, and Santa Ana Haciendas

Wooden canoas transported water to the village. Masonry canoas are upstream and closer to the source. The water passed by the fields of many estates before reaching the handsome fountain in the village's central square.

(Archivo General de la Nación, Mexico City, Tierras section, vol. 888, exp. 20, fol. 26, 1764, by Buenaventura de Arze)

power over water. As we shall see, some farmers downstream rioted or broke waterworks upstream to force an accommodation.

PASSIVE AND ACTIVE RESISTANCE

Within the limitations set by terrain, legal precepts, and relations among farmers, different groups reacted to and resisted encroachment on their resources in ways suited to their situation and the season. Resistance tactics are classified here as passive or active.[18] This taxonomy takes into account the effects and expected results of acts of defiance. Active resistance was direct and unmediated by officials, while passive acts achieved their goal indirectly, often with some intervention by external authorities.

Active resistance included breaking dams, sabotage such as placing rocks in irrigation ditches, and riots. These tactics addressed the problem immediately and worked outside the judicial system. In instances of active resistance, those involved did not ask for Audiencia sanction before they acted.

Passive resistance included acts of malfeasance, noncooperation, and lawsuits. None of these tactics affected the usurpation in an immediate sense. In the case of lawsuits, resistance depended on the Audiencia's mediation and intervention. Categorization of lawsuits as passive may seem inappropriate considering the enormous cost and effort involved. However, it is clear that regardless of the competence of lawyers retained by contestants, prompt results by the court system were impossible.[19]

The choice of one approach did not prevent the use of other tactics if circumstances changed or if the first strategy was ineffective. The village of Santa Ana Quatepec (Atlixco jurisdiction), for example, used three different strategies—rebellion, sabotage, and legal suit—in its battle with the Hacienda La Sabana to retain its water rights.[20] Logically, communities or individuals exerted active resistance at times when irrigation was crucial to the health of a crop, while passive resistance served to enforce gains made previously, ensure the continuity of possession, or weaken opposition with the hope of a later victory.

The cycle of seasons determined the rhythm of agricultural work but also the farmer's need for irrigation. As such, seasonal variations also affected the level of resistance and choice of strategies—active or

Table 5. Incidence of resistance in Puebla employed by indigenous and Spanish populations by type, 1680–1810

Type	Indians	Spanish
Sabotage	6	2
Riot/violence	9	3
Malfeasance	5	3
Noncooperation	1	1
Composition	21	29
Block grant	7	5
Contestation	58	62

Sources: Archivo General de la Nación, Mexico City, Tierras, Indios, Mercedes, and Reforma Agraria sections, and Archivo Judicial de Puebla, Puebla, Mexico.

passive—when farmers upstream appropriated too much water. Active resistance was appropriate before the rains started when farmers planted or at the beginning of the dry season when the winter crops were sown. Passive resistance occurred year round but especially when irrigation was not so vital.

ACTIVE RESISTANCE

Both Iberian and indigenous farmers used acts of defiance such as the destruction of waterworks. Evidently, they felt a certain aloofness from local authorities. They believed that the results of an act outside the boundaries of the law outweighed the potential consequences (i.e., imprisonment, fines, sanctions, and lawsuits). Indeed, the absence of a centralized water authority seems to have allowed the proliferation of alternate authorities such as estate servants as well as the frequent use of resistance strategies outside legal norms. Active resistance was not limited to certain groups but rather was employed by both Indian and Spaniard alike, although each group tended to use certain tactics more than others. (See table 5.) Resistance strategies were also related to the location of farmers vis-à-vis a hydraulic network and their power within the countryside. One such method, attack on waterworks, included breaking dams, ditches, or aqueducts, and placing stones in streams, ditches, or aqueducts to divert the water. These actions reversed water usurpation at a critical moment. Farmers did so without the permission or the blessing of the Audiencia.

The complaint of Don Crisostomo Zubia, owner of the Hacienda Raboso, is one of the most transparent examples. Zubia was himself the subject of many complaints by both Spaniards and Indians, and his estate became a water monopolist by the end of the eighteenth century. In 1789, however, he appealed to the *subdelegado* because someone had destroyed his dam. At the same time, the governor of Izúcar and respective barrios complained that Zubia was taking too much water from the Santiago *acequia*. The *hacendado* left the town and barrios without irrigation for their crops.[21] Clearly, the attack on Zubia's dam was part of a campaign of resistance against his constant appropriation of resources. The Indians of Izúcar and barrios could not rely upon the subdelegado or the Audiencia and so they broke Zubia's dam and recovered the irrigation that they believed was their due. In effect, they relied on active resistance rather than a bureaucratic solution in the short term.

Poblano farmers reacted in different ways to being deprived of their water by their neighbors, but the most successful tactics were direct actions which did not rely on official intervention nor the influence of the law. Sabotage was probably the most effective of these active forms of resistance. The Augustinian monks, owners of the Hacienda de Quatlapanga (Huejotzingo jurisdiction), for instance, took advantage of the fact that the *targea* carrying seven and a half *surcos* to the Hacienda Nanacamilpa crossed their land. In 1783, they broke the targea and took the water, later alleging in legal documents that they objected to its presence on their land because of the risk of *servidumbre*.[22] The Indians of Santa Ana Quatepec placed stones in the irrigation ditch of the Hacienda La Sabana after the strategy of destroying the estate's dam was not sufficient to increase irrigation from the one and a half surcos allotted by law to over five. The hacienda servants removed these obstacles and the Indians put them back. The Indians did not accept the legal rights of the Hacienda nor the authority of its servants. The fact that the Indians' homes were located near an ideal location for such acts was an advantage in their struggle to maintain control over water.[23] Such tactics, when used with some frequency, served to emphasize competitor farmers' vulnerability and possibly to moderate their conduct.[24] In both these examples, farmers destroyed or modified water allotments without legal sanction when they were left without sufficient resources.

When contract enforcement lapsed, the results could be a complex legal mess. In one case, Doña Elena Velásquez de la Cadena raged about the interference with her water supply caused by the destruction of a diversion dam by Santa María Coronango residents. She claimed rights to the water but the Indians asserted that the estate had a longstanding arrangement with them to rent the irrigation for ten pesos annually. Because the Indians had failed to enforce the contract Doña Elena claimed the water rights through servidumbre. The Indians shattered the dam because water was diverted in such a way that its excessive depth near the village caused drowning of livestock and people.[25] The Indians did not accept the servidumbre nor Doña Velásquez's dangerous dam; legally, however, they did not have a case. Therefore, they acted outside the law to resist a situation they considered unjust.

Although victims occasionally complained that acts of sabotage were aimed at destroying their crops and nothing else,[26] the destruction of dams, irrigation ditches, and aqueducts as well as stream diversion typically had a very precise goal: use of irrigation elsewhere. Individuals or groups accused of sabotage frequently offered rationales for their conduct based on tradition; ultimately, however, their actions were the most effective means of ensuring the supply of water at a crucial moment. In 1712, the officials of San Martín Huaquechula detailed longstanding rights to the water of the Guichilac river. The village had first fought over these water rights with neighboring villages in 1550, and then in 1707 with Don Joseph de Espinoza, but had maintained legal possession of the rights despite these challenges. When Don Thomas de Burgos leased the Hacienda of Açicintitlan, water rights conflicts emerged once more. Burgos began appropriating the irrigation held by to Huaquechula "in such as way as to leave them with no water at all." Village residents broke Burgos' dam four or five times, and then lodged an official complaint with the Audiencia.[27] Huaquechula residents and many other Poblano farmers understood that the only method to immediately resolve such problems was to take direct action. Both Indian and Spanish farmers adopted such measures when only prompt action was acceptable, location made direct action viable, and finally, if they believed they could act without direct reprisals.

More drastic acts such as rebellions and physical confrontations, implied a different set of circumstances. The goal of all resistance was the restitution of resources. Although forceful, the *alboroto* or *tumulto* were less immediate than simply redirecting water. Physical intimidation was more commonly used by farmers at a disadvantage because of their location downstream. Intimidation sometimes included the destruction of dams or irrigation ditches.

The series of conflicts between the villages of Santiago Teutlan and Huaquechula demonstrates the usefulness of forceful demonstrations. Because Santiago Teutlan's well—used by residents and to water cattle—was often dry, the village depended on water which belonged to Huaquechula. Teutlan residents provided a loan to Huaquechula to finance a lawsuit, and Teutlan took payment in the form of an agreement allowing access to water. Teutlan nonetheless remained extremely vulnerable to the whims of Huaquechula residents who could easily withhold water, and in 1732 the latter did so.

Huaquechulanos prevented Teutlanos from watering their livestock; Teutlanos attempting to fill water jars in Huaquechula were attacked and their jars broken. Teutlan officials complained to the Audiencia that their fields and cattle were at risk, residents had no drinking water, and that they were facing depopulation. Huaquechula apparently inflicted this punishment on its neighbors because of a land dispute in which a former governor of Huaquechula had aided the people of Teutlan by handing over certain titles. Teutlan residents did not wait for intervention by the Audiencia; instead, they swarmed into the town square of Huaquechula and rioted. The local priest intervened and then the *alcalde mayor* gave Teutlan a composition for the disputed water. Residents of the two villages embraced and promised to maintain peaceful relations.

Yet, in 1734, the same problems resurfaced. When Teutlan residents refused to help the neighboring village with expenses for the church, building a corral for the fiesta, or cleaning the acequia, among others, Huaquechula cut off the water.[28] Huaquechula derived its power through its control over water, but Teutlan was able to temporarily neutralize this control by rioting in Huaquechula. Rebellion was an active and effective method to counteract the loss of access to water (more so than a complaint to the Audiencia), but did not and could not reverse the situation which gave Huaquechula control over the local source of water.

Rebellion as a tactic was used most often by indigenous groups rather than Spaniards perhaps because it required strength in numbers. Although the disparity in numbers provides an explanation of why Spaniards did not engage in such conduct, it should also be emphasized that most Spaniards would not have wished to embrace the disorderly conduct inherent to rebellion. In the case of the estate owners around the village of Tochimilco, why did they not react like the residents of Santiago Teutlan and riot in the town square for access to water? It certainly could not have been less effective than their appeals to the Audiencia, but their comparatively small numbers and the loss of dignity implied upon embracing such a strategy obviated this logical solution. Indians engaged in tumultos nine times whereas Spaniards, although the Iberians often used their servants in an aggressive manner, confronted other Spaniards with direct violence only three times. (See table 5.) When formal complaints did not restore irrigation to the Hacienda Ballinas, Don Pedro Pinto along with one of his leaseholders and other allies went armed to the land of the offending party, the Monastery of Chicuasengo and Quatepec, destroyed some canals and the *toma*, and manhandled three monks who tried to block their way.[29] The Indians of Santa Ana Quatepec reacted in a similar fashion when the servants of the Hacienda La Sabana tried to return the course of irrigation waters to its previous state by removing the stones placed there by the village residents. When the servants did so, Santa Ana Quatepec residents would "come out tumultuously and in numerous bands" using their numbers to frighten the hacienda servants.[30] Essentially, most Indians and Spaniards used strength in numbers to counteract the abuse of control over water at an upstream location. Such demonstrations of force could not change geophysical realities, but could counteract, at least temporarily, the abuses of farmers upstream.

Indigenous groups who were not totally dependent on local hacendados used their capacity to intimidate quite effectively. In the town of Izúcar, the Spanish begrudgingly respected the Indian population because of its long history of rebelliousness. The indigenous popula-

tion of Izúcar rose up at least four times during the eighteenth century, but the rebellion of 1781 was particularly serious. The Audiencia dispatched troops from Mexico City to quell the insurrection,
but not before the Indians destroyed the Casas Reales, the Arca de
Tributos, and the Public Archives. The Indians also released prisoners
from the local jail. At least ninety-eight Indians including four women
were imprisoned, and fourteen died in the revolt. Soldiers killed a few
more during the pacification.[31] These events occurred while news of
the ravages caused by the indigenous army of Tupac Amaru II trickled
back from the viceroyalty of Peru where Indian challenges to Spanish
rule continued unchecked.

Because of the fear caused by the revolt in Peru and Izúcar's history of rebelliousness, the Indians there held some authority when
they acted. They could intimidate without actually engaging in an
uprising. In 1790, the new subdelegado of Izúcar, Don José Uriz y
Armendariz, decided to allot forty surcos of irrigation to the Ingenio
San Nicolás. As a result, both Spaniards and Indians were deprived
of necessary water. According to a letter written by Anastacio José
Benitez to the viceroy, the corresponding attitude of the Indians was
worrisome in the extreme. As he described it, they "turned their
backs [on the Spaniards] with arrogance, they did not remove their
hats, all these were signs that they were disposed to mount a campaign of resistance."[32] Don Crisostomo Zubia, owner of the Ingenio
Raboso, also described the nonremoval of hats, the body language,
and the insolent tone of the indigenous governor's speech, and con-
cluded that these signs indicated a dangerous lack of respect.[33] Lazaro
Josef Figueroa Yañez also predicted a rebellion.[34] Taylor emphasizes
the importance of the removal of hats as a gesture of deference to a
social superior. The omission of such courtesies was a highly charged
symbolic act which signified insubordination.[35] In this instance, there
was no need on the part of the Indians to actually engage in an insurrection, because the effect was the same.

The use of rebellious attitudes or actual insurrectionary tactics
could redress the balance of power in the countryside. The Indians
used their strength in numbers to coerce estate owners and were
sometimes successful in maintaining control of their access to irrigation, a resource vital to their survival. Spaniards also engaged in in-

timidation tactics, albeit typically through their servants (as discussed in the previous chapter). Nevertheless, actual physical confrontations were not a guaranteed method of securing resources.

The rebellion of the indigenous population of San Diego Chalma and respective barrios, located in Tehuacán jurisdiction near Tepapayeca, provides an example of the consequences of failure. In 1730, estate owner Bachiller Don Juan Berdejo, a cleric, complained that Chalma residents prevented him from irrigating his seedlings in the Tochapa region. In 1729, the Indians complained that Berdejo had attempted to usurp their control of four surcos which they had controlled "from time immemorial." The Indians did not wait for a judicial ruling. Whenever Berdejo attempted to shut off their supply of water to use it on his land, they arrived at the irrigation ditch with "algosura y tumulus." The Indians intimidated Berdejo and his workers so much that they deprived him of irrigation and he was unable to plant his fields.[36] Chalma residents seemed to have foiled Berdejo's plan to usurp their water and certain adjacent cropland. If the story ended here, the Indians' actions would be just one more example in a series of others.

On Monday, June 27, 1730, the Indians took their resistance one step further. At about 11:00 in the morning, they went to the lands of Guastla with stones, garrotes, and *coas* and destroyed the dam which directed water to the estate. Although it was not their turn nor time for water, the water was redirected to their village. Two hours later, Berdejo arrived accompanied by many Spaniards and ordered that the irrigation be returned to its normal setting. When the Indians refused, the *Teniente general* destroyed the dam the Indians had built.

Berdejo's group provides a rare example of Spaniards using their strength in numbers to counteract such a demonstration by the Indian village over water rights. The most common strategy was to order servants to serve as enforcers. The Spaniards' presence in this case might indicate how seriously the situation affected Berdejo and worried the other Spaniards. One witness stated that he did not see the Indians lose respect for the Teniente, nor did the Indians attempt to take away his ceremonial baton, nor did they try to drown him. But two witnesses described how the Spaniards beat the Indians with their swords from horseback, and forced them to flee.[37] The stakes must have indeed been high for such violence to occur.

A year later, officials described Calcagualco, one of the barrios involved, as depopulated. The Audiencia first ruled in favor of Berdejo
in 1732, and a Royal Edict in 1734 upheld the verdict. The remaining indigenous population continued to fight in the courts for their
water rights until 1735.[38] Although the many gaps in the documentation conceal the reasons why this struggle escalated from sabotage
and intimidation to a full-fledged confrontation, the fact that success
for Berdejo meant the depopulation of a community shows that the
Indians' rebellion was probably a last ditch effort to ensure survival.
The use of rebellion by Indians implied vulnerability in terms of control over water, but this tactic could help to redress the balance of
power in certain instances. When this strategy failed, however, clearly
the results could be disastrous.

PASSIVE RESISTANCE

Passive resistance, unlike active resistance, was of a more long-term
nature. Campaigns of passive resistance extended throughout the
year, and were often used by practitioners of active resistance between planting cycles, that is, during the interim between campaigns
of active resistance. The judicial system provided the most obvious
solution to remedy illegal appropriations of irrigation rights over the
long term. Both Spaniards and Indians regularly appealed to local
authorities and then, when dissatisfied, launched suits in the Audiencia. Spanish farmers used the court system more frequently, but the
differences between the two ethnic groups in this regard is really inconsequential. (See Table 5.) In ten instances, Indians also used the
Juzgado de Naturales, a court created specifically for their grievances.[39]
Many of these lawsuits continued for years if not for generations, and
often outlasted the original litigants. The judicial solution was extremely costly and also entailed many trips to Mexico City. The many
Poblanos—as individuals or corporate units—who engaged in these
lawsuits evidently believed that they were worthwhile. Retrospec-
tively, however, the outcomes of many such endeavors seem less than
satisfactory. Much of the documentation does not indicate a clear adjudication of resources; final verdicts were not often forthcoming and
compromise seemed to be the order of the day.

The Audiencia's lack of authority to enforce its decisions must
have been quite frustrating for the plaintiffs. In 1771, the villages

of Huilango, Huaquechula, and the town of Atlixco complained to the Audiencia that the mayordomo of the Hacienda Santa Catalina Esteban usurped their portion of the Guichital River. In record time, the Audiencia upheld their position almost immediately. No one, however, could force the Hacienda's mayordomo to accede to the court's decision until the critical period for irrigating seedlings had passed. The crops of the estate were thus relatively safe, and the villages' fields were barren.[40] This type of situation made the strategy of combined active and passive resistance much more effective and practical. For example, when the villages of Necoxtla and San Matheo along with other indigenous villages and Spanish farmers failed to block the water rights grant to Hernan Pérez de Neyra, the indigenous population began to rent, sell, and stockpile its water causing Pérez de Neyra to appeal to the Audiencia once more for an injunction.[41] In reality, dual strategies of active and passive tactics were quite common.[42] As suggested previously, such a blend of active and passive resistance was probably most effective because it combined a recognized and authorized manner of resistance with one that, although not strictly legal, was much more practical.

Farmers also used the judicial system to shore up the defense of communities and to try to prevent further usurpations. Both Indians and Spaniards sued as a means of preempting plans that would be detrimental to their access to water, or to reassert jeopardized legal rights in order to forestall future, unspecified attempts at appropriation.[43] The first strategy included legal objections to the planned construction of new dams, diversion of water to other areas, and new allocations of irrigation rights. These attempts reveal an understanding that it was more onerous to fight a *fait accompli*. The second strategy had the same defensive objective, but lacked a specific target. In many instances, the plaintiffs were trying to prevent the creation of a servidumbre. In addition to simple requests to bolster formal water rights through composition on the part of Spanish and Indians, villages often turned to the courts to enforce rental contracts even if they were of little financial value.[44] Failure to enforce rental contracts, of course, was an invitation to the assertion of squatter's rights.

On two occasions, the village of Chietla, in particular, attempted to compel Spanish residents to comply with their contractual obligations to clean irrigation ditches. The indigenous officials openly stated that they hoped to prevent the creation of a servidumbre resulting from the Spaniards' long-term noncompliance.[45] The Spaniards probably found cleaning duties not only onerous but humiliating since it entailed submission to people they considered their social inferiors. Legal inventiveness allowed the Chietla residents to use the judicial system not just as a means to seek redress after the fact, but to shore up the defense of communal resources. Such passive means of resistance were extremely important, although less dramatic, because they could prevent difficulties.

Other forms of passive resistance existed, which defied those who tried to monopolize water in subtle manners and could be exerted in any season. Both overt noncollaboration and acts of malfeasance on the part of indigenous communities could, in the context of a larger struggle to retain resources, serve as a means to pressure either Audiencia officials or Iberian landholders to respect rights otherwise easily flaunted. In two instances, indigenous groups pressured judicial authorities to restore their water rights by threatening nonpayment of tributes or *obenciones*.[46] In both instances the Indians triumphed, and such victories were not so common as to be dismissed lightly.

Refusal to make customary payments was also used in a more direct fashion by the residents of Huaquechula. When the monastery of San Francisco de Aguella claimed an additional *naranja* of water in 1804, the Indians argued that these were "imaginary rights" lacking any documentary confirmation. Nonetheless, the subdelegado of Atlixco ruled in favor of the monastery. In February 1805, the residents of Huaquechula declared a blockade against the monks; they refused to attend mass or to pay for the "dotaciones, hermandades, fiestas" and other dues which they typically contributed toward the monastery's subsistence.[47] In addition to these economic sanctions, the residents intimidated the clerics so much by their hardly concealed hostility that the monks sought external assistance.

Within the category of passive resistance, a steady encroachment onto the property of neighboring estates was slightly more aggressive, but did not entail direct, immediate access to water.[48] Villages often took advantage of vacant haciendas to encroach on land and water.[49] The communities of Tlapanala, Tepapayeca, Quatepec, Quespala, and Calmectitlán took over some land owned by Don Pedro Pinto's abandoned estate, and also began using the water from a spring called "la sequia jonda." They asserted that Pinto had previously usurped the communities' rights to three surcos from the spring. Pinto's estate was abandoned for many years, and surrounding Spaniards also encroached on estate land and water. The Inquisition eventually took over the estate because of Pinto's debts. The new owners reinstated the indigenous communities' water rights, and in April 1760 the villages celebrated an "act of possession." In 1761, as the Inquisition prepared to sell the estate, the tide turned; when commissioners arrived to inspect and measure the water on January 3, 1761, the "insolent" Indians "formed a tumult" against them.[50] Once again, the combination of several tactics was the most successful for the retention of resources, and thus, continued survival. Like the legal challenges, non-collaboration and acts of malfeasance were forms of passive resistance which strengthened the defense of farmers all year round. If these methods were successful, the farmers who used them did not need to resort to more active means of opposition at planting season. A combination of passive and active forms of resistance was also particularly effective in the struggle to maintain control over irrigation.

Passive resistance was not as dramatic nor as effective as active methods. Lawsuits were usually slow. Even when the Audiencia reached a decision rapidly, its reach was limited. Audiencia officials often could not enforce their verdicts until the crucial period of planting had passed. Legal challenges were not effective over the short term, but over the long term they were important. Without a legal claim and therefore a challenge to a usurpation, the altered arrangement could become regularized through *servidumbre*. Therefore, legal tactics such as lawsuits and other attempts to block grants or enforce rental contracts were vital in the long term. Other methods such as malfeasance and boycotts were also not effective in gaining immediate access to water, but they did weaken the resolve of those who were usurping water. Passive resistance was inscribed in a longer cycle of years, whereas active resistance was located temporally in the cycle of seasons and planting. Yet, both were important and interdependent and for this reason, farmers easily moved from one strategy to another.

RESISTANCE AND SURVIVAL

Poblanos were ingenious in their methods of resisting encroachments of their resources and in the eighteenth century, when the agrarian economy was expanding, their inventiveness was necessary. Resistance—both active and passive—was essential to the survival of indigenous towns and to Spanish estates as economically viable units. Some villages were less successful in their struggle and became *despoblado,*[51] or were transformed into appendages of haciendas who provided them with access to water as a good will gesture.[52]

The stakes in this struggle were high in many cases, and the consequences for Indian villages who could not or did not resist usurpation were dire, ranging from a rapid deterioration of the communal economy to the complete subjugation of a village to a hacendado. For the estate owner, such a failure meant economic hardship, debt, and finally, bankruptcy. Indians and Iberians committed acts of resistance in the face of intimidation and retaliation. Only the owners of particularly powerful and wealthy estates could shield themselves, at least partially, through their servants. Powerful estate owners could compensate for lack of numbers with their servants as well as the collusion of judicial officials to jail "troublemakers," and other acts of intimidation. The resistance of Poblano Indians should be understood in the light of the violence that they could expect from estate servants, neighboring communities, or the authorities. In the context of an agrarian economy in flux, their resistance was all the more important and the consequences of failure all the more critical. Yet, the most dramatic resistance to encroachment of water resources often signified a position of weakness and a losing battle. How long could communities or individuals continue to riot or to pay Mexico City lawyers to sue neighbors? In fact, the least spectacular methods of resistance were probably the most effective in the long term, and individuals and communities who do not appear in the archives were likely the most resistant and successful in retaining water rights.

***

Active and passive resistance were two strategies that Poblano farmers used depending on the season and their geographic location. Farmers used active resistance to save their crops when people upstream usurped water. They broke dams, conduits, and irrigation ditches; they placed stones in the course of water to divert it higher upstream; and they rioted. None of these methods was legal, but those who engaged in active resistance did so because they knew that recourse to the courts was slow, ineffective, and unlikely to save their crops. Passive resistance was a strategy used over the long term. Although less dramatic and immediate, it was important nonetheless. While farmers used active resistance to save the plants they had in the ground, they used passive resistance with future crops in mind. Legal action could block future problems, ensure that *servidumbre* rights did not become a reality, and finally, could give farmers a legal basis to defend themselves when they acted outside the law in active resistance. The two methods were, in fact, interdependent. Passive resistance could not save crops immediately, but it ensured a long-term preservation of legal water rights.

In the face of increasing incidents of water usurpation and the pressures of a growing population and a reduction in available irrigation, Poblano farmers had to try to maintain an adequate level of resources or give up farming. They were caught in the processes that, according to the model, should have led to a centralized irrigation system. The upsurge in conflicts over water rights was, according to the Hunts, the reason for a communal demand for a bureaucracy to govern water usage and alleviate the tensions surrounding irrigation and farming. Yet, Poblano farmers did not favor bureaucratic solutions. Instead of asking for bureaucrats, they took matters into their own hands using active or passive resistance. Only passive resistance implied the involvement of bureaucrats, although the Audiencia was a distant and ineffective force and hardly an example of the centralized water bureaucracy the Hunts envision. Although sugar planters in Izúcar did move to a centralized irrigation system at the beginning of the nineteenth century, they did not do so result of a communal accord nor were their actions an attempt to impose peace. The reaction of Poblano farmers to being deprived of water was much more visceral—they broke dams, they boycotted, they rioted—and only afterwards did they seek approval from bureaucrats.

SEVEN

Urban Survival and Water

Rural society revolved around the demands of farming, the timing of sowing and irrigation, the needs of growing plants and then, finally, the hope for a plentiful harvest. Poblano farmers—whether Spanish or Indian—shared these aspirations and constraints even if they approached farming in different manners and planted on different scales. But these farmers, particularly the indigenous population, usually lived grouped together in small villages or towns. Their existence was rooted in the community and their fortunes were intermingled with those of their neighbors. These small communities depended upon agriculture and they were also never greatly separated from their crops. Urban limits did not stop the intrusion of commercial plantings and even in Puebla de los Angeles, the metropolis of the region, individuals used their gardens to raise crops. Water shortages meant many things to these small farming communities: lack of food, inability to pay tributes, disruption of everyday life, and in extreme cases, crisis and depopulation.

The intimate connection between these rural communities and access to water was manifested on an internal/external axis[1] but also within the village limits themselves. The problems faced by these communities were the consequences of trends discussed in the previous chapters: reduction in water supplies, theft of irrigation, and unsuccessful resistance to appropriations. Essentially, their difficulties were an extension of the struggle over water that was occurring in the countryside but one which affected them in their homes. This chapter examines the effects of water shortages on the small towns in the Poblano countryside.

RURAL/URBAN CONTINUITIES

No strict boundaries existed between the rural and the urban in colonial Puebla. Even when many village residents worked land outside the town limits, others farmed in *solares* or urban gardens, and still others worked orchards adjacent to their homes. Urban planting may

127

have been an extension or an addition to other crops but, by the eighteenth century, these plots became central to the survival of towns whose populations had lost cropland. The town of Chietla is a good example of the importance of farming within town boundaries and how community members responded to water shortages. Located in the *tierra caliente* jurisdiction of Izúcar, Chietla was a very small village surrounded by hills on all sides but the west. At the end of the eighteenth century, it was composed of only three streets and had a population of 2,037. In 1792, Indian residents, the church, and some *cofradías* maintained about 500 orchards within the village proper. According to Ignacio Maneyra, the groves formed "a delicious thicket of fruit trees that are so dense that their shade rather than a vice can be called glory of the earth."[2] The residents grew the fruits mamey and zapote as well as a great quantity of dates that they sold in Puebla de los Angeles and Mexico City. Accounts regarding water supplies were contradictory. Official descriptions indicated that in 1792 water from the Izúcar river, into which the Agueguello and the Tilapa rivers emptied nearby, was still abundant.[3] However, in 1703 the residents noted a decrease in the level of the river.[4] Since the late seventeenth century, the Indians had progressively lost control of their irrigation to local sugar estates and a wheat flour mill. Already in 1705 community residents complained that because their orchards' yields had declined due to a water shortage, they were unable to pay their tributes.[5] In 1725, Chietla inhabitants complained that their *cacique* had sold both their communal lands and their irrigation rights.[6] Chietla officials petitioned for redress and access to irrigation for their orchards again in 1736 and 1808 when they specified that they cultivated bananas and mameys.[7] The Indians of Chietla did not mention fields outside the boundaries of their community in the documentation on irrigation; their orchards were their primary concern in terms of water and seem to have been their major source of income. For Chietla residents, the fruit trees surrounding them in their household compounds and daily lives were their livelihood. Problems of inadequate water affected them quite directly within the boundaries of the community because their farming was urban.

Other communities also farmed within their boundaries although they were not always dependent on fruit trees. The residents of Tochimilco, as discussed in the previous chapter, used lots inside the

Fig. 11. Convent Church in Tochimilco
The atrium of the Tochimilco church held a healthy crop of beans in the summer
of 1988.
(Photo by Sonya Lipsett-Rivera)

town to grow wheat. In the 1980s, the people of Tochimilco still
farmed within the town limits; avocado trees could be seen peeking
out over the high stone walls surrounding homes, and a very healthy
crop of beans was found in the atrium in front of the church. (See
Fig. 11.)

In Puebla de los Angeles, inspections in 1702 turned up many illegal reservoirs that residents used for their gardens.[8] The problem
of water appropriation for gardens was not resolved. In 1808, Don
Sebastián de Ochoa de Echagueu protested that he had not received
any of the water granted to him for six years because his neighbor,

Doctor Don José Suárez, used all available water in his garden, especially in the dry season.[9] In 1809 Don Joseph Ponze complained that
he lacked water because Don Pedro de la Rosa depleted it to irrigate
his wheat.[10]

An eighteenth-century map of Puebla de los Angeles clearly shows
the presence of cultivated fields on the edges of the city. (See Fig. 12.)
Farming was also close to the barrios of Puebla. Such proximity between farms and city residents caused problems for Doña Leocadia
Gertrudis Ramírez and Don Nicolás de Toledo when, in 1762 and
1765, residents of the Santiago barrios blocked the water intakes
for their farms.[11] The residents of various communities, whether
small like Chietla and Tochimilco or imposing such as Puebla de los
Angeles, farmed where they could, and lack of irrigation in fields outside the city limits or in gardens and orchards meant a crisis of subsistence. But water deprivation, as discussed previously, depended to
a great extent on hydrology and geographical location. Thus, if a town
like Chietla was vulnerable to usurpation, others such as Tochimilco
were less so. Therefore, the strategy of in-town gardens worked well
for the latter but not for the former. Some villages and towns were
susceptible to the appropriation of water by farmers upstream, while
others were the bane of farmers downstream.

As indigenous communities lost their lands or were relegated to
marginal fields, urban planting became more important. But farming within village boundaries did not mean an escape from the problems faced by those who cultivated fields in the countryside. When
streams, rivers, or aqueducts no longer carried sufficient water, urban
plots suffered and so did the community. Urban farmers depended no
less upon the vagaries of hydrology, and hoped that farmers upstream
did not abuse their irrigation rights. The division between urban and
rural, however, was not clearly delineated in activities nor in the fate
of communities because their fortunes were very much connected.

EXTERNAL CAUSES OF WATER SHORTAGES

When farmers appropriated water, even further up the course of waterways, they affected both the crops of Spaniards and Indians and
the towns in which they lived. Stopping such abuses was difficult
for farmers in the hinterland as well as their urban counterparts. Although a few Poblano towns were large enough that they suffered

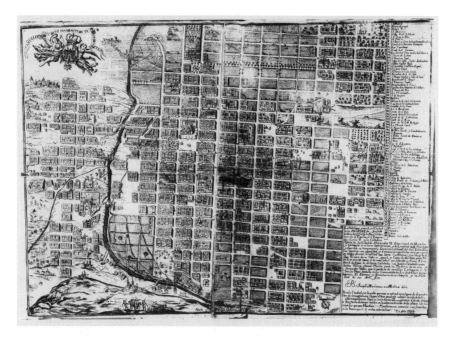

Fig. 12. Colonial Map of Puebla de los Angeles
Plots of land dedicated to farming are on the edges of the city. Some are located next to the Almoloya river, but many others are not.
(Archivo General de la Nación, Mexico City, Tierras section, vol. 2673, exp. 1, fol. 29, 1754, by José Mariano de Medina)

internal problems of water allocation, most shortages occurred on an internal/external axis. In other words, either villages consumed too much water and deprived others downstream or farmers upstream usurped water and affected a community further down. In essence, because the culprits were external, control over their movements was difficult. In legal terms, town councils had broad jurisdiction which went beyond urban boundaries, but as discussed below, community leaders found that they did not possess the power to impose their authority. Despite knowing quite clearly who was responsible for their water shortages, village officials frequently could not prevent nor even stop such abuses.

Small villages were not the only victims of external water theft. In 1764, the Convent of Santa Clara, as the owner of the Hacienda Tlaytec, complained that it no longer received its allotted four *surcos* of water from the Atoyac river because of the condition of the canal, but mostly because the village of Tetela stole water.[12] The village of Santa María Coyoaco (San Juan de los Llanos jurisdiction), on the other hand, suffered because the employees of the Hacienda Amajaque broke the village's conduits and used all the water on the estate's fields and to water its livestock. The entire village, Indians and others, were feeling the effects of the lack of water.[13] These problems of usurpation support the image of a system in which authority over water distribution was not enforced and the external problems of villages were beyond their reach and scope of action.

For both village residents and those operating outside the villages, water shortage problems highlighted the questions of jurisdiction and enforcement. As seen in previous chapters, by the eighteenth century, Poblanos had a precise idea of the quantity of water to which they held rights, but without representation by a central authority on location, power devolved upon the individual or persons who could wield it. Thus, in these contentious times, water rights rarely equated to actual access to the resource.

The officials of the town of Cholula found the contradictory relationship between rights and usage particularly frustrating. A major urban center and site of religious significance before the Spanish conquest, during the colonial period Cholula was situated in the heart of a prime wheat production area. Its location seems to have been the root of its water problems. The town residents had used water coming down the Sierra Nevada since at least 1537 and were given formal rights to do so in 1543. In 1593, Juan de Pineda wrote a series of reports to the Spanish crown, and Cholula was one of his subjects. He waxed eloquent on many aspects of the town and the surrounding region but with one reservation. According to de Pineda, the town lacked an adequate water supply, highlighted by the fact that Spanish and Indian residents were limited to drinking from a basin "in which if water is present one day, for three it does not come." Pineda believed that the solution to this deficiency was simple: build a proper aqueduct and construct an elegant fountain in the main square which "would adorn it properly."[14] No doubt such urban landmarks would beautify any community, but if it was indeed built, its frequent barrenness must have simply reminded the townspeople of their impotence.

Because of Cholula's regular water shortages, the Audiencia reiterated the community's water rights in 1646, 1669, and 1714. On this last occasion, the *oidores* added the threat of a fine of 500 pesos imposed on anyone who impeded the free flow of water to Cholula.[15] As elsewhere, however, these governmental decrees were relatively toothless. Cholula's authority over water matters, even strengthened by Audiencia decrees, was not sufficient to protect its residents from water shortages.

The officials of Cholula had the same problems experienced by many other Poblano communities: farmers irrigated their wheat by breaking the canals which brought water to the town. The Hacienda Buenavista, owned by the Augustine monastery, was a major culprit.[16] The officials of Cholula dealt with these difficulties in timeworn ways: inspection and prosecution, appeal to the Audiencia, and probably a lot of hand wringing.

But one aspect of Cholula's problem was unusual and highlights one of the difficulties in a decentralized water system. According to Cholula's officials, many of the people responsible for the usurpation of the town's water lived outside Cholula's jurisdiction—usually in the rich wheat-producing districts. The river network connected jurisdictions and did not respect political boundaries. Spanish law, however, did not make allowances for expanded jurisdiction to correct water usage abuses occurring upstream in another political jurisdiction. In 1704, to correct their lack of authority, Cholula officials complained in the *Juzgado de Naturales* and asked for additional authority to prosecute farmers who usurped their water even if they did so in another jurisdiction. Apparently, the farmers of Atlixco, one of the major wheat producing areas in Puebla, regularly took excess irrigation and left Cholula without a drop.[17]

Cross-jurisdictional blame for water shortages was not limited to Cholula. The village of San Gregorio Xacapexico in the same jurisdiction also complained that farmers outside the jurisdiction broke water conduits to irrigate their wheat and *chilares;* orders to the contrary from any level of government were ineffective.[18] The village of Huejotzingo requested a Royal Provision in 1742 to prevent farmers upstream from impeding the course of water.[19] The administrator of the Ingenio San Nicolás in Izúcar blamed farmers in the Atlixco jurisdiction for using too much irrigation and thus reducing the water supply for the *ingenio's* fields as well as the town.[20] Spanish law provided town councils a broad jurisdiction within the surrounding countryside but did not make allowances for hydraulic systems. The people of Cholula clearly understood the root of their water shortages but also appreciated that a reinforced authority was the only means to resolve the situation to their satisfaction. Yet, within this decentralized system, no such solution was forthcoming.

Because the water shortages affecting rural communities at times originated outside their immediate surroundings and may have occurred at quite a distance from their political jurisdiction, their authority was hollow. In theory the Audiencia had political jurisdiction which superseded these limitations and it could have imposed an equitable allocation of water. Yet, as seen in previous chapters, the Audiencia's power to enforce settlements was negligible and its speed in resolving disputes was appallingly slow. The solution to water rights problems facing many rural Poblano communities could only come from a political body that had authority across jurisdictional boundaries and the power to enforce its decisions. In essence, Poblano communities needed a centralized irrigation system. But, in the eighteenth century, the victims of water shortages did not clamor for the creation of such a bureaucracy.

EFFECTS OF WATER SHORTAGES

The internal problems of rural communities caused by the external appropriation of water were frequently quite serious. In the case of

Cholula, the diversion of streams meant that when the rainy season ended and the normal sources of water were dry, the wells were brackish and foul, and obtaining water for normal everyday chores and necessities meant that residents had to walk three-quarters of a league to the nearest available source.[21] Their situation was by no means unique. In fact many Poblano communities had similar complaints about the lack of drinking water.[22]

Internal water shortages caused a host of problems. What remained of the water was usually stagnant and contaminated and thus officials believed that it caused disease. In 1799 the flow of water to Cholula ceased for twenty-four days; their remaining supplies were fetid "from which the whole city could be infected and thus depopulated."[23] Water shortages occurring at the same time as food shortages because of crop failure constituted a recipe for disaster. An example is a crisis described by the town council of Santa María Toxtepec (Tecali jurisdiction) in 1800. Originally, the town had access to a stream that passed through a nearby ravine, but the owners of the Rancho Tepalcatepeque successfully took control of it. The village then built a conduit across the *monte* to secure water for the community. But Don Francisco Gómez responded by building a dam at a higher elevation and thereby obtained most of the water. By the end of the eighteenth century, the villagers' crops languished; the residents went hungry and suffered various afflictions.[24]

During the wheat irrigation period, the flow of water to the village of San Gregorio Xacapesico (Cholula jurisdiction) would suddenly be reduced to a trickle for up to twenty-four days. Officials protested that these mere drops were fetid and could cause illness.[25] The understanding of the relationship between sickness and contaminated or polluted water should not be equated with a contemporary equivalent. Scientists recognized waterborne bacterium in the early twentieth century. However, in the late eighteenth century, people associated stagnant, poor quality water, as well as garbage, with disease because of the "miasmas" they were thought to engender.[26] The residents and officials of Poblano communities understood that stagnant, stale water was not healthy, not only because of miasmas, but also because it signified food shortages resulting from inadequate irrigation and a plethora of other problems.

In most Poblano villages, farming families kept livestock, such as cattle, pigs, sheep, and even goats. These animals might simply supplement farmers' incomes and/or diets, but in some areas, they formed an important part of the community's livelihood. When streams ran low, water was scarce not only for humans but also for their animals, and livestock often played the role of scapegoat.[27] For example, in 1708 lack of sufficient water in town forced the residents of San Andrés Chalchicomula to take their livestock to drink at a source about a league away because pigs had broken water conduits while drinking.[28] In 1723, officials of the same community reported that not only was the human population lacking sufficient water but their cattle went thirsty. They blamed the *haciendas* upstream whose cattle broke the conduits that carried water to the town.[29] By 1763, the authorities had progressed from grievance to action; owners of mule pairs watered in town were charged two reales every time the animals drank.[30]

Santiago Teutlan town officials also complained in 1732 that they had no water for people, plants, and livestock. A well was excavated to ensure that village residents' cattle could drink, but the well occasionally ran dry.[31] In a conflict between the residents of Aguatepeque and an estate administrator, the latter cut off the town's traditional access to water from the barranca Tesaguapan where residents watered their livestock. The administrator demanded money every time a mule drank from the barranca, and confiscated the animals of those who could not pay.[32] These problems occurred during times of normal rainfall; if such usurpations continued in periods of drought, the results could be disastrous. In 1711, Don Martín Calvo, the owner of the Ingenio San Nicolás Tolentino, reported the loss of 500 head of cattle, 120 mules, and 250 horses because of a combination of conflicts over irrigation and drought.[33] The lack of water for animals was simply another aggravation for most residents if they were themselves facing a crisis of subsistence. It was another manner in which communities found that their survival was compromised by the prospect of dry wells and aqueducts.

Water shortages caused the failure of crops, sickness, and parched animals. These problems compounded the difficulties many communities were undergoing in the eighteenth century in their attempts to survive as viable entities. The extent of such hardship is difficult to assess. Spokespersons for some villages, such as Ahuehuezingo, stated that they could not pay tributes or other levies because of the associated difficulties caused by the lack of water.[34] Although such declarations may have been made for dramatic effect, the very real effect of such changes upon communities became evident when they began to disintegrate. In 1798, Tototepeque village officials warned that if water was not restored to them, their community would be destroyed.[35] Necoxtla's leaders also warned of grave consequences for the town if their water was not restored.[36] When Huaquechula deprived it of water, Santiago Teutlan brought up the specter of depopulation.[37] As seen in previous chapters, a few villages simply ceased to exist after being depopulated as residents left for greener pastures. Other, more fortunate villages lost many residents to emigration, but managed to survive as viable communities. Several villages complained that they were losing young folk and linked the pattern of migration to water shortages.[38] The loss of population in eighteenth-century Poblano villages was part of a larger trend described by other scholars.[39]

The diversion of streams to fields above Poblano villages upset these communities in many ways but water shortages also unbalanced the patterns of daily life. When water no longer flowed into the central fountain, livestock could be driven to another supply source, but the domestic tasks involved with running households were not so mobile. Thus the arduous task of fetching water usually fell to the daughters—*doncellas* or maidens—who went to nearby ravines or other sources to carry water to the household. The image of women fetching water is not uncommon even in many contemporary societies, and thus although it may be drudgery, it may not seem a catastrophe. It was, however, a major concern for many Poblano communities because the young women who left the confines of the village to fetch water in the countryside were sometimes seduced, raped, or assaulted.[40] The village officials who complained to the Audiencia presented the fetching of water outside urban limits as a problem with moral dimensions. The officials of San Rafael and associated villages (Huejotzingo jurisdiction), for example, noted that they no longer had drinking water or water for cooking and cleaning in their homes. Consequently, they had to walk at least a quarter league, and on the way cross deep ravines. As a result, young maidens' "honesty was endangered in the depth and roughness of the ravines" where "they were sacrificed to the licenses and desires of many cattle drovers who watered their animals there and many types who come and go in these parts."[41] Women were indeed vulnerable to attack when they left the comparative security of the village not only to fetch water but also when they worked in *milpas*, gathered edibles, or traveled. Indian officials expressed their concern over water shortages inside the villages through the example of attacks on their daughters and wives in part because it was an exemplary demonstration of the way in which water shortages forced community life out of balance. These women were attacked because inadequate water forced them to leave the security of the village.

Preconquest Nahuas defined peripheral, external space as dangerous, in contrast to the center. Persons, such as prostitutes, who moved into and out of the center transgressed community standards.[42] These metaphors of center and periphery/moral and immoral are still used by the contemporary Poblano communities studied by James Taggart.[43] Water shortages in the villages forced young women to leave the internal moral space and travel through dangerous areas; it forced them to transgress codes of safety and expose themselves to danger. The plight of young women who were attacked or seduced at the side of streams was real. However, its evocation by community leaders was not only a protest against water shortages and corresponding dangers faced by women, but also a metaphor for the disequilibrium the water shortages caused the community. Their use of this symbol—attacks on the virtue of *doncellas*—was perhaps the most eloquent manner in which these communities could portray the distress these shortages caused their members.

When the fountain in the village square was dry, wells contained only foul, brackish water, and aqueducts were empty, the effects upon towns were extensive. Poor quality water was not only distasteful, it was associated with disease (even if for the wrong reasons). Livestock and humans needed water to survive. Water shortages constituted attacks on rural communities' livelihoods, and resulted in an inability to pay dues and taxes, as well as an incentive for young men and women to leave for greener pastures. Fundamentally, however, water shortages unbalanced daily life in rural communities and made their survival as viable entities a much more difficult enterprise.

INTERNAL COMPETITION FOR WATER

Contention over water and its attendant problems did not occur only on the internal/external axis described previously, although such situations were indeed most frequent in the documentation. Within a large city like Puebla de los Angeles, the water allocation system was quite extensive and complex. Drinking water was channeled directly into many homes and public buildings, which created a two-tier system of allocation along class lines. Access to water was not guaranteed for any user, and there were many breakdowns of the system.[44] But even in smaller towns, such as Izúcar and Tehuacán, internal complications existed, albeit they were not as common as in Puebla de los Angeles.

The smaller towns of the Poblano countryside also had various barrios, all with claims on water. In comparison to Puebla de los Angeles, the data for small towns do not provide much detail are not nearly as voluminous, although they are intriguing. In 1716, for example, the alcalde mayor of Chietla reported that the Indians of an unnamed barrio were not receiving the water allotted to them. The water shortage led to the usual problems, including dried out plants. Barrio residents launched an *alboroto* and a *tumulto* which led to imprisonment of the Indian Diego Melchor for rebellion and mistreatment in words and action of the Indian Nicolás de Castillo. Because Melchor did not contribute money from his *derrames* (unused water that was often sold to another party), his recalcitrance provoked the ire of others in the community.[45]

In Izúcar several barrios issued formal complaints. In 1787, the barrios of Izúcar along with the Ingenio Raboso accused the Santiago Miahuacán barrio of abusing its position as first on the irrigation ditch by taking more than its allotted share of water and using it on its seedlings.[46] Ten years later, Indians residing in Santiago stated that the water no longer reached them. For 150 years, they held rights to six surcos from the Rio Grande called "de Izúcar," which passed through haciendas in the Atlixco valley and then ingenio land in the Izúcar jurisdiction. The Santiago barrio population at this time totaled 200 families or more than 500 individuals who held various plots of land, including *solares*. With the crops raised on this land they paid for tributes and church upkeep. Initially, the barrio's lawyer, Don Bartolomé Díaz Borrego, reported the Indians' charge that outlying farms were retaining the irrigation water in reservoirs rather than returning it to the river, thereby causing the shortages experienced by barrio residents. But it was later discovered that the problem was a *caja ladrón* or rogue dam much closer to the barrio. Barrio residents were able to thwart this usurpation of their water with a new canal.[47]

In 1792, Don Francisco Iraeta inspected and regulated the usage of the Atoyac river. His work included examination of the water intakes of the various neighborhoods in Izúcar. Iraeta ordered the closing of the *contraacequias* in all areas except the lower barrio. Later the owner of the Ingenio San Nicolás protested that the new arrangement allowed residents of these neighborhoods unrestricted access to water. In brief, smaller quantities of water were available to the ingenio.[48]

Finally, Indian residents of Santa María Tlalteca (Izúcar jurisdiction) protested in 1721 that a mere twenty-five couples residing in the nearby San Martín barrio had usurped the three surcos of water allotted to Santa María.[49] What this and the previous two examples indicate is that like larger urban centers such as Puebla de los Angeles, the barrios of smaller towns had identities separate from the town as water users. They were willing to rebel to protest water shortages; they aggressively appropriated resources as dictated by their interests; and they suffered as a community if their sources dried up. Different groups competed for water within the same urban jurisdiction (town and barrios).

The internal difficulties of smaller towns were not only at the neighborhood level; in some cases, individuals fought for access to resources. Many people broke pipes or diverted running water which passed by their homes, and sometimes stored it in reservoirs. Such informal retention of resources was not always appreciated by households downstream and officials responsible for regulating the flow. In San Andrés Chalchicomula a 1708 grant specified that water should not be diverted to individual homes.[50] The ban was not permanent, however; by 1745 individuals were requesting private access to domestic water.[51]

Nevertheless, in many villages and towns, in-house water was a perk for some households. Few squabbles over this privilege are documented for towns or villages, although in Puebla de los Angeles they were quite common. In the village of Santo Domingo Izúcar, the alcalde mayor Don Miguel Raboso used his position to usurp the community's water, leaving the village and its seven barrios bereft.[52] Private squabbling of a more individualistic and personal nature occurred over in-house water in small communities. In Tehuacán in 1784, Don Isidoro de Arizaga bought a house in the San Lazaro barrio. The house had received running water for over forty years. The canalization of water first passed through a house belonging to Licenciado Don Luis Murguis. All was fine until Don José Mariano de Castro purchased the Murguis house and hired a carpenter to block the passage of the water, thereby leaving Arizapa without a drop.[53] Of course, water was most probably available to the Arizapa household at the communal fountain or elsewhere, but there was also an element of prestige to having running water in one's home. It meant that the female members of the household would not be forced to leave the safety and modesty of the home in order to travel the streets to fetch water.[54] The element of personal or familial prestige associated with in-house water gives the conflict between Arizapa and Castro undertones of personal enmity, but unfortunately such information as well as any final official determinations do not exist. The story of the Arizapa household's loss of running water is, of course, but one example. In comparison to the extensive similar documentation available for Puebla de los Angeles, it is a tantalizing glimpse at some of the internal workings of smaller towns. Alongside the information on Puebla de los Angeles, it pales in comparison but does indicate a similar pattern: a movement toward privatization of water rights and internal conflict over water rights.

Resources controlled by indigenous communities were generally understood to be communal resources divided among the residents. The community fought together for retention and preservation of their irrigation and they generally showed a common front to the outside world. But, as discussed in chapter five, divisions did exist within Indian communities. Some officials and caciques betrayed the trust of their villages and sold off or appropriated communal resources.

Another type of conflict was manifest in Izúcar, where individual Indians fought for private rights to water within urban limits. Bernardino José, an Indian resident of the San Bernardino barrio, inherited land which he used as a fruit orchard. He later added land in the Asumpción barrio to his inheritance. Bernardino José needed water for his orchard and he believed that, as a native of the town, access to water was his birthright. His cousin Antonio Chimboro, however, prevented the flow of irrigation water to his land. In turn,

Chimboro claimed that it was Bernardino José who had impeded the flow of water, and that Bernardino's claim to the land was false. The tensions between the two seem to have been rooted in family squabbles over inheritance, but they also raised the issue of individual rights of access to communal resources. In the end, the *subdelegado* ruled in favor of Bernardino José,[55] but this case is instructive in that it shows a trend toward a sense of private ownership of water rights within indigenous society. The conflict between Bernardino José and his cousin points to a movement away from communal values regarding water rights to a privatized concept. Bernardino José used the rhetoric of communal rights inherent to a native of the town. In his private conflict with an individual, however, he appealed to the subdelegado rather than indigenous officials. Bernardino José's actions show that privatization of water rights was replacing the communal nature of control over water in indigenous communities.

Another similar case, also from Izúcar, reinforces the impression that water rights were being privatized. Alexandro Josef Coyote, an Indian of the Santa María Magdalena barrio, inherited a house and *solar* from his father. Before his death Coyote's father introduced running water into the property and had reached an arrangement with his neighbors Nicolás Ordás de Amarilla and Manuel Sánchez, who ran a tannery, to receive water from the same canal. In 1801, the tanners began to cause difficulties for Coyote. They attempted to impede his access to the water he used to irrigate the wheat planted in his *solar*. Tensions mounted when the tanners sent a boy into the *solar* to trample the wheat, thereby destroying the harvest. Arguments flew back and forth over the ownership of irrigation rights. Among other things, the tanners asserted that they held rights by virtue of *servidumbre*, or the historical nature of their water reservoirs, rather than written documentation. The subdelegado ruled in favor of Coyote.[56] In this instance, an Indian defended his private water rights against Spaniards rather than other Indians, and he did not appeal to the community for assistance. In fact, he ably defended himself and he did so on the basis of private rights through antiquity of possession to water within the town.

These examples of private conflicts over urban water rights would be lost in the documentation for Puebla de los Angeles, but stand out in Tehuacán and Izúcar. Do they have a particular significance in the small countryside village that they would not in the large center? They point to an ethos of water rights which was at odds with the traditional indigenous philosophy of resource distribution. They also show a strategy of individual defense of rights unmediated by the community. Water rights were becoming private matters and their protection was also a personal concern. Furthermore, the impression of privatization of water rights lends itself to the notion of a breakdown of the traditional alliances among Indians. Chapter five discussed the complaints of many Indians that their caciques and officials had sold the community's resources—land or water—and pocketed the income. Coupled with this type of betrayal, the self-reliance of Bernardino José and Alexandro Josef Coyote makes more sense.

Complaints by residents of the village of Quautlazingo (Cholula jurisdiction) also fall into this category. In 1718 they protested that they carried the burden of cleaning the irrigation system without assistance or adequate compensation, and without sufficient access to the water carried in the ditches they cleaned.[57] The annual repair and cleaning of ditches was a responsibility communities shared to ensure that their irrigation network functioned properly. Without such maintenance, ditches caved in, conduits silted up, and water did not flow freely. When one group felt that the annual chore was unfair and insufficiently rewarded, it meant a breakdown of the notion that irrigation was a community privilege and therefore maintenance of the ditches was everyone's responsibility. When Quautlazingo complained about their cleanup duties, they presented themselves as outside the communal values pertaining to irrigation. All these elements indicate a deterioration of the communal ties that united the indigenous community. These communal values became weaker in the wake of structural changes in the Poblano countryside, but as solidarity declined, so too did the community's viability and chances for survival at the end of the eighteenth century.

Apart from rivalry between individuals, struggles over water rights also occurred between farmers and enterprises. The countryside was primarily agrarian, but as seen in chapter four some processing of harvests occurred *in situ*. Rural towns were a hub in regional commerce networks and the location of preliminary transformation of agricultural products into manufactured goods. Wheat mills were the most common type of agricultural industry. According to various reports and official descriptions, most agricultural towns in the Poblano countryside had at least one mill.[58] Because these mills were typically powered by running water, mill operators sometimes competed for the rights to divert the flow of streams and rivers. Such dual usage of water led to occasional conflicts. The mills' practice of washing grain also adversely affected water quality.[59]

There was very little other industrial activity: Cholula had a saltpeter factory, and San Juan de los Llanos, Tepeaca, Huamantla, and Cholula had textile workshops.[60] Most manufacturing activity was centered around wheat or textiles, but in the sugar producing areas, there was at least one *aguardiente* factory. In 1703, Indians and other residents of Chietla complained that when the canals were not cleaned the cane alcohol producer obstructed their use of water.[61] Most of these activities complemented the agrarian orientation of small rural centers, but when they appropriated water, they caused difficulties in residents' daily lives.

Other urban activities compromised the quality of drinking water. Again, drinking water quality problems were common in Puebla de los Angeles where the activities of many industries as well as the sheer demographic density meant that waterways were often the most convenient repository for human, household, and industrial waste. In smaller centers, the level of contamination from such sources was minor but did exist. In San Andrés Chalchicomula and Tecamachalco, women who washed clothes upstream caused an ongoing water pollution problem; in the latter village, the cleaning of wool was a related problem.[62] In 1740 town officials harkened back to a Royal Decree of April 4, 1618, which stated that "no person should wash any clothes or other items in the principal irrigation ditch because people drink this water and such practices cause harm and disease because of all the filthy rubbish which is deposited there."[63] When livestock—generally pigs and cattle—drank from nearby aqueducts or wooden conduits, they often damaged these structures but also dirtied the water as well. Pigs, in particular, were prone to bathing in the streams or irrigation ditches.[64] Water remained problematic whether it flowed in abundance or only in a trickle. Its quantity, cleanliness, and accessibility were vital to the viability and survival of these communities.

Problems of access to water that were internal to rural Poblano communities raise a series of questions. These conflicts seem to have arisen not so much because of an absolute absence of water, but rather because of disagreements over its allocation. In this sense such internal problems over water resemble those documented for larger cities. Internal squabbles over water also signal a shift away from communal values shared by both Spanish and Indian cultures. The privatization of water rights led to confrontations between individuals over access to water but also to a lack of concern over water quality by many in the community. The individualistic approach to water concerns weakened the community and prevented it from acting as a group to resolve its problems.

***

The rural villages and towns of the Poblano countryside were not divorced from the problem of access to water. Whether individual residents were farmers or day laborers on estates, the usage of water upstream affected their level of consumption. Urban life was not divorced from the vagaries of farming; agriculture took place inside and outside town limits, but more importantly activities outside villages affected urban life and vice versa because waterway networks connected the urban and rural. The consequences of shortages of irrigation or drinking water for households and for livestock were far-reaching. The effects ranged from the inability to pay tributes, sickness, death of animals, depopulation of certain communities, and finally, the imbalance of normal patterns of daily life. All these difficulties, of course, were simply an extension of the problems faced by local farmers because these villages generally depended on agriculture for their livelihood. The authority of town councils was not sufficient, even in the Hispanic system of broad jurisdiction, to counter the threat of external usurpation, nor was it sufficiently influential to resolve all internal allocation problems. By the end of the colonial period these trends contributed to the broader shift toward privatization of water resources and the creation of water monopolists independent of officialdom within the Poblano countryside. Quite clearly, the decentralized irrigation system prevalent in eighteenth-century Puebla did not provide the level of intervention required to address the problems caused by water shortages in rural communities. Moreover, Hispanic water law did not take into account the connection between distant towns and farmers on the same hydrological network. According to the centralization model, those most affected by these shortages should have demanded a centralized irrigation system with an effective bureaucracy. That the victims of water shortages did not do so was probably the result of the trend toward water rights privatization. Just as rural Poblanos needed to act together to create institutions that could protect their rights to irrigation, the communal values associated with water were disappearing.

EIGHT

The Last Drop

By the end of the colonial period the Poblano countryside had been spatially redefined and fundamentally altered. The indigenous *señorios* had disappeared along with the predominance of corn and cotton crops. In their place the Spanish carved out jurisdictions which concentrated on the production of wheat, sugar, and livestock. Indian farmers were frequently relegated to marginal lands without irrigation, farmed orchards within their villages, or survived by cutting down trees to produce charcoal. Water was a fundamental part of the new agrarian economy and, therefore, those who did not have adequate access to irrigation did not prosper.

The theory of centralization provides an explanation for the rise in the level of conflicts which occurred in eighteenth-century Puebla. Demographic, economic, and environmental factors contributed to an increased demand for irrigation beyond system capacity. Centralization theory explains that conditions such as population growth, the extension of cultivation, and urban demand for agrarian goods, lead to constant struggles over water. Eighteenth-century Puebla fits this part of the model.

As population in the region rose in the late seventeenth and early eighteenth centuries, and the colonywide demographic recovery stimulated demand for wheat and sugar, the expansion of cultivated land, and the increased planting of profitable but thirsty crops led to conflicts between estate owners and their neighbors—both Spanish and Indian—and pitted village against village. The decline in available resources due to poor ecological practices such as deforestation, unchecked pastoralism, and improper use of the plow led to a lowering of the water table and aggravated the competition for scarce resources. With such a recipe for conflict, it is not surprising that eighteenth-century Puebla farmers struggled to control water.

What came after, however, could not be explained by the centralization model. According to the model, such an increase in the level of conflict eventually provokes the affected communities to call for a bureaucracy to manage water affairs. The body of officials that would then administer irrigation matters represents a centralization of authority over water. Centralization theory posits that a structure (the centralized bureaucracy) emerges from a process, that is, the rise in conflicts over water rights. In eighteenth-century Puebla, although power over water did increasingly come under the control of a few large landowners, no bureaucratic structures evolved from a community-based desire for centralization. Indeed, the call for a water bureaucracy at the end of the colonial period was made by those who had become water monopolists and not the indigenous communities.

Under a system in which central authority was not effective, those with advantages, either in location upstream or local political power, or simply a band of servants, were able to exert their strength and gradually obtain control over available irrigation. Several water monopolists emerged from the process through which large landowners acquired rights to irrigation. In a system wherein water rights were not centralized, individuals or communities with access to the means to intimidate were able to secure greater access to resources which, in turn, reinforced their economic and political power. The absence of a central authority in the matter of access to irrigation allowed large estates to use their own means of water allocation enforcement— bands of servants. Their power to usurp irrigation led to their appropriation of the majority of resources. The decentralized system failed to protect the integrity of resources controlled by indigenous communities and smaller Spanish estates.

Such incursions on irrigation rights did not go unchecked, and Spaniards as well as Indians used both passive and active methods of resistance. Recourse to the courts is the most striking strategy to the historian because the voluminous records of these complaints and lawsuits form the central core of documentation on water matters. But, within these legal documents, there are indications of other more direct and active forms of resistance: sabotage, stream diversion, and, finally, rebellions. These forms of resistance were particularly effective at times when irrigation was immediately necessary for the health of crops. During other periods, when irrigation was not directly vital, passive means of resistance were employed such as lawsuits, boycotts, and gradual appropriation. Resistance to the usurpation of water kept in check the process by which certain farmers appropriated more and more water rights. But it could not entirely stop the momentum of the trend to monopolization of water rights.

Although the doctrine of prior appropriation inherently put Spanish estates at a judicial disadvantage at the beginning of the colonial period, *hacendados* were able to circumvent the limitations imposed by laws which emphasized previous usage of irrigation. These large landowners slowly acquired legal rights to water by various means, including purchase, rental, squatter's rights, and outright usurpation. The owners of large estates were also at a disadvantage numerically when compared to indigenous communities. Yet, by hiring servants who were on the front lines of the battle for water rights, they leveled the playing field.

Political influence allowed many estate owners to debilitate the resistance of indigenous communities despite their greater numbers. Spanish estate owners used the court system effectively against both rival indigenous communities and other estate owners who were in competition with them for water. Cunning hacendados sometimes even pitted two opponents against each other in order to reap the rewards of a fight in which they had not participated. Alliances between indigenous communities and Spanish estate owners occurred at times but the estates which became water monopolists simply used such partnerships to gain greater allocations of water. The accumulation of irrigation rights was gradual and continued over generations and even through changes of ownership, but it is clear from the documentation that the consolidation of rights by water monopolists had reached a watershed at the end of the colonial period.

Within a decentralized system, powerful individuals or institutions were able to impose their agenda. In the documentation, certain names constantly crop up: the Pintos, the Rabosos, or the Ingenio San Nicolás, for example. These were either families or estates who were perpetually in conflict with neighbors over water allocation. Over the course of many decades, these estate owners gradually acquired extensive water rights and became "water monopolists." It is hard to determine exactly which factors distinguished these particular estates but the explanation cannot be a solely geographic one. In other words, the owners of these estates did not manage to accumulate extensive water rights simply because they lived upstream and could appropriate water. Instead many of these estates were owned by people who managed to orchestrate their advantages on a variety of fronts. For example, they used political position along with alliances with other neighbors. They did not hesitate to intimidate local indigenous communities nor to pit neighbor against neighbor. But these water monopolists were not created by a single strong individual; what is striking is that the accumulation of water rights continued over generations and sometimes, even when an estate changed hands, the new owners continued the same traditions. These men were, by and large, ruthless—they struck fear in the hearts of the surrounding population while simultaneously manipulating ecological advantages along with political and social privileges.

The alteration in the Poblano countryside weakened many of the Spanish-owned estates but also debilitated the resource base of many indigenous communities. Some, like Tochimilco, were well positioned to resist encroachments, but many others suffered a gradual reduction in water allocations. Such reduced access to irrigation severely limited the types of crops they could plant, whether they could plant over the dry season, and finally, in years of scarce rainfall, the success of their harvests. By the end of the colonial period small estates were similarly affected. The consequences of this deterioration were felt not only in the *milpas* but also in the small villages which dotted the countryside. Many such communities farmed almost entirely within their boundaries and when competition for water became too fierce, they were left without a drop. Deprived of water, their orchards languished, their gardens wilted, and the social fabric of these towns became unbalanced. In essence the process of water resource monopolization which was possible in the decentralized system characteristic of Puebla, made it difficult for small farmers and the people who lived in the rural communities to survive.

By the end of the colonial period the process of monopolization was well established. According to the Hunts, who first proposed the theory of centralization, the unbalancing of the equation of land-population-water leads to conflict. Out of these battles, the need for a centralized system whose bureaucrats will adjudicate disagreements becomes apparent to those involved in the struggle. In effect, water system users will be ready to forego a certain degree of independence in order to have peace and a regular, dependable access to water. In

Puebla, at the end of the colonial period, the decentralized system had borne fruit for a few estates. Not surprisingly, in 1808 one of the water monopolists, the Ingenio San Nicolás, called for the creation of an official water police. The proposed system would crystallize the divisions of water as they had developed over three centuries of colonialism and one century of unabashed usurpation. No such constabulary was created in the sixteenth or seventeenth centuries when competition for irrigation was minimal, nor did the owner of the Ingenio San Nicolás make such a request at the beginning of the eighteenth century when the estate was by no means a water monopolist.

The ingenio's petition makes sense only if it is seen as the culminating act of those who profited from a decentralized system which allowed them to create their own informal water guards and to usurp or acquire their neighbors' resources. It is also not surprising that the request came from large landowners in Izúcar whose concentration on sugarcane production implied great need for irrigation while they were downstream from the Atlixco farmers. Once they had acquired an informal water guard, the estate required more formal authority to protect their resources. A water bureaucracy would legalize an informal situation. In 1816 several communities in the Izúcar region requested the imposition of an accord to determine an adequate and fair division of water.[1] Also in 1816 an unspecified group in Izúcar elected a *guarda aguas*[2] and by 1820, the control of the new water bureaucracy was clearly in the hands of the Ingenio San Nicolás.[3]

The 1808 petition by the Ingenio San Nicolás seems to have inaugurated a new era of water management in Puebla in which official guards rather than servants patrolled the canals and made sure that all respected irrigation allocations. But these officials seem to have been merely a formalization of the band of servants previously used by the estates. The water guards, although official, were controlled by the Ingenio San Nicolás.

This study ends in 1810, but certain significant processes in the nineteenth and early twentieth centuries indicate the outcome of these late colonial processes. During the nineteenth century, the process of water rights consolidation continued but federal officials began to call for greater central authority in the realm of water management. The Mexican government reformed the legal framework which governed the use of irrigation in 1856 with the Ley Lerdo which, among other things, prohibited corporate ownership of village lands and waters.[4] During the *Porfiriato,* the government reasserted its authority over water but also expanded the rights of estate owners to appropriate land and water. The concentration of resources simply continued with a renewed veneer of legality. But the Porfirian bureaucrats detected some problems of water usage and they used the new laws to try to bring order to irrigation management. Commentators believed that the state had an important role in the management of water. In effect these individuals were advocating the centralization of control over irrigation. Water engineers inspected and adjusted the usage of several river systems including the Atoyac in Puebla.[5] But it was only after the Mexican Revolution that the state finally created a central bureaucracy governing water matters which had some teeth. The 1917 Constitution reasserted the state's ownership of any waters which ran across two properties and made public welfare central to irrigation usage. By the mid-twentieth century a bureaucracy had emerged which held authority over irrigation throughout the nation.[6] Power over water rights was finally centralized.

The processes which began with the breakdown of the population-land-water equation in Puebla culminated in the creation of national bureaucracies. Yet it is not clear that the centralization of control over water rights alleviated the inequities in rural Puebla or Mexico in general. This book began with the story of Rafaela who died upon falling into a barranca when she was fetching water. A twentieth-century Rafaela might still have to walk to the stream to fetch water. The choice to centralize control over water is beneficial for the social peace but it cannot guarantee social justice.

Notes

CHAPTER ONE

1. Archivo General de la Nación, Mexico City (hereinafter cited as AGN), Tierras section, vol. 1436, exp. 1, 1740–43. Similar complaints are found in AGN, Indios, vol. 47, fol. 136–140, 1723; AGN, Tierras, vol. 612, exp. 4, fol. 3v–106v, 1740; AGN, Tierras, vol. 1263, exp. 1, 1795; and AGN, Mercedes, vol. 67, fol. 118–120, 1708.

2. In "Prehispanic Irrigation Agriculture in Nuclear America," *Latin American Research Review* 6(1971):46, Barbara Price states that strategic resources for a fundamentally agrarian population are land and water.

3. Thomas Glick, *Irrigation and Society in Medieval Valencia* (Cambridge, 1970); *The Old World Background of the Irrigation System of San Antonio, Texas* (El Paso, 1972); Kjell Enge and Scott Whiteford, *The Keepers of Water and Earth: Mexican Rural Organization and Irrigation* (Austin, 1989); Robert A. Fernea, "Conflict in Irrigation," *Comparative Studies in Society and History* 6(1963–64):76–83; Eva Hunt, "Irrigation and the Socio-Political Organization of the Cuicatec Cacicazgos," in Johnson, ed., *The Prehistory of the Tehuacán Valley*, pp. 162–259; E. R. Leach, "Hydraulic Society in Ceylon," *Past and Present* 15(April 1959):2–26; and Michael Meyer, *Water in the Hispanic Southwest: A Social and Legal History, 1550–1850* (Tucson, 1984).

4. Some examples of studies of arid regions include Richard E. Greenleaf, "Land and Water in Mexico and New Mexico," *New Mexico Historical Review* 47(1972):85–112; Hutchins C. Wells, "The Community Acequia: Its Origins and Development," *Southwestern Historical Review* 47(1972):85–112; and Marc Simmons, "Spanish Irrigation Practices in New Mexico," *New Mexico Historical Review* 47(1972):135–50.

5. Carlos Salvador Paredes Martínez, *La región de Atlixco, Huaquechula y Tochimilco: La sociedad y la agricultura en el siglo XVI* (Mexico City, 1991), pp. 30, 79–80, 95–96.

6. Ibid., pp. 85, 90, 93, 121.

CHAPTER TWO

1. Angel Palerm, *Obras hidraúlicas prehispánicas en el sistema lacustre del Valle de México* (Mexico City, 1973); Barbara Price, "Prehispanic Irrigation in Nuclear America," *Latin American Research Review* 6(1971):3–60; William Sanders, Jeffrey Parsons, and Robert Santley, *The Basin of Mexico: Ecological Processes in the Evolution of a Civilization* (New York, 1979); Pedro Carrasco, "La economía prehispánica de México," in Florescano, ed., *Ensayos sobre el desarrollo de México y América Latina,*

pp. 15–53; and William E. Doolittle, *Canal Irrigation in Prehistoric Mexico: The Sequence of Technological Change* (Austin, 1990).

2. Teresa Rojas Rabiela, "La tecnología agrícola mesoamericana en el siglo XVI," in Rojas Rabiela and Sanders, *Historia de la agricultura prehispánica-siglo XVI,* pp. 139, 141, 143, 153, and Carrasco, "La economía prehispánica," p. 15. In *Tepeaca en el siglo XVI: Tenencia de la tierra y organización de un señorio* (Mexico City, 1984), p. 13, Hildeberto Martínez notes that before the Conquest indigenous communities stored water over the dry season in *jagüeyes.*

3. Doolittle, *Canal Irrigation,* pp. 115–16.

4. Richard Woodbury and James Neely, "Water Control Systems of the Tehuacán Valley," in Johnson, ed., *The Prehistory of the Tehuacán Valley,* pp. 81–161; Doolittle, *Canal Irrigation,* pp. 25–27; and Melvin Fowler, "Early Water Management at Amalucan, State of Puebla, Mexico," *National Geographic Research* 3(1987):52–68.

5. Angel Palerm, "The Agricultural Basis of Urban Civilization in Mesoamerica," in Steward, et al., eds., *Irrigation Civilizations,* p. 36.

6. Donald Robertson, "The Relaciones Geográficas of Mexico," *Proceedings of the 33rd International Congress of Americanists* 2–3(1958):541–42.

7. Palerm, "The Agricultural Basis of Urban Civilization," p. 34.

8. Joseph Raymond, "Water in Mexican Place Names," *The Americas* 9(1952–53):201–05.

9. Francisco del Paso y Troncoso, *Papeles de Nueva España,* Tomo III, Suplemento (1569; reprint, Mexico City, 1947), p. 16.

10. Victor M. Castillo F., *Estructura económica de la sociedad mexica, según las fuentes documentales* (Mexico City, 1972), p. 76.

11. Teresa Rojas Rabiela, *Las siembras de ayer: La agricultura indígena del siglo XVI* (Mexico City, 1988), pp. 130–147, 172.

12. Ibid., pp. 151–52.

13. Ibid., pp. 141–42.

14. In *Estructura económica* (p. 58), Castillo reproduces the following quote from the *Florentine Codex:* "Aquí, los hombres decían de éstos [de los ríos], que de allá vienen del Tlalocan, puesto que son su propriedad, puesto que de él sale la diosa cuyo nombre es Chalchiuhtlime, 'La de la falda de jade.' Y decían que los cerros son sólo fingidos, sólo por encima son terrosas, pedregosos, que sólo son como vasijas, como casa que están repletas de agua. Si en algún tiempo se quisiera destruir los cerros [pensaban que] se anegaría su mundo."

15. Charles Gibson, *The Aztecs Under Spanish Rule: A History of the Indians of the Valley of Mexico, 1519–1810* (Stanford, 1964), p. 315; Rojas Rabiela, "La tecnología agrícola mesoamericana en el siglo XVI," in Rojas Rabiela and Sanders, eds., *Historia de la agricultura,* p. 143; Alain Musset, *De l'eau vive à l'eau morte: Enjeux techniques et culturels dans la vallée de Mexico (XVIe–XIXe s.)* (Paris, 1991), pp. 202–04. In "Conflict in the Modern Teotihuacán Irrigation System," *Comparative Studies in Society and History* 4(1963):518, René Millon et al. state that this preHispanic practice continued within appeals to Christ, "El Divino Redentor," in modern Teotihuacán.

16. Musset, *De l'eau vive à l'eau morte*, p. 215.

17. Eva Hunt, "Irrigation and the Socio-Political Organization of Cuicatec Cacicazgos," in Johnson, ed., *The Prehistory of the Tehuacán Valley*, pp. 200, 237.

18. John B. Glass, "A Survey of Native Middle American Pictorial Manuscripts," in *Handbook of Middle American Indians*, vol. 14 (Austin, 1975).

19. Carrasco, "La economía prehispánica," p. 22.

20. Hunt, "Irrigation," p. 234.

21. Ronald Spores, *The Mixtecs in Ancient and Colonial Times* (Norman, 1984), p. 67.

22. Woodrow Borah, *Justice by Insurance: The General Court of the Naturales in Colonial Mexico and the Legal Aides of the Half-Real* (Berkeley, 1983), p. 43, and Hunt, "Irrigation," p. 235.

23. Comments on this phenomenon appear in Kjell Enge and Scott Whiteford, *The Keepers of Water and Earth: Mexican Rural Social Organization and Irrigation* (Austin, 1989), p. 30, and Luis Emilio Henao, *Tehuacán: Campesinado e irrigación* (Mexico City, 1980), p. 35.

24. "[S]in que español mestizo mulato ni otro genero de gente se les quite o ympiden repartiendo esta agua por las asequias o contrasequias que ellos quizieron. Y en este uso y aprovechamiento tienen de entrar las Indias viudas y en comun todos los Indios que viven en el Pueblo y pagan tributos y tienen tierras." In AGN, Tierras, vol. 3330, exp. 12, 1685.

25. Archivo Judicial de Puebla (hereinafter cited as AJP), #44, Izúcar, 1801.

26. AGN, Tierras, vol. 430, exp. 2, 1724; AGN, Indios, vol. 38, exp. 51bis, 1712; AGN, Indios, vol. 38, exp. 60, 1712; AGN, Tierras, vol. 2710, exp. 1, 1712; and AGN, Tierras, vol. 1449, exp. 12, 1725. In the village of Santa Isabel Tecali, the *cacicas* were often in conflict with the rest of the population over special water rights, as seen in documentation found in the Biblioteca Nacional-Colección Tenencia de la Tierra en Puebla (hereinafter cited as BN-TTP), caja 36, 1742; AGN, Indios, vol. 47, exp. 24, 1723; and AGN, Indios, vol. 47, exp. 82, 1723.

27. AGN, Tierras, vol. 3661, exp. 4, 1717.

28. Francisco de Solano, *Cedulario de tierras: Compilación de legislación agraria colonial (1497–1820)* (Mexico City, 1984), pp. 207–08.

29. Michael Murphy, *Irrigation in the Bajío Region of Colonial Mexico* (Boulder, 1986), pp. 281–82.

30. AGN, Mercedes, vol. 65, fol. 50v, 1699; AGN, Mercedes, vol. 73, fols. 88v–92, 1733; Archivo del Ayuntamiento de Puebla (hereinafter cited as AAP), vol. 42, L. 324, 1706; and Viceregal and Ecclesiastical Mexican Collection, Special Collections (VEMC), Tulane University, New Orleans, Louisiana, Leg. 36, exp. 47, 1730.

31. AGN, Tierras, vol. 612, exp. 4, 1740; AGN, Tierras, vol. 880, exp. 1, 1762; and AGN, Mercedes, vol. 73, fol. 88v–92, 1733.

32. See, for example, AGN, Tierras, vol. 299, exp. 2, 1713; AGN, Tierras, vol. 901, exp. 1, 1679–1788; AGN, Tierras, vol. 1084, exp. 3, 1782; BN-TTP, caja 15, 1708; AGN, Tierras, vol. 3681, exp. 3, 1754; AJP, 1795, #76; AJP, 1737 #6; AJP, 1796 #83; BN-TTP, caja 7, 1717; AJP, 1808 sin clasificar; AGN, Mercedes, vol. 59,

fol. 372–373v, 1686; AGN, Tierras, vol. 2122, exp. 1, 1787; and AGN, Mercedes, vol. 67, fol. 128–128v, 1709.

33. AGN, Mercedes, vol. 60, fol. 155–56, 1686.

34. The work titled *Claridad de la acequia de la villa de Elche* and the subsequent historiographical battle are best described in Thomas Glick, *Irrigation and Society in Medieval Valencia* (Cambridge, 1970), pp. 149–74. See also S. M. Immamudin, *Muslim Spain, 711–1492,* A.D.: A Sociological Survey (Leiden, 1981), p. 81.

35. In *The Spanish Element in Texas Water Law* (Austin, 1959), p. 75, Betty Earle Dobkins says that Roman law allowed a servitude to be formed in the case of water, when the resource was used daily in the owner's presence over the course of ten years. In *Tehuacán*, p. 36, Henao provides a different and probably more localized definition of *servidumbre* as a *tanda* or turn of water.

36. Glick, *Irrigation in Medieval Valencia*, p. 13, and Glick, *Islamic and Christian Spain in the Early Middle Ages* (Princeton, 1979), p. 73.

37. Glick, *The Old World Background of the Irrigation System of San Antonio, Texas* (El Paso, 1972), p. 4.

38. Francisco de Solano, *Cedulario de tierras, Compilación de legislación agraria colonial (1497–1820)* (México, 1984), pp. 15–16, 61, 273–74; Michael Meyer, *Water in the Hispanic Southwest* (Tucson, 1984), p. 118; Dobkins, *The Spanish Element*, p. 95; and Richard Greenleaf, "Land and Water in Mexico and New Mexico," *New Mexico Historical Review* 47(1972):94.

39. Manuel Fabila, *Cinco siglos de legislación agraria (1493–1940)* (Mexico City, 1941).

40. Ley 2, titulo 18 del libro IV, cited by J. M. Ots Capedequí, *España en América: El régimen de tierras en la época colonial* (Mexico City, 1959), p. 59.

41. Glick, *Irrigation in Medieval Valencia*, p. 150.

42. In "Land and Water Rights in the Viceroyalty of New Spain," *New Mexico Historical Review* 50(1975):191, William Taylor mentions the paternalistic concerns of the Recopilación.

43. BN-TTP, caja 37, #1001, 1736.

44. Glick, *Irrigation in Medieval Valencia*, pp. 12–13.

45. Ibid., p. 73.

46. Theodore Downing, "Irrigation and Moisture-Sensitive Periods: A Zapotec Case," in Downing and Gibson, eds., *Irrigation's Impact on Society*, pp. 117–19.

47. Taylor, "Land and Water," p. 198.

48. AGN, Tierras, vol. 1352, exp. 4, 1803; AGN, Tierras, vol. 2078, exp. 6, 1797; AGN, Tierras, vol. 2679B, exp. 7, 1779; and AGN, Tierras, vol. 2704, exp. 32, 1704.

49. AGN, Tierras, vol. 1352, exp. 4, 10 March 1803.

50. AGN, Tierras, vol. 485, 2a parte, exp. 1. fol. 25v, 1730. For other examples, see AGN, Tierras, vol. 3659, exp. 1, fols. 2v–3v, 1775; AGN, Tierras, vol. 888, exp. 1, 1773; BN-TTP, caja 40, #1017, 1717; and AGN, Reforma Agraria, caja 11, exp. 4, 1822, no. 3923.

51. AGN, Tierras, vol. 3043, exp. 4, 1760, Izúcar. Other examples include AJP, 1763 sin clasificar, Izúcar, and AJP, #36, 1801.

52. AGN, Tierras, vol. 3324, exp. 6, 1754.

53. AGN, Tierras, vol. 1263, exp. 1, 1745, 1795.

54. Greenleaf, "Land and Water," p. 99.

55. Murphy, *Irrigation in the Bajío,* pp. 320–21; Taylor, "Land and Water Rights," p. 204.

56. Murphy, *Irrigation in the Bajío,* p. 320.

57. One description of such a ceremony in the case of the restitution of water rights to Don Pedro Pinto is found in AGN, Tierras, vol. 3043, exp. 4, fol. 41v–43, 1760. In *Cedulario de tierras,* p. 27, Solano says that this ceremony derived from the formality used to declare sovereignty over land.

58. Instituto Nacional de Antropología e Historia (INEH), 3a serie, Reg. 12, carpeta XIV.

59. Some examples where objections to the granting of water rights caused delay, compromise, or rejection of the appropriation are described in BN-TTP, caja 36, 1742; AGN, Mercedes, vol. 63, fol. 88v–90v, 1694; AGN, Mercedes, vol. 63 fol. 101–104, 1695; and AGN, Mercedes, vol. 73, fol. 100–101, 1734.

60. BN-TTP, caja 36, 1742.

61. AGN, Mercedes, vol. 63, fol. 88v–90v, 1694, and AGN, Mercedes, vol. 63, fol. 101–104, 1695.

62. AGN, Mercedes, vol. 73, fol. 100–101, 1734.

63. For an example of a denunciation, see BN-TTP, caja 32, 1749.

64. AGN, Tierras, vol. 1063, exp. 2, 1781, and AGN, Tierras, vol. 939, exp. 2.

65. AGN, Tierras, vol. 540, exp. 3, 1732.

66. BN-TTP, caja 40, 1071, 1718.

67. BN-TTP, caja 3, 1717.

68. In *Cedulario de tierras,* p. 52, Solano says that in 1646 the farmers of Atlixco offered the Crown 20,000 pesos, while farmers of Huejotzingo offered 16,000 pesos for collective compositions of their landholdings and water rights. The other references were found in BN-TTP, caja 5, 1716, Cholula, and in the Archivo General de Indias, Spain (hereinafter cited as AGI), Indiferente, 1661, 1757 for San Juan de los Llanos.

69. José Lameiras, "Relación en torno a la posesión de tierras y aguas: un pleito entre indios principales de Teotihuacán y Acolman en el siglo XVI," in Rojas Rabiela, ed., *Nuevas noticias,* p. 177.

70. AGN, Indios, vol. 32, exp. 145, 1693.

71. BN-TTP, caja 3, 1710, and AJP, 1736, #8.

72. AGN, Tierras, vol. 1084, exp. 3, 1782, Chietla; AGN, Tierras, vol. 1034, exp. 1, 1778, Izúcar; AGN, Tierras, vol. 3659, exp. 1, fol. 2v–3, 1775, San Juan de los Llanos; and AGN, Indios, vol. 64, exp. 42, fol. 54, 1772, Izúcar.

73. AGN, Tierras, vol. 1459, exp. 5, 1738.

74. AGN, Mercedes, vol. 67, fol. 118–118v, 1708.

75. AGN, Tierras, vol. 959, exp. 1.

76. Fray Joseph Sánchez de Leon to the Prior Provincial, Izúcar, AGN, Tierras, vol. 3681, exp. 3, fol. 2, 1754, and BN-TTP, caja 32, 1749.

77. The villagers of Santiago Teutlan lent money to Huaquechula in return for

water. (See AJP, 1732, #8.) The inhabitants of Tepapaeca rented water to Lic. Don Carlos Antonio de Vergara when they owed tribute. (AJP, 1732, #19, 1731, Izúcar.) The Naturales of Atlixco sold water rights to the Hacienda de la Puríssima Concepción for a censo of 1,000 pesos in 1749. (AGN, Tierras, vol. 299, exp. 2.)

78. Marc Simmons, "Spanish Irrigation Practices in New Mexico," *New Mexico Historical Review* 47(1972):135–50. See also Meyer, *Water in the Hispanic Southwest*, and Greenleaf, "Land and Water Rights."

79. This pattern is very similar to the institution of water guards described for Valencia by Glick in *Irrigation in Medieval Valencia*, passim.

80. On the estate of the Convent of the Carmelitas Descalzas, for example, certain members of the staff were called *guarda aguas*. (AGN, Tierras, col. 1300, exp. 8, 1798.)

81. AJP, 1808, #56, sin clasificar.

82. AGN, Padrones, vol. 38, exp. 1, 1791.

83. AGN, Indios, vol. 47, exp. 75, fol. 136–40, 1723; and AGN, Tierras, vol. 888, exp. 4, 1763.

84. AGN, Mercedes, vol. 73, fol. 98v–99, 1739; BN-TTP, caja 41, #1078, 1750; BN-TTP, caja 42, #1160, 1742; AGN, Mercedes, vol. 60, fol. 160, 1686; AGN, Tierras, vol. 1321, exp. 15, 1800; AGN, Indios, vol. 47, exp. 24, 1723; AGI, Indiferente leg. 1659, 1753; AGN, Indios, vol. 64, exp. 138, 1773; and AGN, Tierras, vol. 1084, exp. 3, 1782.

85. Monica Barnes and David Fleming, "Filtration-gallery Irrigation in the Spanish New World," *Latin American Antiquity* 2(1991):48–51.

86. Insight into the maintenance work of these ditches can be found in Stanley Crawford's *Mayordomo: Chronicle of an Acequia in Northern New Mexico* (Albuquerque, 1988).

87. AGN, Tierras, vol. 1084, exp. 3, 1782.

88. Don Pedro de Santiago, alcalde of the village of Quexpala (Izúcar jurisdiction), complained of the Spaniards who contributed to the *limpia*. (See AJP, 1741 #1, fol. 1–1v.) On the other hand, the Indians of San Juan Quautalzingo complained that they were forced to clean the water cajas in Cholula three or four times per year. (AGN, Indios, vol. 42, exp. 45, fol. 66v–68v., 1718.) Other examples are AGN, Indios, vol. 64, exp. 42, fol. 54, 1772; AGN, Tierras, vol. 1404, exp. 21, 1809; AJP, 1736, #8, fol. 1–6v; AGN, Tierras, vol. 565 (2a parte), exp. 2, 1736; AJP, 1732, #8, fol. 29–31; and AGN, Tierras, vol. 1034, exp. 1, 1778.

89. AGN, Indios, vol. 67, exp. 223, fol. 282–282v, 1789.

90. Don José Díaz Colombres intentionally allowed conduits to silt up so that water overflowed onto his fields and not those of the Indians of Santa María Malacatepec. (AGN, Tierras, vol. 1404, exp. 21, 1809.) Other examples include AGN, Tierras, vol. 1236, exp.1, 1792; AGN, Indios, vol. 64, exp. 42, fol. 54, 1772; and AGN, Tierras, vol. 3659, exp. 1, fol. 1–22, 1775.

91. AGN, Tierras, vol. 3324, exp. 6, 1754.

CHAPTER THREE

1. Karl Wittfogel, *Oriental Despotism: A Comparative Study of Total Power* (New Haven, 1957), and "The Hydraulic Civilizations," in Thomas, ed., *Man's Role in*

Changing the Face of the Earth, vol. 1 (Chicago, 1956); "The Hydraulic Approach to Pre-Spanish Mesoamerica," in Johnson, ed., *The Prehistory of the Tehuacán Valley, Chronology and Irrigation,* vol. 4 (Austin, 1972), pp. 59–80.

2. In "Prehispanic Irrigation Agriculture in Nuclear America," *Latin American Research Review* 6(1971):45, Barbara Price characterizes this debate as "sterile when asked in so simplistic a way." On the other hand, Michael E. Smith, in "New World Complex Societies: Recent Economic, Social, and Political Studies," *Journal of Archaeological Research* 1(1993):8, argues that the essential element of Wittfogel's theory—that large complex irrigation systems affected political centralization—is correct.

3. See William Sanders, Jeffrey Parsons, and Robert Santley, *The Basin of Mexico, Ecological Processes in the Evolution of a Civilization* (New York, 1979), pp. 392–400, or Angel Palerm, *Obras Hidraúlicas en el sistema lacustre de Valle de México* (Mexico City, 1973), p. 19. More recently, in *Las siembras de ayer: La agricultura indígena del siglo XVI* (Mexico City, 1988), pp. 123–27, Teresa Rojas Rabiela accepts whole-heartedly the applicability of the Wittfogel model for preHispanic central Mexico simply on the basis that irrigation systems existed in this area.

4. William E. Doolittle, *Canal irrigation in Prehistoric Mexico: The Sequence of Technological Change* (Austin, 1990), pp. 146–48.

5. Pedro Carrasco, "La economía prehispánica de México," in Florescano, ed., *Ensayos sobre el desarollo de México y América Latina (1500–1975)* (Mexico City, 1979), p. 22.

6. Carlos Salvador Paredes Martínez, *La región de Atlixco, Huaquechula y Tochimilco: La sociedad y la agricultura en el siglo XVI* (Mexico City, 1991), pp. 95–96.

7. In "Irrigation, Conflict, and Politics: A Mexican Case," in Downing and Gibson, *Irrigation's Impact on Society,* pp. 153–54, Eva and Robert Hunt argue that a "power elite" is essential for the efficient administration of irrigation systems. This notion is also confirmed in Kjell Enge and Scott Whiteford, *The Keepers of Water and Earth: Mexican Rural Social Organization and Irrigation* (Austin, 1989). However, although the Tehuacán system appears to be egalitarian, it provides a means to monopolize water, and therefore, power for a small group.

8. See Hunt, "Irrigation and the Socio-Political Organization of Cuicatec Cacicazgos," and Hunt and Hunt, "Irrigation, Conflict, and Politics."

9. Hunt and Hunt, "Irrigation, Conflict, and Politics," p. 132.

10. Ibid., p. 150.

11. Ibid., p. 152.

12. Ibid.

13. Susan Lees, "The State's Use of Irrigation in Changing Peasant Societies," in Downing and Gibson, eds., *Irrigation's Impact on Society,* p. 125.

14. R. Daniel Powell, "Centralization of Irrigation Systems: A Case on the Argentine Frontier," *Canadian Journal of Latin American and Caribbean Studies* 10(1985):57.

15. In *Canal Irrigation,* p. 151, Doolittle states the following: "Assuming that all of the water flowing through a canal is used, a functioning canal—with a given gradient, cross-sectional area, and shape—can carry only so much water, and, therefore, irrigate only so much land. The excavation of a second canal, intended

to take water out of the first will not normally increase the total size of the irrigated areas. The second canal will result in some previously unused land being irrigated for the first time, but will also result in water shortages on lands previously cultivated."

16. Lees, "The State's Use of Irrigation," p. 125. In "Centralization of Irrigation Systems," p. 57, Powell adds that centralization could follow short-term degradation of the environment.

17. Hunt and Hunt, "Irrigation, Conflict, and Politics," p. 152.

18. In *Rivers of Empire: Water, Aridity, and the Growth of the American West* (New York, 1985), pp. 78, 80–81, Donald Worster says that the Mormons actually decentralized a previously very centralized irrigation system to avoid increasing federal control. In *Irrigation in the Bajío Region of Colonial Mexico* (Boulder, 1985), p. 26, Michael Murphy argues that control of waterworks drifted away from central authorities as landowners took on the construction of irrigation systems in the Bajío.

19. Woodrow Borah and Sherburne Cook, *Essays in Population History: Mexico and the Caribbean, Vol. 1* (Los Angeles, 1971), p. viii.

20. Gunter Völlmer, "La evolución cuantitativa de la población indígena en la región de Puebla (1570–1810)." *Historia Mexicana* 23(1973):46–47.

21. Hunt and Hunt ("Irrigation, Conflict, and Politics," p. 148) state that "within each city-state [of Mesoamerica] clear unification of authority existed, with marked differences in rights of water control and other political privileges between social classes. The functions of the elite were a monopoly."

22. Carrasco, "La economía prehispánica de México," p. 22; Paredes Martínez, *La región de Atlixco*, pp. 21–37, 57; Enge and Whiteford, *The Keepers of Water*, p. 71.

23. See Michael Meyer, *Water in the Hispanic Southwest: A Social and Legal History, 1550–1850* (Tucson, 1984), passim; Richard Greenleaf, "Land and Water in Mexico and New Mexico, 1700–1821," *New Mexico Historical Review* 47(1972):85–112; Wells C. Hutchins, "The Community Acequia: Its Origins and Development," *Southwestern Quarterly* 31(1927–28):261–84; and Marc Simmons, "Spanish Irrigation Practices in New Mexico," *New Mexico Historical Review* 47(1972):135–50. Murphy (*Irrigation in the Bajío Region*, p. 32) says that water officials played a very minor role in Celaya, while in Querétaro (p. 99), the role of water judges was merged into the position of the alcalde mayor, although water guards existed outside the town.

. 24. Paredes Martínez (*La región de Atlixco*, p. 137) states that many Indians abandoned their irrigation rights because they were too labor intensive in a situation of population decline.

25. As stated in "Atlixco: L'eau, les hommes et la terre dans une vallée mexicaine, 15e–17e siècles," *Annales HSS* 6(November–December 1995):1343, Juan Carlos Garavaglia agrees.

26. In *Morfología social de la hacienda Mexicana* (Mexico City, 1988), p. 193, Herbert Nickel also comments on the rising level of conflicts over land and water. For neighboring Morelos, Gisela Von Wobeser, "El uso del agua en la región de Cuernavaca, Cuautla durante la época colonial," *Historia Mexicana* 32(1983):467–

95, and Cheryl English Martin, *Rural Society in Colonial Morelos* (Albuquerque, 1985), p. 109, note a similar rise in conflicts in the eighteenth century.

27. Völlmer, "La evolución cuantitativa," pp. 43–51.

28. AGN, Tierras, vol. 635, exp. 1, 4 December 1742.

29. Arij Ouweneel and Catrien Bijleveld. "The Economic Cycle in Bourbon Central Mexico: A Critique of the *Recaudación del diezmo líquido en pesos*," *Hispanic American Historical Review* 69(1989):505. Ouweneel and Bijleveld note a parallel between conflicts over land and population growth.

30. Nickel, *Morfología*, p. 193.

31. Plaintiffs singled out the flight of families from their villages because of water shortages in AGN, Indios, vol. 41, exp. 224, 1717; BN-TTP, caja 5, 1790; AGN, Tierras, vol. 2691, exp. 9, 1799; AJP, 1732, #8; and AGN, Tierras, vol. 3512, exp. 2, fol. 4–8, 1775. Secondary sources for this general trend in migration can be found in Guy Thomson, "The Cotton Textile Industry in Puebla During the Eighteenth and Early Nineteenth Centuries" in Jacobsen and Puhle, eds., *The Economies of Mexico and Peru During the Late Colonial Period, 1760–1810*, pp. 175–76; Miguel Angel Mateos Cuenya, "Evolución demográfica de una parroquía de la Puebla de los Angeles," *Historia Mexicana* 35(1987):458–62; and F. J. de Villa Sánchez, *Puebla Sagrada y Profana* (Puebla, 1835), p. 42.

32. Mercedes Olivera, *Pillis y macehuales: Las formaciones sociales y los modos de producción de Tecali del siglo XII al XVI* (Mexico City, 1978), p. 206.

33. In *Morfología*, p. 193, Nickel estimates that around 1650 the growing Indian and colonywide population began to have an effect on the use of land and water.

34. The following authors make the same argument for the Mexican economy in general: Eric Van Young, "The Age of Paradox: Mexican Agriculture at the End of the Colonial Period, 1750–1810," in Jacobsen and Puhle, eds., *The Economies of Mexico and Peru During the Late Colonial Period: 1760–1810*, p. 67, and Gisela Landázari Benítez and Verónica Vásquez Mantecón, *La industria paraestatal en México: Azúcar y estado (1750–1880)* (Mexico City, 1988), p. 32.

35. Enrique Florescano, *Origen y desarrollo de los problemas agrarios de México* (Mexico City, 1986), p. 92; Juan Carlos Garavaglia and Juan Carlos Grosso, "La región de Puebla/Tlaxcala y la economía novohispana (1670–1821)," *Historia Mexicana* 35(April–June 1986):549–600; Aristides Medina Rubio, *La iglesia y la producción agrícola de Puebla, 1540–1795* (Mexico City, 1983), pp. 123, 247–50; François Chevalier, *Land and Society in Colonial Mexico: The Great Estate* (Berkeley, 1963), p. 59; Alejandra Moreno Toscano, "Regional Economy and Urbanization: Three Examples of the Relationship between Cities and Regions at the End of the Eighteenth Century," in Richard Schaedel, ed., *Urbanization in the Americas from its Beginnings to the Present*, p. 401; Antonio Diego Bermúdez de Castro, *Theatro angelopolitano: Historia de la ciudad de Puebla de los Angeles* (1746; reprint, n.p., 1835); 1st ed., 1746), p. 64; and Guadalupe Albi Romero, "La sociedad de Puebla de los Angeles en el siglo XVI," *Jahrbuch fur Gesischte von Staat, Wirschshaft und Gesellschaft Lateinamerikas* 7(1970):76–145.

36. Von Wobeser, "El uso del agua," p. 492, and Martin, *Rural Society*, p. 109,

describe a similar pattern between the sugar planters of Cuernavaca and the surrounding indigenous communities.

37. AGN, Tierras, vol. 1436, exp. 1, 1715; AGN, Tierras, vol. 1869, exp. 7,
1802; AGN, Tierras, vol. 3681, exp. 3, 1754; AGN, Mercedes, vol. 65, fol. 14v–15,
1698; AGN, Tierras, vol. 188, exp. 3, 1700; AJP, 1736, #8, fols. 4–5, Chietla; AGN,
Reforma Agraria, caja 4, exp. 2, 1783 (Epatlán); AGN, Tierras, vol. 2691, exp. 9,
1799; AGN, Tierras, vol. 635, exp. 1, 1742; AGN, Tierras, vol. 959, exp. 1, 1772;
AJP, 1701, #3; and AGN, Tierras, vol. 1097, exp. 1, 1783.

38. AGN, Tierras, 1097, exp. 1, fol. 3, 1783; and AGN, Reforma Agraria, caja
4, exp. 2, fol. 37v, 1783–1900.

39. AGN, Tierras, vol. 3706, exp. 1, fols. 3–3v, 1749.

40. AGN, Tierras, 1097, exp. 1, fol. 3, 1783.

41. Charles Gibson, *The Aztecs Under Spanish Rule: A History of the Indians of the
Valley of Mexico, 1519–1810* (Stanford, 1964), p. 310, and Enge and Whiteford, *The
Keepers of Water*, pp. 78, 81.

42. AGN, Tierras, vol. 1772, exp. 13, 1799; AGN, Historia, vol. 578 B, fol. 18–
21, 1770; AGN, Tierras, vol. 3324, exp. 6, 1754; AJP, fol. 11–11v, 1716; AGN,
Padrones, vol. 38, exp. 1, 1791; AGN, Historia, vol. 74, exp. 10, 1790.

43. AGN, Tierras, vol. 635, exp. 1, 4 December 1742.

44. Eric Van Young, *Hacienda and Market in Eighteenth-Century Mexico: The Rural
Economy of the Guadalajara Region, 1675–1820* (Berkeley, 1981), pp. 207–20, 223–
24, and David Frye, *Indians into Mexicans: History and Identity in a Mexican Town*
(Austin, 1996), pp. 108–09, show a similar scenario. In the area of Mexquitic in
the state of San Luis Potosí, population growth in the eighteenth century led to a
shortage of land and especially irrigable land. Because irrigation was controlled
by hacienda owners, the Indians could not expand their production to compensate
for increased numbers.

45. AGN, Tierras, vol. 1263, exp. 1, 1795; AGN, Tierras, vol. 3324, exp. 6,
1754; AGN, Tierras, vol. 1313, exp. 16, 1798; AGN, Tierras, vol. 635, exp. 1, 1742;
and AGN, Indios, vol. 47, exp. 140, fols. 291–298, 1723.

46. AGN, Tierras, vol. 901, exp. 1, 1679–1788; AGN, Tierras, vol. 222, 2a
parte, exp. 2, 1705; AGN, Indios, vol. 40, exp. 10, 1716; AGN, Tierras, vol. 566,
2a parte, exp. 2, 1736; AGN, Indios, vol. 38, exp. 51 bis, 1712; AGN, Tierras, vol.
273, exp.4, 1709–1711; and Yale Library-Puebla Collection (hereinafter cited as
YL-PC), box 46, series 4, folder 1126, 1703.

47. Arij Ouweneel, "The Agrarian Cycle as a Catalyst of Economic Development in Eighteenth-Century Central Mexico: The Arable Estate, Indian Village
and Proto-Industrialization in the Central Highland Valleys," *Ibero-Amerikanishes
Archiv* 15(1989):404–05.

48. Jack Licate, *Creation of a Mexican Landscape: Territorial Organization and Settlement in the Eastern Puebla Basin, 1520–1605* (Chicago, 1981), p. 106; Gibson, *The
Aztecs*, p. 305; and Ursula Ewald, *Estudios sobre la hacienda colonial en México: Las
propriedades rurales del Colegio Espíritu Santo en Puebla* (Wiesbaden, 1976), p. 143.

49. Arnold J. Bauer, "La cultura mediterránea en las condiciones del Nuevo

Mundo: elementos en la transferencia del trigo a las Indias," *Historia/Santiago* 21(1986):37.

50. Alfred Crosby, *Ecological Imperialism: The Biological Expansion of Europe, 900–1900* (Cambridge, 1986), p. 290.

51. Crosby, *The Columbian Exchange: Biological and Cultural Consequences of 1492* (Westport, 1972), pp. 110–11.

52. Garavaglia, "Atlixco," p. 1326.

53. Ewald, *Estudios*, p. 143.

54. Paredes Martínez, *La región de Atlixco*, p. 140, and Ewald, *Estudios*, p. 144.

55. Paredes Martínez, *La región de Atlixco*, pp. 136–37.

56. Ewald, *Estudios*, p. 143.

57. Rojas Rabiela, *Las siembras de ayer*, pp. 145–48, and Ewald, *Estudios*, pp. 143–44, also concur that environmental damage must have been reduced in Indian lands because they farmed smaller plots, with mixed crops and less plowing, and used terracing with maguey cacti.

58. Enge and Whiteford, *The Keepers of Water*, p. 50. In "Hydraulic Development as a Process of Response," *Human Ecology* II(1974):170, Susan Lees suggests that increased exploitation of land contributed to environmental degradation, and associates increased salinity with the use of canal irrigation.

59. Paredes Martínez, *La región de Atlixco*, pp. 72–73.

60. Crosby, *The Columbian Exchange*, p. 111.

61. For general studies, see Elinor Melville, *A Plague of Sheep: Environmental Consequences of the Conquest of Mexico* (Cambridge, 1994), and Crosby, *Ecological Imperialism* and *The Columbian Exchange*. For Puebla, see Hunt, "Irrigation and the Socio-Political Organization of Cuicatec Cacicazgos," p. 235; Paredes Martínez, *La región de Atlixco*, p. 118; and Ewald, *Estudios*, p. 143. These authors note the problems caused by livestock.

62. Paredes Martínez, *La región de Atlixco*, pp. 71–76, and Garavaglia, "Atlixco," pp. 1344–45.

63. Licate, *Creation of a Landscape*, p. 106.

64. Ewald, *Estudios*, p. 143.

65. Sanders et al., *The Basin of Mexico*, p. 409.

66. Ronald Spores, *The Mixtecs in Ancient and Colonial Times* (Norman, 1984), p. 221.

67. Gibson, *The Aztecs*, p. 303, and "The Role of the Environment in the Valley of Mexico," in Wauchope, ed., *The Indian Background of Latin American History: The Maya, Aztec, Inca, and Their Predecessors*, pp. 42–43.

68. Melville, *A Plague of Sheep*, pp. 108–09. See also Melville's article, "Environmental and Social Change in the Valle del Mezquital, Mexico, 1521–1600," *Comparative Studies in Society and History* 32(1990):24–53. Her work convincingly contradicts the argument advanced by Sherburne Cook in *The Historical Demography and Ecology of the Teotlalpan* (Berkeley and Los Angeles, 1949), pp. 53–54, that preconquest population levels were responsible for the worst ecological degradation.

69. Melville, *A Plague of Sheep*, p. 72.

70. Ewald, *Estudios*, p. 143, and Hunt, "Irrigation," p. 235. In "The Use of Forest Resources in New Spain," paper presented at the Humans and Ecosystems Before Global Development: Problems, Paradigms, and Prospects for Early Environmental History Conference, 1996, p. 10, María de la Luz Ayala calculates that most families burned ten kilos of wood daily.

71. Garavaglia, "Atlixco," p. 1344, and Paredes Martínez, *La región de Atlixco*, p. 90.

72. Wolfgang Trautmann, *Las transformaciones en el paisaje cultural de Tlaxcala durante la época colonial* (Wiesbaden, 1981), p. 227.

73. Ayala, "The Use of Forest Resources," p. 4.

74. AGN, Historia, vol. 578B, fol. 18–20.

75. AGN, Tierras, vol. 1263, exp. 1, 1795, and AGN, Tierras, vol. 2772, exp. 13, 1799.

76. AJP, 1790, #4; AJP, 1710, no exp. number; AGN, Padrones, vol. 38, exp. 1, 1791; AGN, Tierras, vol. 1772, exp. 13, 1799; and AGN, Tierras, vol. 1436, exp. 1, 1740.

77. AGN, Tierras, vol. 3324, exp. 6, 1754.

78. AJP, 1780, #80, fol. 1v.

79. Bermúdez de Castro, *Theatro angelopolitano*, p. 37.

80. William Cronon, *Changes in the Land, Indians, Colonists, and the Ecology of New England* (New York, 1983), p. 126. In "The Use of Forest Resources," p. 5, Ayala associates the decrease in water in New Spain with deforestation, but flooding was another result.

81. Ewald, *Estudios*, p. 143.

82. Sanders et al., *The Basin of Mexico*, p. 409. These authors state that the population decline led to abandonment of land and the replacement of cropland with pasture, and thus, the elimination of vegetation.

83. Hunt, "Irrigation and Socio-Political Organization," p. 235.

84. Garavaglia, "Atlixco," p. 1347.

85. Paredes Martínez, *La región de Atlixco*, p. 127.

86. Claude Morin, *Michoacán en la Nueva España del siglo XVIII: Crecimiento y desigualdad en una economía colonial* (Mexico City, 1979), p. 256.

87. Garavaglia and Grosso, "La región de Puebla/Tlaxcala," p. 108.

88. Hans Aeppli and Ernst Schönhals, *Los suelos de la cuenca de Puebla-Tlaxcala: Investigaciones acerca de su formación y clasificación* (Wiesbaden, 1975), pp. 8, 111, 116–17.

89. Luis Emilio Henao, *Tehuacán: Campesinado e irrigación* (Mexico City, 1980), p. 17. Unfortunately, Henao does not provide any more details.

90. Excellent descriptions of Spanish irrigation systems and their administration can be found in Thomas Glick's *Irrigation and Society in Medieval Valencia* (Cambridge, 1970).

91. Glick, *The Old World Background of the Irrigation System of San Antonio, Texas* (El Paso, 1972), pp. 8–10.

92. AJP, 1808, #56, 23 November 1808.

CHAPTER FOUR

1. Cortés assigned Huejotzingo to Diego de Ordaz, Tehuacán to Antonio de Ruiz, Tepeaca to Pedro Almíndez Chirinos, and Tecali to Francisco de Orduño. Cuautinchan may have been part of the Tecali *encomienda*. Pedro de Alvarado received the Izúcar region in encomienda, but when he and his wife died in 1549, the encomienda reverted to the Spanish Crown. See Kjell Enge and Scott Whiteford, *The Keepers of Water and Earth: Mexican Rural Social Organization and Irrigation* (Austin, 1989), p. 78; Carlos Salvador Paredes Martínez, *La región de Atlixco, Huaquechula y Tochimilco: La sociedad y la agricultura en el siglo XVI* (Mexico City, 1991), p. 38; Mercedes Olivera, *Pillis y macehuales: Las formaciones sociales y los modos de producción de Tecali del siglo XII al XVI* (Mexico, 1978), pp. 123–24; and Peter Gerhard, *Geografía histórica de la Nueva España, 1519–1821* (Mexico City, 1986), pp. 166, 227, 286.

2. Paredes Martínez, *La región de Atlixco,* pp. 38, 70–71, and Hanns Prem, "Early Spanish Colonization and Indians in the Valley of Atlixco, Puebla," in Prem and Harvey, *Explorations in Ethnohistory: Indians of Central Mexico in the Sixteenth Century,* p. 210.

3. Clara Elena Suárez, *La política cerealera y la economía novohispana: El caso del trigo* (Mexico City, 1985), p. 62, and François Chevalier, *Land and Society in Colonial Mexico: The Great Hacienda* (Berkeley, 1963), p. 61. In 1632, 90 haciendas in the same valley produced 150,000 fanegas of wheat (Chevalier, *Land and Society,* p. 64).

4. Alejandra Moreno Toscano, "Regional Economy and Urbanization: Three Examples of the Relationship Between Cities and Regions in New Spain at the End of the Eighteenth Century," in Schaedel, ed., *Urbanization in the Americas,* p. 405.

5. Chevalier, "La Signification sociale de la fondation de Puebla de los Angeles," *Revista de historia de América* 23(June 1947):128–29; Suárez, *La política cerealera,* p. 27; and Julia Hirschberg, "A Social History of Puebla de los Angeles, 1531–1560," Ph.D. diss., University of Michigan, 1976.

6. Prem, "Early Spanish Colonization," p. 211.

7. Paredes Martínez, *La región de Atlixco,* p. 42.

8. Ibid., p. 65.

9. Ibid., p. 49.

10. Ibid., p. 41.

11. Prem, "Early Spanish Colonization," p. 215.

12. Juan Carlos Garavaglia and Juan Carlos Grosso, "Mexican Elites of a Provincial Town: The Landowners of Tepeaca (1700–1870)," *Hispanic American Historical Review* 70(1990):260–61.

13. Luis Emilio Henao, *Tehuacán: Campesinado e irrigación* (Mexico City, 1980), p. 56, and Enge and Whiteford, *The Keepers of Water and Earth,* p. 79.

14. Prem, "Early Spanish Colonization," p. 213; Prem, *Milpa y hacienda: Tenencia de la tierra indígena y española en la cuenca del Alto Atoyac, Puebla, México (1520–1650)* (Wiesbaden, 1978), p. 146, and Paredes Martínez, *La región de Atlixco,* pp. 118–19.

15. Enge and Whiteford, *The Keepers of Water and Earth,* p. 79; Herbert Nickel,

Morfología social de la hacienda mexicana (Mexico City, 1988), p. 57; and William E. Doolittle, *Canal Irrigation in Prehistoric Mexico: The Sequence of Technological Change* (Austin, 1990), pp. 115–16.

16. Moreno Toscano, "Regional Economy and Urbanization," p. 401; Antonio Diego Bermúdez de Castro, *Theatro Angelopolitano, Historia de la Ciudad de la Puebla* (n.p., 1835), p. 64; Nickel, *Morfología social*, p. 206; and Aristides Medina Rubio, *La iglesia y la producción agrícola en Puebla, 1540–1795* (Mexico City, 1983), p. 123.

17. Reinhard Liehr, *Ayuntamiento y oligarquía en Puebla, 1787–1810*, vol. 1 (Mexico City, 1971), pp. 22–23.

18. Guy Thomson, *Puebla de los Angeles: Industry and Society in a Mexican City, 1700–1850* (Boulder, 1989), pp. 9–10.

19. Ibid., p. 10, and Garavaglia and Grosso, "Marchands, hacendados et paysans à Tepeaca: Un marché local mexicain à la fin du XVIIIe siècle," *Annales ESC* (May–June 1989):569.

20. Thomson, *Puebla de los Angeles*, pp. 14–32; Garavaglia and Grosso, "La región de Puebla/Tlaxcala y la economía novohispana (1670–1821)," *Historia Mexicana* 35(1986):549–600.

21. Sonya Lipsett-Rivera, "Puebla's Eighteenth-Century Agrarian Decline: A New Perspective," *Hispanic American Historical Review* 70(1990):479.

22. Suárez, *La política cerealera*, p. 71.

23. Medina Rubio, *La iglesia y la producción agrícola*, p. 122.

24. Nickel, *Morfología social*, p. 186.

25. Moreno Toscano, "Regional Economy and Urbanization," p. 401.

26. Ibid.; Bermúdez de Castro, *Theatro Angelopolitano*, p. 64; Nickel, *Morfología social*, p. 206; and Medina Rubio, *La iglesia y la producción agrícola*, p. 123.

27. Thomson, *Puebla de los Angeles*, pp. 15, 17.

28. Bermúdez de Castro, *Theatro Angelopolitano*, p. 64.

29. Ibid. In *Puebla de los Angeles*, p. 14, Thomson puts the count at fourteen mills. He also states that such a large number of mills in a single city was unique in Spanish America.

30. Medina Rubio, *La iglesia y la producción agrícola*, p. 123.

31. Olivera, *Pillis y macehuales*, p. 159. See also AGN, Historia, vol. 74, exp. 10, fol. 412v, 1794.

32. Garavaglia and Grosso, "Marchands," pp. 558, 569. See also AGN, Historia, vol. 74, exp. 10, fol. 414, 1794.

33. AGN, Historia, vol. 74, exp. 10, fol. 412–414v, 1794.

34. Ibid.

35. Arnold J. Bauer, "La cultura mediterránea en las condiciones del Nuevo Mundo: elementos en la transferencia del trigo a las Indias," *Historia/Santiago* 21(1986):45, and Karl W. Butzer, "Spanish Regionalism and Its Simplification in the New World," paper presented at the 15th International Congress of the Latin American Studies Association, 1989, p. 9.

36. Bauer, "La cultura mediterránea," p. 39; Michael Murphy, *Irrigation in the Bajío Region of Colonial Mexico* (Boulder, 1986), p. 123; and Butzer, "Spanish Regionalism," p. 9.

37. Chevalier, *Land and Society in Colonial Mexico*, p. 60.

38. Paredes Martínez, *La región de Atlixco*, pp. 124–27, and Arij Ouweneel, "The Agrarian Cycle as a Catalyst of Economic Development in Eighteenth-Century Central Mexico: The Arable Estate, Indian Village and Proto-Industrialization in the Central Highland Valleys," *Ibero-Amerikanishes Archiv* 15(1989):408.

39. Medina Rubio, *La iglesia y la producción agrícola*, pp. 123–24, and Suárez, *La política cerealera*, p. 83.

40. Butzer, "Spanish Regionalism," pp. 10–11.

41. Because the *blanquillo* yields were so high, it pushed down the price of wheat. As a result, *blanquillo* was the target of a defamation campaign in the seventeenth century. In March 1677, the *Protomedicato* (medical guild) issued a report which stated that *blanquillo* was unhealthy for human consumption. Two months later, the viceroy forbade the planting of *blanquillo* for human use. Punishments ranged from confiscation of land, exile to the Philippines, and six years of hard labor in the galleys for Spaniards or six years of work in an *obraje* for Indians. The viceroy reversed the prohibition in 1692 after the publication of a book which denied the previous charges of the *Protomedicato*. His decision also came a year after an infestation of the fungus *chahuistle* affected much of the wheat crop. Of course, 1692 was the year of great famines in Mexico which led to a major riot in the capital. See Suárez, *La política cerealera*, pp. 85–89, and Gustavo Rafael Alfaro Ramírez, "El abasto de cereales en la Puebla del siglo XVII," paper presented to the Seminario de Historia Urbana, Puebla, 1996.

42. Paredes Martínez, *La región de Atlixco*, p. 138.

43. AGN, Mercedes, vol. 65, foja 14v–15, 1698; AGN, Tierras, vol. 1869, exp. 7, 1802; AGN, Historia, vol. 578B, fol. 16–17v and fol. 22v–24, 1779; and AGN, Tierras, vol. 188, exp. 3, 1700. In *La región de Atlixco*, p. 138, Paredes Martínez also comments on the cultivation of wheat by Indians in Tochimilco.

44. AGN, Historia, vol. 578B, fol. 3–24, 1770.

45. AGN, Tierras, vol. 3681, exp. 3, 1754; AGN, Tierras, vol. 1363, exp. 5, 1805; and AGN, Tierras, vol. 2691, exp. 9, 1799.

46. Sidney Mintz, *Sweetness and Power: The Place of Sugar in Modern History* (New York, 1985), pp. 24, 32.

47. Felipe Ruiz de Velasco, *Historia y evoluciones del cultivo de la caña y de la industria azucarera en México hasta el año de 1910* (Mexico City, 1937), pp. 118–24.

48. Ward Barrett, *The Sugar Hacienda of the Marqueses of del Valle* (Minneapolis, 1970), p. 4.

49. Liehr, *Ayuntamiento*, p. 16.

50. J. H. Galloway, *The Sugar Cane Industry: An Historical Geography from its Origins to 1914* (Cambridge, 1989), pp. 14–15; and Enge and Whiteford, *The Keepers of Water and Earth*, p. 49.

51. Gisela Landázuri Benítez and Verónica Vázquez Mantecón, *La industria paraestatal en México: Azúcar y estado (1750–1880)* (Mexico City, 1988), p. 90. For information on other sugar production regions, see Richard Sheridan, *Sugar and Slavery: An Economic History of the British West Indies, 1623–1775* (Baltimore, 1973), p. 108, and Mintz, *Sweetness and Power*, p. 21.

52. Landázuri Benítez and Vázquez Mantecón, *Azúcar y estado,* p. 90.

53. Ibid. In *The Sugar Hacienda,* pp. 45–46, Barrett says that the *criolla* variety was quite disease resistant and, as a result, disease was insignificant in Morelos and in Puebla. This author also states that flooding killed rats and ants (p. 44).

54. Landázuri Benítez and Vázquez Mantecón, *Azúcar y estado,* p. 89. In *The Sugar Hacienda,* p. 46, Barrett states that over the course of the colonial period sugar planters in Morelos shifted planting time away from the month of June because the indigenous communities were planting their own *temporal* corn crops.

55. Sheridan, *Sugar and Slavery,* p. 115.

56. Landázuri Benítez and Vázquez Mantecón, *Azúcar y estado,* pp. 36–39, 43. Gisela Von Wobeser, "El uso del agua en la región de Cuernavaca, Cuautla durante la época colonial," *Historia Mexicana* 32(1983):494, comments on the growth of the sugar industry in the eighteenth century.

57. Mintz, *Sweetness and Power,* p. 45.

58. AGN, Indios, vol. 25, exp. 146, 1676, Tepejojuma.

59. AGN, Historia, vol. 74, exp. 10, fol. 413, 1794.

60. Paredes Martínez, *La región de Atlixco,* pp. 102–03.

61. Garavaglia and Grosso, "Marchands," p. 570.

62. Ouweneel, "The Agrarian Cycle," p. 408.

63. Ibid., pp. 404–05.

64. In *La región de Atlixco,* p. 102, Paredes Martínez lists olives, apples, pomegranates, oranges, figs, limes, quince, melons, and cucumbers as Spanish introductions to the Atlixco region.

65. AGN, Historia, vol. 578B, fol. 21–21v, 1770 (Informe de Tochimilco del General Don Francisco Xavier Bernal de Aguayo, Alcalde mayor). A similar dependence on orchards by indigenous communities as well as the cofradías and churches is mentioned in the padrón of Chietla (AGN, Padrones, vol. 28, exp. 2, 1792; see also AGN, Indios, vol. 44, exp. 47, fol. 52–54, 1720).

66. AGN, Tierras, vol. 225, 2a parte, exp. 2 1705, and AGN, Tierras, vol. 565, 2a parte, exp. 2, 1736. A similar example is the town of Chietla (AJP, 1736, #8; AJP, 1808 #61 sin clasificar).

67. Paredes Martínez, *La región de Atlixco,* pp. 71–76. Juan Carlos Garavaglia, "Atlixco: L'eau, les hommes et la terre dans une vallée mexicaine, 15e–17e siècles" *Annales HSS* 6(November–December 1995):1344–45.

68. Ouweneel, "The Agrarian Cycle," p. 410, and Garavaglia and Grosso, "Mexican Elites," p. 259.

69. In *Morfología social,* p. 186, Nickel comments on Tepeaca. See also AGN, Tierras, vol. 1404, exp. 21, 1809; AGN, Mercedes, vol. 73, fol. 98–99v, 1734; BN-TTP, caja 31, 1787; and AGN, Tierras, vol. 888, exp. 4, 1763.

70. Garavaglia and Grosso, "Marchands," pp. 567–68. For Tecali, see Olivera, *Pillis y macehuales,* p. 159.

71. Thomson, *Puebla de los Angeles,* p. 15.

72. Garavaglia and Grosso, "Mexican Elites," p. 259.

73. Liehr, *Ayuntamiento,* pp. 24–25.

74. Thomson, *Puebla de los Angeles*, p. 38, and Liehr, *Ayuntamiento*, p. 25. According to Olivera in *Pillis y macehuales*, p. 162, leather work was also performed in Tecali.

75. Paredes Martínez, *La región de Atlixco*, p. 72, and Liehr, *Ayuntamiento*, p. 25.

76. Liehr, *Ayuntamiento*, p. 25.

77. Garavaglia and Grosso, "Marchands," p. 563.

78. Thomson, *Puebla de los Angeles*, pp. 33–37, and Paredes Martínez, *La región de Atlixco*, p. 42. See also Jan Bazant, "Evolution of the Textile Industry of Puebla, 1544–1845," *Comparative Studies in Society and History* 7(1964–1965):56–69.

79. Paredes Martínez, *La región de Atlixco*, p. 42, and Garavaglia and Grosso, "Marchands," p. 569.

80. Thomson, *Puebla de los Angeles*, p. 11. According to AGN, Historia, vol. 74, exp 19, fol. 413–413v, 1794, there were forty-five textile workshops in San Juan de los Llanos.

81. Archivo Judicial de Tecali (Museo de Antropología), roll #2, #69, 1739, Tecali.

82. AJP, 1732, #8. Other such examples are found in AGN, Tierras, vol. 1088, exp. 1, 1783; AGN, Tierras, vol. 612, exp. 4, 1740; AGN, Tierras, vol. 1152, exp. 1, 1787; AGN, Tierras, vol. 57, exp. 3, 1795; AGN, Indios, vol. 47, exp. 75, fol. 136–140, 1723; AGN, Tierras, vol. 888, exp. 4, 1763; AGN, Mercedes, vol. 67, fol. 118–118v, 1708; BN-TTP, caja 31, 1787; AGN, Indios, vol. 64, exp. 138, 1773; AGN, Tierras, vol. 1404, exp. 21, 1809; and AGN, Mercedes, vol. 73, fol. 98v–99v.

CHAPTER FIVE

1. Preconquest conflicts were mentioned in lawsuits about water in a few instances that have been documented. See José Lameiras, "Relación en torno a la posesión de tierras y aguas: un pleito entre indios principales de Teotihuacán y Acolman en el siglo XVI," in Rojas Rabiela, et al., eds., *Nuevas noticias sobre las obras hidraúlicas prehispanicas y coloniales en el valle de México*, and Ralph Roys, *The Titles of Ebtun* (Washington, 1939).

2. AGN, Tierras, vol. 3295, exp. 3, 1711; AGN, Tierras, vol. 273, exp. 4, 1709–1711; AGN, Tierras, vol. 901, exp. 1, 1679–798; AGN, Mercedes, vol. 59, fol. 369v, 1684.

3. AGN, Tierras, vol. 1123, exp. 1, 1759; AGN, Tierras, vol. 901, exp. 1, 1679–1788.

4. In 1694, for example, Joseph de Arévalo petitioned the Audiencia for a water grant. The neighboring indigenous community lodged a protest; the Audiencia overturned the protest with the argument that Arévalo had presented twelve Spanish witnesses and four *ladino* Indian witnesses, in contrast to the village's indigenous witnesses. In brief, the preponderance of Spanish and Hispanized witnesses outweighed the greater numbers of a village. (AGN, Mercedes, vol. 63, fol. 88v–90v, 1694.)

5. AGN, Tierras, vol. 952, exp. 2, 1769. It is not clear if they believed that a compromise over water would be instrumental in the return of their land or that

they simply worried that further encroachments would follow if they continued to resist. The connection between these two cases is nonetheless mentioned in the document.

6. AGN, Intendentes, vol. 40, fol. 100, Tehuacán, 10 June 1790.

7. AGN, Tierras, vol. 2679B, exp. 1, 1730.

8. AJP, 1736, #8, fol. 5v–6v, Chietla, 6 November 1736.

9. AGN, Tierras, vol. 959, exp. 1, 1772.

10. AGN, Tierras, vol. 110, exp. 6, 1784. John Lloyd Stephens, *Incidents of Travel in Central America, Chiapas, and Yucatán* (London, 1841), p. 402, describes a similar bondage in the Yucatán among peons who worked without pay on a hacienda in return for access to the only cenote in the region during the dry season.

11. In Chietla, the servants of Don José Bringas Manzaneda beat and mistreated any unfortunate who tried to take irrigation water before five or six o'clock in the afternoon. (AGN, Tierras, vol. 1084, exp. 3, 27 April 1782.) In "Environmental and Social Change in the Valle del Mezquital, Mexico, 1521–1600," *Comparative Studies in Society and History* 32(January 1990):30, Elinor Melville shows that the violence of estate slaves aimed at Indians was part of the struggle to establish pastoralism.

12. AGN, Tierras, vol. 515, exp. 1, 1731–1741.

13. AGN, Tierras, vol. 1097, exp. 1, fol. 3, 1783.

14. AGN, Tierras, vol. 2161, exp. 3, 1645–1784; AGN, Tierras, vol. 57, exp. 3, 1795–1799; AGN, Tierras, vol. 1284, exp. 1, 1797–1801; and AGN, Reforma Agraria, vol. 4, exp. 2, 1783, fol. 1–36v. In *The Aztecs Under Spanish Rule: A History of the Indians of the Valley of Mexico, 1519–1810* (Stanford, 1964), pp. 340–41, Charles Gibson also mentions conflicts over the right to fish in the Valley of Mexico.

15. Archivo Judicial de Tecali, Museo de Antropología, rollo 2, no. 69, fol. 1–1v, Tecali, 21 January 1739.

16. AGN, Tierras, vol. 645, segunda parte, exp. 2, 1743.

17. AGN, Tierras, vol. 2122, exp. 1, 1782. Another example, although less blatant, is found in Cholula's gift of the leftovers of the public fountain to their Alguacil Mayor, Don Manuel Antonio Rubin de Celis. (AGN, Mercedes, vol. 75, fol. 62v–63v, 1746.)

18. See AGN, Indios, vol. 38, exp. 51bis, 1712, and AGN, Tierras, vol. 2710, exp. 1, 1712.

19. AGN, Indios, vol. 30, exp. 188, 1688.

20. Zubia was eventually denounced, not for his practice of using so-called criminals (some were sent there by priests for such offenses as leaving their wives), but rather because of work conditions, which ultimately led to the deaths of several Indians working on the sanjas. (AGN, Criminal, vol. 393, exp. 1, fol. 1–8, 1794.)

21. Four individuals of Huilango were imprisoned after challenging the legitimacy of water rights of people in San Miguel Aguacomoluican. (AGN, Tierras, vol. 1869, exp. 5, 1802.) Other occurrences can be found in AGN, Indios, vol. 40, exp. 10, fol. 9–10, 1716; AGN, Indios, vol. 100, fol. 183–184, 1811; AGN, Tierras, vol.

1284, exp. 1, fol. 185–185v., 1799; and AGN, Tierras, vol. 2672B, exp. 31, fol. 525–525v, 1790. In *The Keepers of Water and Earth: Mexican Rural Social Organization and Organization* (Austin, 1989), p. 80, Kjell Enge and Scott Whiteford recount that Indians of the Tehuacán region often abstained from protesting water usurpations by the *hacendado* for fear of imprisonment because they refused to labor on the very same estate.

22. AGN, Tierras, vol. 2078, exp. 6, 1797. Alliances with officials could also benefit one Spanish landowner to the detriment of another. Dons José and Andrés Gómez, owners of the Hacienda Señor San José and San Diego Tepalcatepec in Tecali complained in 1800 that the *subdelegado* took away their rights to water from the Amozoque barranca and gave them to the subdelegado's ally, Don José Manuel Gómez. (AGN, Tierras, vol. 1321, exp. 15, 1800.)

23. AGN, Tierras, vol. 3681, exp. 3, 1754.

24. AGN, Tierras, vol. 412, exp. 5, 1723.

25. AJP, 1701, #3, Izúcar.

26. AGN, Tierras, vol. 2710, exp. 1, 1787; AJP, 1793, 1a parte sin clasificar; AGN, Tierras, vol. 1064, exp. 6, 1781; AGN, Tierras, vol. 1321, exp. 17, 1802; AJP, 1808, sin clasificar; AGN, Tierras, vol. 626, exp. 1, 1741; and AGN, Tierras, vol. 1152, exp. 1, 1787.

27. AGN, Tierras, vol. 370, exp. 4, 1719; BN-TTP, caja 4, 1695.

28. AGN, Tierras, vol. 818, exp. 4, 1755.

29. AGN, Tierras, vol. 1321, exp. 17, June 1802; AGN, Tierras, vol. 299, exp. 2, October 1713; AGN, Tierras, vol. 645, 2a parte, exp. 2, October 1743; AGN, Tierras, vol. 888, exp. 3, October 1763; AGN, Mercedes, vol. 80, fol. 127v–128, December 1781; AGN, Tierras, vol. 1064, exp. 6, December 1781; and AGN, Tierras, vol. 3295, exp. 3, November 1711.

30. AGN, Tierras, vol. 1903, exp. 2, 1809.

31. AGN, Tierras, vol. 3398, exp. 2, fol. 33, November 1788.

32. AGN, Tierras, vol. 818, exp. 4, 1755; AJP, 1793, 1a parte, sin clasificar; AGN, Tierras, vol. 515, exp. 1, 1731; AJP, 1763, sin clasificar; and AGN, Mercedes, vol. 80, fol. 127v–128, 1781.

33. AGN, Mercedes, vol. 80, fol. 85, 1777; AGN, Tierras, vol. 2672, 2a parte, exp. 31, 1790; and AGN, Tierras, vol. 612, exp. 4, 1740.

34. AGN, Tierras, vol. 540, exp. 3, 1734; and BN-TTP, caja 32, 1749.

35. AGN, Tierra, vol. 2698, exp. 1, 1789.

36. AGN, Tierras, vol. 299, exp. 2, 1713.

37. AJP, 1793, 1a parte, sin clasificar; AGN, Tierras, vol. 515, exp. 1, 1752; AGN, Tierras, vol. 273, exp. 4, 1709–11; and AGN, Tierras, vol. 3324, exp. 6, 1754.

38. AGN, Tierras, vol. 3681, exp. 3, fol. 1, 1754.

39. AGN, Tierras, vol. 3681, exp. 3, fol. 3–3v. 1, 1754.

40. "[S]olo quiere pleitos, o que otros no siembren: pues son tantas las amenazas que ya no tengo quien quiera sembrar mis tierras." (AGN, Tierras, vol. 3324, exp. 6, fol. 1v., 1754.)

41. AGN, Mercedes, vol. 79, fol. 172, 1754; AGN, Tierras, vol. 888, exp. 3,

1763; AGN, Tierras, vol. 626, exp. 1, 1741; AGN, Tierras, vol. 1062, exp. 1, 1731; AJP, 1761, #3; AGN, Mercedes, vol. 80, fol. 127v–128, 1781; and AGN, Tierras, vol. 612, exp. 4, 1740.

42. AGN, Tierras, vol. 540, exp. 3, 1734; AGN, Tierras, vol. 1132, exp. 2, 1785; and AGN, Tierras, vol. 880, exp. 1, 1762.

43. AGN, Tierras, vol. 626, exp. 1, 1741; AGN, Tierras, vol. 645, 2a parte, exp. 2, 1743; and AGN, Tierras, vol. 2710, exp. 1, 1787.

44. "En el y en particular la casica como más principal y el gobernador y alcaldes tendrán particular cuydado de que así se cumpla." (AGN, Tierras, vol. 3330, exp. 12, 1685.)

45. AGN, Tierras, vol. 1123, exp. 1, 1759; and BN-TTP, caja 14, 1708.

46. AGN, Tierras, vol. 1123, exp. 1, 1759.

47. Documentation on this conflict is plentiful. See AGN, Tierras, vol. 1123, exp. 1, 1759; AGN, Tierras, vol. 2684, exp. 4, 1793; AGN, Tierras, vol. 3031, exp. 6, 1796; AGN, Tierras, vol. 1320, exp. 9, 1800; AJP, 1796, #1; AJP, 1796, #83; and BN-TTP, caja 41, #1110, 1789.

48. BN-TTP, caja 41, #110, 1789.

49. In the Relación de Acatlán in *Papeles de Nueva España* (Mexico City, 1947), Francisco del Paso y Troncoso reports that Chila warred with Atoyaque, Petlalcingo, and Tonalá before the conquest (p. 67), that Piastla fought Tepexi and Acatlán (p. 78), and that Acatlán made war with Izúcar and Tepexi (p. 60). In the Relación de Ocopetlayuca, he reports that Tochimilco made war with Calpa, Atlixco, Huejotzingo, Choluca, and Tlaxcala (pp. 252–57), that Tetela made war with Tacatlan and Tlaxcala (p. 147), and that Ayutla made war with Nespa and the Yopes (p. 260).

50. AGN, Tierras, vol. 1436, exp. 1, 1715; AGN, Tierras, vol. 939, exp. 2, 1769; AGN, Tierras, vol. 959, exp. 1, 1772; AGN, Tierras, vol. 1869, exp. 5, 1802; AGN, Tierras, vol. 1313, exp. 16, 1798; AJP, 1737, #6; and AJP, 1732 #8. I am omitting the lengthy references to the Ayutla/Putla conflict because they appear in other notes.

51. AJP, 1732, #8.

52. AGN, Tierras, vol. 391, exp. 1, 1721, and AGN, Tierras, vol. 1063, exp. 2, 1781.

53. AGN, Indios, vol. 38, exp. 51bis, 1712; AGN, Indios, vol. 38, exp. 60, 1712; AGN, Tierras, vol. 2710, exp. 1, 1712; and AGN, Tierras, vol. 1449, exp. 12, 1725–1726.

54. AGN, Tierras, exp. 4, 1803, and AGN, Tierras, vol. 2078, exp. 6, 1797.

55. AGN, Tierras, vol. 2679B, exp. 1, 1779.

56. AGN, Tierras, vol. 2704, exp. 32, 1709.

57. AGN, Indios, vol. 38, exp. 51 bis, 1712.

58. AGN, Indios, vol. 38, exp. 51 bis, 1712; AGN, Indios, vol. 38, exp. 60, 1712; and AGN, Tierras, vol. 2710, exp. 1, 1712.

59. AGN, Indios, vol. 38, exp. 51 bis, 1712.

60. AGN, Indios, vol. 64, exp. 118, fol. 176v–178v, 1773.

61. For informative analyses of class divisions within indigenous communities, see Karen Spalding, *Huarochirí: An Andean Society Under Inca and Spanish Rule* (Stanford, 1986), and Steven J. Stern, *Peru's Indian Peoples and the Challenge of Spanish Conquest: Huamanga to 1640* (Madison, 1982).

62. AGN, Indios, vol. 47, exp. 24, 1723, and AGN, Indios, vol. 47, exp. 82, fol. 144v–159v, 1723.

63. BN-TTP, caja 36, 1742.

64. AJP (Ant.), rollo 32, 1789.

65. AJP, 1801, #4.

66. AGN, Indios, vol. 40, exp. 10, 1716.

67. AGN, Tierras, vol. 3158, exp. 5, 1699.

68. From a report by the inquisitors Barzena, Arias, and Tagle in AGN, Tierras, vol. 3339, exp. 3, fols. 79–80, 1753.

69. AGN, Tierras, vol. 1123, exp. 1, 1759.

70. AGN, Mercedes, vol. 80, fols. 127v–128, 1781; AGN, Tierras, vol. 1064, exp. 6, 1781; AGN, Tierras, vol. 3295, exp. 3, 1711; AGN, Tierras, vol. 2672, 2a parte, exp. 31, 1790; and AGN, Mercedes, vol. 80, fol. 85, 1777.

71. AGN, Mercedes, vol. 80, fol. 85, 1777, and AGN, Tierras, vol. 2672, segunda parte, exp. 31, 1790.

72. AJP, 1808, #56, sin clasificar.

73. AJP, 1816, #42; AJP, 1820, no exp. number; and AJP, 1844, no exp. number. Don Cosme Olavarrieta, administrator of the Hacienda San Nicolás, reported in 1844 that every year those with irrigation rights gathered to elect a person to the position of water guardian.

CHAPTER SIX

1. Eric Wolf, *Peasant Wars of the Twentieth Century* (New York, 1969); Barrington Moore Jr., *Social Origins of Dictatorship and Democracy: Lord and Peasant in the Making of the Modern World* (Boston, 1966); and Jeffrey Paige, *Agrarian Revolution: Social Movements and Export Agriculture in the Underdeveloped World* (New York, 1975).

2. William Taylor, *Drinking, Homicide, and Rebellion in Colonial Mexican Villages* (Stanford, 1979), p.128.

3. Ibid., chapter 4.

4. James Scott, *Weapons of the Weak: Everyday Forms of Peasant Resistance* (New Haven, 1985), pp. 29–32.

5. I take this concept of the continuum of resistance from August Meier and Elliot Rudwick, *From Plantation to Ghetto*, 3rd ed. (New York, 1976), pp. 80–86.

6. In *Water in the Hispanic Southwest: A Social and Legal History, 1550–1850* (Tucson, 1984), p. 58, Michael Meyer also mentions this phenomenon.

7. Enrique Florescano and Isabel Gil Sánchez, *Descripciones económicas generales de Nueva España, 1784–1817* (Mexico City, 1973), p. 17; and Enrique Florescano, *Descripciones económicas regionales de la Nueva España: Provincias del Centro, Sureste, y Sur, 1766–1827* (Mexico City, 1976), p. 168.

8. Florescano and Sánchez, *Descripciones económicas generales de Nueva España,* p. 17; Florescano, *Descripciones económicas regionales,* p., 168; and AGN, Historia, vol. 578B, fol. 3v, 1770.

9. AGN, Historia, vol. 578B, fol. 3–24, 1770.

10. AGN, Tierras, vol. 635, exp. 1, 1742, and AGN, Tierras, vol. 1864, exp. 7, 1802. These walled-in gardens still existed in Tochimilco when I visited the town in 1989.

11. AGN, Mercedes, vol. 65, fol. 14v–15, 1698.

12. Ibid.; AGN, Tierras, vol. 188, exp. 3, 1700; AGN, Tierras, vol. 635, exp. 1, 1742; AGN, Tierras, col. 1342, exp. 5, 1802; and AGN, Tierras, vol. 1869, exp. 7, 1802.

13. Florescano, *Descripciones económicas regionales,* pp. 172–73.

14. AGN, Indios, vol. 47, exp. 75, fol. 136, exp. 140, 1723.

15. Ibid.; AGN, Tierras, vol. 888, exp. 4, 1763; AGI, Indiferente, vol. 1659, 1753; AGN, Mercedes, vol. 67, fol. 118–118v, 1708; and AGN, Mercedes, vol. 77, fol. 39–39v, 1745.

16. Meyer, *Water in the Hispanic Southwest,* p. 58; Taylor, *Landlord and Peasant in Colonial Oaxaca* (Stanford, 1972), p. 92; and Susan Ramírez, *Provincial Patriarchs: Land Tenure and the Economics of Power in Colonial Peru* (Albuquerque, 1986), p. 198, also mention this pattern.

17. In *Shadows over Anáhuac: An Ecological Interpretation of Crisis and Development in Central Mexico, 1730–1800* (Albuquerque, 1996), p. 92, Arij Ouweneel makes the rather dubious statement about Puebla that "most Indian townships, situated up-stream as they were, did not face any problem in water disputes." He seems to ignore the hydraulic system and also the presence of many estates in the higher reaches of the mountains and volcanoes.

18. Although this terminology is used frequently, I found Herman Konrad's discussion of active and passive resistance in *A Jesuit Estate in Colonial Mexico: San Lucia, 1576–1767* (Stanford, 1980) to be particularly useful.

19. In *Drinking, Homicide,* p. 138, Taylor says that "The leisurely legal process was not, however, a satisfactory means of coping with this kind of real emergency." In *Provincial Patriarchs,* p. 248, Ramírez quotes from a colonial era Peruvian document: "The damage is irreparable and the appeals difficult, because while they [indigenous groups] address themselves to higher courts of law, the crops die."

20. AGN, Tierras, vol. 1300, exp. 8, 1798.

21. AJP, Museo de Antropología, Rollo 32, 1789.

22. AGN, Tierras, vol. 888, exp. 3, 1783.

23. AGN, Tierras, vol. 1300, exp. 8, 1798.

24. In *Rural Society in Colonial Morelos* (Albuquerque, 1985), p. 113, Cheryl English Martin states that the fear of sabotage acted as a deterrent or moderating influence on the hacendados of Morelos.

25. AGN, Tierras, vol. 1459, exp. 5, 1738.

26. AGN, Mercedes, vol. 73, fol. 172, 1754; AGN, Tierras, vol. 515, exp. 1,

1731; AGN, Tierras, vol. 1404, exp. 21, 1809; and AGN, Tierras, vol. 225, 2a parte, exp. 2, 1705.

27. AGN, Indios, vol. 38, exp. 37, fol. 49–50v, 1712. In "Agrarian Social Change and Peasant Rebellion in Nineteenth-Century Mexico: The Example of Chalco," in Katz, ed., *Rural Social Conflicts in Mexico*, p. 111, John Tutino reports a similar situation.

28. AJP, 1732 #8, fol. 7–7v.

29. AGN, Tierras, vol. 3681, exp. 3, fol. 3–3v, 1754.

30. AGN, Tierras, vol. 1300, exp. 8, 1798.

31. AGN, Reales Cédulas Originales, vol. 123, exp. 58, fol. 1, 1782; AGN, Reales Cédulas Originales, vol. 127, exp. 64, fols. 1–1v, 1784; and AGN, Correspondencia de Virreyes, Primera serie, vol. 129, fol. 279–289, 1781. In *Drinking, Homicide*, p. 120, Taylor also mentions the rebellion of 1781.

32. AGN, Tierras, vol. 2672, parte 2, exp. 31, fol. 512v, 1790.

33. AGN, Tierras, vol. 2672, parte 2, exp. 31, fol. 531–532, 1790.

34. AGN, Tierras, vol. 2672, parte 2, exp. 31, fol. 586–587, 1790. In *Rural Society*, p. 110, Martin documents an instance in 1797 when a rumor that the Oaxtepec Indians were about to rebel forced the owners of the Hacienda Pantitlán to reach a compromise with them on irrigation.

35. Taylor, *Magistrates of the Sacred: Priests and Parishioners in Eighteenth-Century Mexico* (Stanford, 1996), pp. 230–32.

36. AGN, Tierras, vol. 485, 2a parte, exp. 1, fol. 4–4v, 1729.

37. AGN, Tierras, vol. 485, 2a parte, exp. 1, fol. 112, fol. 122v., 1729.

38. AGN, Tierras, vol. 485, 2a parte, exp. 1, fol. 162–165v and fol. 166, 1729.

39. For a description of the workings of this court, see Woodrow Borah, *Justice by Insurance: The General Indian Court of Colonial Mexico and the Legal Aides of the Half-Real* (Berkeley, 1983).

40. AGN, Tierras, vol. 13, exp. 2, 1771.

41. AGN, Mercedes, vol. 73, fol. 101v, 102v, 1734.

42. AGN, Tierras, vol. 1363, exp. 5, 1805; AGN, Tierras, vol. 1300, exp. 8, 1790; AGN, Indios, vol. 38, exp. 37, 1717; AGN, Tierras, vol. 1459, exp. 5, 1738; AGN, Tierras, vol. 901, exp. 1, 1679–1788; and AGN, Tierras, vol. 2672, segunda parte, exp. 31, 1740. Taylor, *Drinking, Homicide*, p. 120, and Tutino, "Agrarian Social Change," pp. 111, 113, also show the use of similar strategies.

43. AGN, Tierras, vol. 1349, exp. 5, 1803; AGN, Tierras, vol. 1058, exp. 2, 1780; AGN, Indios, vol. 25, exp. 414, fol. 291, 1670; AGN, Indios, vol. 38, exp. 37, 1717; AGN, Tierras, vol. 412, exp. 5, 1723; AGN, Tierras, vol. 13, exp. 2, 1771; AGN, Mercedes, vol. 63, fol. 88v–90v, 1694; AGN, Indios, vol. 64, exp. 138, 1773; AGN, Tierras, vol. 1084, exp. 3, 1782; AGN, Indios, vol. 64, exp. 42, 1772; AJP, 1736, no. 8; and AGN, Tierras, vol. 1263, exp. 1, 1795.

44. AGN, Indios, vol. 64, exp. 138, 1773; AGN, Tierras, vol. 1263, exp. 1, 1795; AGN, Tierras, vol. 3330, exp. 12, 1685; AGN, Indios, vol. 64, exp. 42, 1772; AGN, Tierras, vol. 1084, exp. 3; and AJP, 1736, no. 8.

45. AGN, Tierras, vol. 1084, exp. 3, 1782.

46. AGN, Tierras, vol. 565, 2 parte, exp. 2, 1736, and AGN, Tierras, vol. 635, exp. 1, 1742.

47. AGN, Tierras, vol. 1354, exp. 7, 1804. Taylor, "Conflict and Balance in District Politics: Tecali and Sierra Norte de Puebla in the Eighteenth Century," in Spores and Hassig, eds., *Five Centuries of Law and Politics in Central Mexico,* reports a similar strategy in the Tecali area when Santa María Toxtepec and many neighboring villages refused to make the regular payments to the *corregidor* and *cacique* in protest over tribute and tithes. In *Drinking, Homicide,* p. 137, Taylor also documents an incident in Almoloya when the villagers refused to attend mass in response to the local priest's unwillingness to preach in their language.

48. Konrad, *A Jesuit Estate,* pp. 165–69, also notes this phenomenon.

49. AGN, Tierras, vol. 3324, exp. 6, 1754; AGN, Tierras, vol. 3034, exp. 4, 1760; AGN, Tierras, vol. 1122, exp. 1, 1759; AGN, Tierras, vol. 1179, exp. 2, 1789; AGN, Tierras, vol. 2684, exp. 4, 1793; AGN, Tierras, vol. 939, exp.2, 1769; AGN, Tierras, 959, exp. 1, 1772; AGN, Tierras, vol. 1063, exp. 2, 1781; AGN, Tierras, vol. 1869, exp. 5, 1802; and BN-TTP, caja 12, 1780.

50. AGN, Tierras, vol. 3042, exp. 4, fol. 10v–47, 1755–1761.

51. Some of the communities that suffered this fate either partially or totally included the Barrio of Xaxalpa (AGN, Tierras, vol. 635, exp. 1, 1742), the barrio of Calcagualco (AGN, Tierras, vol. 485, segunda parte, exp. 1, 1725), and the town of San Juan Ajalpa (AGN, Indios, vol. 41, exp. 224, 1717).

52. Two examples of this fate are Santa María Toxtepec in the Tecali jurisdiction (AGN, Tierras, vol. 1321, exp. 15, 1800), and San Gerónimo Coyula in the Atlixco jurisdiction (AGN, Tierras, vol. 110, exp. 6, 1784).

CHAPTER SEVEN

1. Puebla de los Angeles was an exception to this internal/external axis; in fact, its problems of access to water were rooted more in the flawed bureaucratic strategy of water allocation. See Sonya Lipsett-Rivera, "Water and Bureaucracy in Colonial Puebla de los Angeles," *Journal of Latin American Studies* 25(1993):25–44.

2. AGN, Padrones, vol. 28, exp. 2, 1792.

3. Ibid., and AGN, Historia, vol. 74, exp. 10, 1794. In 1720, the residents of Chietla stated that they depended on their harvests of palms and dates, but that their alcalde stole their fruit and sold it in Mexico City along with his own. Consequently, they could not pay their tributes and *obenciones.* (AGN, Indios, vol. 44, exp. 47, fol. 52–54, 1720.)

4. YL-PC, Box 46, series 4, folder 1126, fol. 8, 1703.

5. AGN, Mercedes, vol. 63, fol. 88v–90v, 1694; AGN, Mercedes, vol. 63, fol. 101–104, 1695; and AGN, Tierras, vol. 225, 2a parte, exp. 2, 1705.

6. AGN, Tierras, col. 1449, exp. 12, 1725.

7. AJP, 1736, #8, and AJP, 1808, #61, sin clasificar.

8. AAP, vol. 42, L. 323, 1704, and Guy Thomson, *Puebla de los Angeles: Industry and Society in a Mexican City* (Boulder, 1989), pp. 7–9. In *¿Relajados o reprimidos? Las diversiones públicas y vida social en la ciudad de México durante el siglo de las luces* (Mexico City, 1987), pp. 132, 134, Juan Pedro Viqueira Albán also mentions that

poor people in Mexico City sometimes had an orchard or a plot within city limits, and states that the division between country and city was not at all clear cut.

9. AAP, vol. 44, L. 367, 1808.

10. AAP, vol. 44, L. 374, 1809.

11. AGN, Tierras, vol. 2244, exp. 4, fol. 3, 1796.

12. BN-TTP, caja 13, 1764. For other such examples, see AGN, Tierras, vol. 1097, exp. 1, 1783; AGN, Mercedes, vol. 83, fol. 52v, 1792; and AGN, Mercedes, vol. 73, fol. 102–102v, 1734.

13. AGN, Indios, vol. 64, exp. 138, 1773. For another such example, see AGN, Tierras, vol. 3029, exp. 10, 1778; AGN, Tierras, vol. 1321, exp. 15, 1800; Archivo Judicial de Tecali, rollo 2, #67, 1739; AGN, Tierras, vol. 952, exp. 2, fol. 13, 1764; AGN, Tierras, vol. 484, 2a parte, exp. 1, 1729; AGN, Indios, vol. 38, exp. 37, 1712; and AGN, Tierras, vol. 299, exp. 2, 1713.

14. Juan de Pineda, "Carta al Rey sobre Cholula," in Carrasco, ed., *Tlalocan: Revista de Fuentes para el Conocimiento de las Culturas Indígenas de México*, 7(1970): 176–92.

15. BN-TTP, caja 5, 1790.

16. AGN, Tierras, vol. 1088, exp. 1783, and BN-TTP, caja 5, 1790.

17. AGN, Indios, vol. 36, exp. 153, 1704.

18. AGN, Tierras, vol. 2691, exp. 9, 1799.

19. AGN, Tierras, vol. 2122, exp. 1, 1782.

20. AGN, Mercedes, vol. 80, fol. 85, 1777.

21. BN-TTP, caja 5, 1790.

22. AGN, Indios, vol. 64, exp. 138, 1773; AGN, Indios, vol. 47, exp. 75, fol. 136–144, 1723; AGN, Indios, vol. 47, exp. 140, 1723; AGN, Tierras, vol. 888, exp. 4, 1762; AGN, Mercedes, vol. 67, fol. 118–118v, 1708; AGN, Tierras, vol. 1313, exp. 16, 1798; AJP, 1737, #6; AGN, Tierras, vol. 3029, exp. 10, 1778; AGN, Indios, vol. 30, exp. 188, 1688; AGN, Tierras, vol. 1321, exp. 15, 1800; AGN, Tierras, vol. 612, exp. 4, 1740; AGN, Padrones, vol. 38, exp. 1, 1791; AGN, Indios, vol. 38, exp. 37, 1712; AGN, Tierras, vol. 2691, exp. 9, 1799; and AGN, Tierras, vol. 3324, exp. 6, 1754.

23. AGN, Tierras, vol. 2691, exp. 9, 1799. In 1808, the Señores del Tribunal de Fiel Executoria in Puebla indicated a connection between water pollution and disease. (AAP, vol. 44, L. 370, fol. 198v–201, 1808.)

24. AGN, Tierras, vol. 1321, exp. 15, 1800.

25. AGN, Tierras, vol. 2691, exp. 9, 1799. In *The Conquest of Water: The Advent of Health in the Industrial Age* (Princeton, 1989), p. 110, Jean-Pierre Goubert states that the popular notion of water purity in Europe was in flux from about 1770 to 1940. Generally, standing water was deemed harmful while running water was equated with purity.

26. Goubert, *Advent of Health,* p. 45.

27. In a rare example of cooperation, the owner of an estate in the Cholula jurisdiction gave residents of the village of Sanctorum permission to water their cattle at a spring on his land. (BN-TTP, caja 10, 1757.) In a document confirming their ownership of water, the residents of the village of San Francisco Chietla

specified that it was for their maintenance as well as livestock, and then for the irrigation of their fields. (YL-PC, Box 46, series 4, folder 1126, 1807, copy of a document dated 1703.)

28. AGN, Mercedes, vol. 67, fol. 118–118v, 1708.

29. AGN, Indios, vol. 47, exp. 75, fol. 136–140, 1723, and AGN, Indios, vol. 47, exp. 140, 1723.

30. AGN, Tierras, vol. 888, exp. 4, 1763.

31. AJP, 1732, #8.

32. Archivo Judicial de Tecali (Ant.), roll 2, #69, 1739.

33. AGN, Tierras, vol. 3295, exp. 3, 1711.

34. AGN, Tierras, vol. 225, 2a parte, exp. 2, 1705. See also AGN, Tierras, vol. 565, 2a parte, exp. 2, 1736.

35. AGN, Tierras, vol. 1313, exp. 16, 1798.

36. AJP, 1737, #6.

37. AJP, 1732, #8.

38. AGN, Indios, vol. 41, exp. 224, 1717; BN-TTP, caja 5, 1790; AGN, Tierras, vol. 2691, exp. 9, 1799; AGN, Tierras, vol. 3512, exp. 2, fols. 4–8, 1775; and AGN, Padrones, vol. 38, exp. 1, 1791.

39. See Thomson, "The Cotton Textile Industry in Puebla During the Eighteenth and Early Nineteenth Centuries," in Jacobsen and Puhle, eds., *The Economies of Mexico and Peru During the Late Colonial Period, 1760–1810,* pp. 175–76, and Miguel Angel Cuenya Mateos, "Evolución demográfica de una parroquía de la Puebla de los Angeles, 1660–1800." *Historia Mexicana* 37(January–March 1987):443–64.

40. Complaints of such attacks during attempts to fetch water are found in AGN, Tierras, vol. 1436, exp. 1, 1740–42; AGN, Tierras, vol. 612, exp. 4, fol. 3v–106v, 1740; AGN, Tierras, vol. 1263, exp. 1, 1795; AGN, Indios, vol. 47, fol. 136–140, 1723; and AGN, Mercedes, vol. 67, fol. 118–120, 1708. Many cases which document this pattern of violence can be found in the Criminal section of the AGN. They are too numerous to list here.

41. AGN, Tierras, vol. 1436, exp. 1, 1740.

42. Louise Burkhart, *The Slippery Earth: Nahua-Christian Moral Dialogues in Sixteenth-Century Mexico* (Tucson, 1989), pp. 61, 63–64.

43. James Taggart, "Metaphors and Symbols of Deviance in Nahuat Narratives," *Journal of Latin American Lore* 3(1977):291–92.

44. Lipsett-Rivera, "Water and Bureaucracy." For a similar study of another colonial city, see Stephen Webre, "Water and Society in a Spanish American City: Santiago de Guatemala, 1555–1773," *Hispanic American Historical Review* 70(1990):57–84.

45. AGN, Indios, vol. 40, exp. 10, 1716.

46. AJP, 1787, #3.

47. AGN, Tierras, vol. 1154, exp. 4, 1787.

48. AGN, Mercedes, vol. 83, fol. 52v, 1792.

49. AGN, Tierras, vol. 391, exp. 1, 1721.

50. AGN, Mercedes, vol. 67, fol. 118–118v, 1708.

51. AGN, Mercedes, vol. 77, vol. 39–39v, 1745. A similar petition is found in AGN, Mercedes, vol. 80, fol. 120v–121, 1780.

52. AGN, Indios, vol. 30, exp. 188, 1688.

53. AGN, Tierras, vol. 1139, exp. 2, 1786.

54. For discussions of the prestige associated with in-house water in colonial Latin America, see Lipsett-Rivera, "Water and Bureaucracy," p. 32, and Webre, "Water and Society," pp. 75–76. For Europe, see Goubert, "The Conquest of Water," p.22. A good analysis of the image of the streets as dangerous can be found in Sandra Lauderdale Graham, *House and Street: The Domestic World of Servants and Masters in Nineteenth-Century Rio de Janeiro,* 2nd ed. (Austin, 1992).

55. AJP, 1801, #44.

56. AJP, 1801, #36, fol. 1–15.

57. AGN, Indios, vol. 42, exp. 45, fol. 66v–68v, 1718. See also AGN, Indios, vol. 64, exp. 42, 1772.

58. AGN, Historia, vol. 74, exp. 10, fol. 412–414v, 1794 [Tehuacán, 3 mills; Izúcar, 3 mills; Chietla, 1 mill; Tecali, 1 mill; San Juan de los Llanos, 2 mills for making oil from turnips; Cholula, 5 mills; Atlixco, 4 mills; Tepeaca, 3 mills; and Tochimilco, 1 mill. Acatlán, Tepeji de la Seda, and Chiautla de la Sal did not have mills]. AGN, Padrones, vol. 3, exp. 2, 1791 [Villages of San Antonio, San Bernardino, and Santa Catalina in Tehuacán jurisdiction had 2 mills]. AGN, Padrones, vol. 28, exp. 2, 1792 [Chietla had one wheat mill].

59. Alain Musset, *De l'eau vive à l'eau morte. Enjeux techniques et culturels dans la vallée de Mexico (XVIe–XIXe s.)* (Paris, 1991), p. 159.

60. AGN, Historia, vol. 74, exp. 10, fol. 412v, fol. 413–413v, 1794, and Thomson, *Puebla de los Angeles,* p. 11.

61. YL-PC, Box 46, series 4, folder 1126, 1703.

62. AGN, Tierras, vol. 888, exp. 4, 1763?; AGN, Mercedes, vol. 67, fol. 118–118v, 1708; and AGN, Tierras, vol. 612, exp. 4, 1740. In *De l'eau vive,* p. 160, Musset reports similar problems for Mexico City.

63. AGN, Tierras, vol. 612, exp. 4, fol. 21–21v, 1740.

64. AGN, Tierras, vol. 888, exp. 4, 1763; AGN, Mercedes, vol. 67, fol. 118–118v, 1708; AGN, Indios, vol. 47, exp. 75, fol. 136–140, 1723; and AGN, Indios, vol. 47, exp. 140, 1723.

CHAPTER EIGHT

1. AJP, 1816, #68.

2. AJP, 1816, #42.

3. AJP, 1820, no exp. number (autos de nombramiento). This trend was still apparent in 1844. See AJP, 1844, no exp. number (Don Cosme Olavarrieta).

4. Kjell Enge and Scott Whiteford, *The Keepers of Water and Earth: Mexican Rural Social Organization and Irrigation* (Austin, 1989), pp. 83–84.

5. Clifton B. Kroeber, *Man, Land and Water: Mexico's Farmland Irrigation Policies, 1885–1911* (Berkeley, 1983), pp. 31–61, 110–18.

6. Enge and Whiteford, *The Keepers of Water and Earth,* pp. 96–97.

Glossary

Acequia	Irrigation ditch.
Agrimensor	Surveyor.
Buey	Unit of measurement used for the assessment of irrigation corresponding to the quantity of water which flows through the area of one square vara.
Caja	In rural areas, a reservoir from which water was distributed.
Canoa	Wooden pipe used to channel water.
Hydromensor	Water surveyor.
Jaguey	Artificial water reservoir.
Mercedado	Owner of a grant or *merced* of water.
Naranja	Unit of measurement used for the assessment of irrigation corresponding to one-third of a surco.
Padrón	Census.
Partidor	Device used to allocate water; a sluice gate.
Presa	Dam.
Remanientes	Water left over when all users with valid claims had taken their shares.
Repartimiento de aguas	Document formally allocating water to users along a canal system, stream, or river.
Sanja	Irrigation ditch.
Surco	Unit of measurement used for the assessment of irrigation corresponding to 1/48th of a buey.
Tanda	System of turns in an irrigation system.
Targea	Masonry conduits for transporting water.
Tomas	Moveable dams serving to divert irrigation away from the main watercourse.
Vara	Unit of measurement, approximately .838 of a meter; may also refer to the measuring stick as in the *vara hydromensor.*

Bibliography

ARCHIVAL SOURCES

AGN   Archivo General de la Nación, Mexico City
AGI   Archivo General de Indias, Spain
AJP   Archivo Judicial de Puebla
AAP   Archivo del Ayuntamiento de Puebla
BN-TTP Biblioteca Nacional-Colección Tenencia de la Tierra en Puebla
YL-PC   Yale University Library-Puebla Collection

REPORTS AND PUBLISHED SOURCES

Aeppli, Hans and Ernst Schönhals. *Los suelos de la cuenca de Puebla-Tlaxcala: Investigaciones acerca de su formación y clasificación.* Wiesbaden: Franz Steiner Verlag, 1975.

Albi Romero, Guadalupe. "La sociedad de Puebla de los Angeles en el siglo XVI." *Jahrbuch fur Gesischte von Staat, Wirtschaft und Gesellschaft Lateinamerikas* 7(1970):6–145.

Alfaro Ramírez, Gustavo Rafael. "El abasto de cereales en la Puebla del siglo XVII." Paper presented at Seminario de Historia Urbana, Puebla, Puebla, 1996.

Ayala, María de la Luz. "The Use of Forest Resources in New Spain." Paper presented at the "Humans and Ecosystems Before Global Development: Problems, Paradigms, and Prospects for Early Environmental History Conference," York University, North York, Ontario, Canada, April 1996.

Barnes, Monica and David Fleming. "Filtration-gallery Irrigation in the Spanish New World." *Latin American Antiquity* 2(1991):48–68.

Barrett, Ward. *The Sugar Hacienda of the Marqueses del Valle.* Minneapolis: University of Minnesota Press, 1970.

Bauer, Arnold J. "La cultura mediterránea en las condiciones del Nuevo Mundo: elementos en la transferencia del trigo a las Indias." *Historia/Santiago* 21(1986):31–53.

Bazant, Jan. "Evolution of the Textile Industry of Puebla, 1544–1845." *Comparative Studies in Society and History* 7(1964–1965):56–69.

Bermúdez de Castro, Antonio Diego. *Theatro Angelopolitano, Historia de la Ciudad de la Puebla.* 1746. Reprint, n.p., 1835.

Borah, Woodrow. *Justice by Insurance: The General Indian Court of Colonial Mexico and the Legal Aides of the Half-Real.* Berkeley: University of California Press, 1983.

Borah, Woodrow and Sherburne Cook. *Essays in Population History: Mexico and the Caribbean, Vol. 1.* Los Angeles: University of California Press, 1971.

Burkhart, Louise. *The Slippery Earth: Nahua-Christian Moral Dialogues in Sixteenth-Century Mexico.* Tucson: University of Arizona Press, 1989.

Butzer, Karl W. "Spanish Regionalism and Its Simplification in the New World." Paper presented at the 15th International Congress of the Latin American Studies Association, San Juan, Puerto Rico, September 1989.

Carrasco, Pedro. "La economía prehispánica de México." In Florescano, ed., *Ensayos sobre el desarollo de México y América Latina,* pp. 15–53.

———, ed. *Tlalocan: Revista de Fuentes para el Conocimiento de las Culturas Indígenas de México.* 7(1970).

Castillo F., Victor M. *Estructura económica de la sociedad mexica, según los fuentes documentales.* Mexico City: Universidad Nacional Autónoma de México, 1972.

Chevalier, François. *Land and Society in Colonial Mexico: The Great Hacienda.* Trans. Alvin Eustis. Berkeley: University of California Press, 1963.

———. "La Signification sociale de la fondation de Puebla de los Angeles." *Revista de historia de América* 23(June 1947):128–29.

Cline, Howard F., ed. *Handbook of Middle American Indians,* vol. 14. Austin: University of Texas Press, 1975.

Cook, Sherburne. *The Historical Demography and Ecology of the Teotlalpan.* Ibero-Americana, No. 33. Berkeley and Los Angeles: University of California Press, 1949.

Crawford, Stanley. *Mayordomo: Chronicle of an Acequia in Northern New Mexico.* Albuquerque: University of New Mexico Press, 1988.

Crosby, Alfred. *The Columbian Exchange: Biological and Cultural Consequences of 1492.* Westport: Greenwood Press, 1972.

———. *Ecological Imperialism: The Biological Expansion of Europe, 900–1900.* Cambridge: Cambridge University Press, 1986.

Cronon, William. *Changes in the Land, Indians, Colonists, and the Ecology of New England.* New York: Hill and Wang, 1983.

Cuenya Mateos, Miguel Angel. "Evolución demográfica de una parroquía de la Puebla de los Angeles, 1660–1800." *Historia Mexicana* 35(1987): 443–64.

Dobkins, Betty Earle. *The Spanish Element in Texas Water Law.* Austin: University of Texas Press, 1959.

Doolittle, William E. *Canal Irrigation in Prehistoric Mexico: The Sequence of Technological Change.* Austin: University of Texas Press, 1990.

Downing, Theodore. "Irrigation and Moisture-Sensitive Periods: A Zapotec Case." In Downing and Gibson, eds., *Irrigation's Impact on Society,* pp. 113–22.

Downing, Theodore and McGuire Gibson, eds. *Irrigation's Impact on Society.* Tucson: University of Arizona Press, 1974.

Enge, Kjell and Scott Whiteford. *The Keepers of Water and Earth: Mexican Rural Social Organization and Irrigation*. Austin: University of Texas Press, 1989.

Ewald, Ursula. *Estudios sobre la hacienda colonial en México: Las Propriedades rurales del Colegio Espíritu Santo en Puebla*. Wiesbaden: Franz Steiner Verlag, 1976.

Fabila, Manuel. *Cinco siglos de legislación agraria (1493–1940)*. 2 vols. Mexico City: Talleres Gráficos de la Nación, 1941.

Fernea, Robert A. "Conflict in Irrigation." *Comparative Studies in Society and History* 6(1963–1964):76–83.

Florescano, Enrique and Isabel Gil Sánchez. *Descripciones económicas generales de Nueva España, 1784–1817*. Mexico City: Secretaría de Educación Pública, 1973.

Florescano, Enrique. *Descripciones económicas regionales de Nueva España: Provincias del Centro, Sureste, y Sur, 1766–1827*. Mexico City: Secretaría de Educación Pública-Instituto Nacional de Antropología e Historia, 1976.

———. *Ensayos sobre el desarrollo de México y América Latina (1500–1975)*. Mexico City: Fondo de Cultura Económica, 1979.

———. *Origen y desarollo de los problemas agrarios de México*. Mexico City: Ediciones Era, 1986.

Fowler, Melvin. "Early Water Management at Amalucan, State of Puebla, Mexico." *National Geographic Research* 3(1987):52–68.

Frye, David. *Indians into Mexicans: History and Identity in a Mexican Town*. Austin: University of Texas Press, 1996.

Galloway, J. H. *The Sugar Cane Industry: An Historical Geography from its Origins to 1914*. Cambridge: Cambridge University Press, 1989.

Garavaglia, Juan Carlos and Juan Carlos Grosso. "La región de Puebla/Tlaxcala y la economía novohispana (1670–1821)." *Historia Mexicana* 35(1986):549–600.

———. "Marchands, hacendados et paysans à Tepeaca: Un marché local mexicain à la fin du XVIIe siècle." *Annales ESC* (May–June 1989): 553–80.

———. "Mexican Elites of a Provincial Town: The Landowners of Tepeaca (1700–1870)." *Hispanic American Historical Review* 70(1990):255–91.

Garavaglia, Juan Carlos. "Atlixco: L'eau, les hommes et la terre dans une vallée mexicaine, 15e–17e siècles." *Annales HSS* 6(November–December 1995):1309–49.

Gerhard, Peter. "Un censo de la diócesis de Puebla en 1681." *Historia Mexicana* 30:4(1981):530–60.

———. *Geografía Histórica de la Nueva España, 1519–1821*. Mexico City: Universidad Nacional Autónoma de México, 1986.

Gibson, Charles. *The Aztecs Under Spanish Rule: A History of the Indians of the Valley of Mexico, 1519–1810*. Stanford: Stanford University Press, 1964.

———. "The Role of the Environment in the Valley of Mexico." In Wauchope, ed., *The Indian Background of Latin American History,* pp. 37–49.

Glass, John B. with Donald Robertson. "A Survey of Native Middle American Pictorial Manuscripts." In Cline, ed., *Handbook of Middle American Indians.*

Glick, Thomas. *Irrigation and Society in Medieval Valencia.* Cambridge: Belknap Press, 1970.

———. *The Old World Background of the Irrigation System of San Antonio, Texas.* Monograph no. 35, Southwestern Studies. El Paso: Texas Western Press of University of Texas, 1972.

———. *Islamic and Christian Spain in the Early Middle Ages.* Princeton: Princeton University Press, 1979.

Goubert, Jean-Pierre. *The Conquest of Water: The Advent of Health in the Industrial Age.* Trans. Andrew Wilson. Princeton: Princeton University Press, 1989.

Graham, Sandra Lauderdale. *House and Street: The Domestic World of Servants and Masters in Nineteenth-Century Rio de Janeiro.* 2nd ed. Austin: University of Texas Press, 1992.

Greenleaf, Richard E. "Land and Water in Mexico and New Mexico, 1700–1821." *New Mexico Historical Review* 47(1972):85–112.

Henao, Luis Emilio. *Tehuacán: Campesinado e irrigación.* Mexico City: Ediciones Edicol, 1980.

Hirschberg, Julia. "A Social History of Puebla de los Angeles, 1531–1560." 2 vols. Ph.D. diss., University of Michigan, 1976.

Hunt, Eva. "Irrigation and the Socio-Political Organization of Cuicatec Cacicazgos." In Johnson, ed., *The Prehistory of the Tehuacán Valley,* vol. 4, pp. 162–259.

Hunt, Eva and Robert Hunt. "Irrigation, Conflict, and Politics: A Mexican Case." In Downing and Gibson, eds., *Irrigation's Impact on Society,* pp. 129–57.

Immamudin, S. M. *Muslim Spain, 711–1492,* A.D.: *A Sociological Survey.* Leiden: E. J. Brill, 1981.

Jacobsen, Nils and Hans-Jürgen Puhle, eds. *The Economies of Mexico and Peru During the Late Colonial Period, 1760–1810.* Berlin: Colloquium Verlag, 1986.

Johnson, Frederick, ed. *The Prehistory of the Tehuacán Valley: Chronology and Irrigation,* vol. 4. Austin: University of Texas Press, 1972.

Katz, Friedrich, ed., *Rural Social Conflicts in Mexico.* Princeton: Princeton University Press, 1988.

Konrad, Herman. *A Jesuit Hacienda in Colonial Mexico: Santa Lucia, 1576–1767.* Stanford: Stanford University Press, 1980.

Kroeber, Clifton B. *Man, Land and Water: Mexico's Farmland Irrigation Policies, 1885–1911.* Berkeley: University of California Press, 1983.

Landázari Benítez, Gisela and Verónica Vásquez Mantecón. *La industria par-*

aestatal en México: Azúcar y estado (1750–1880). Mexico City: Fondo de Cultura Económica, 1988.

Lameiras, José. "Relación en torno a la posesión de tierras y aguas: un pleito entre indios principales de Teotihuacán y Acolman en el siglo XVI." In Rojas Rabiela, Strauss K., and Lameiras, eds., *Nuevas noticias sobre las obras hidraúlicas,* pp. 177–228.

Leach, E. R. "Hydraulic Society in Ceylon." *Past and Present* 15 (April 1959): 2–26.

Lees, Susan. "Hydraulic Development as a Process of Response." *Human Ecology* II(1974):159–75.

———. "The State's Use of Irrigation in Changing Peasant Societies." In Downing and Gibson, eds., *Irrigation's Impact on Society,* pp. 123–28.

Licate, Jack. *Creation of a Mexican Landscape: Territorial Organization and Settlement in the Eastern Puebla Basin, 1520–1605.* Chicago: University of Chicago Press, 1981.

Liehr, Reinhard. *Ayuntamiento y oligarquía en Puebla, 1787–1810.* 2 vols. Trans. Olga Hentsche. Mexico City: SepSetentas, 1971.

Lipsett-Rivera, Sonya. "Puebla's Eighteenth-Century Agrarian Decline: A New Perspective." *Hispanic American Historical Review* 70(1990):463–81.

———. "Water and Bureaucracy in Colonial Puebla de los Angeles." *Journal of Latin American Studies* 25(1993):25–44.

Martin, Cheryl English. *Rural Society in Colonial Morelos.* Albuquerque: University of New Mexico Press, 1985.

Martínez, Hildeberto. *Tepeaca en el siglo XVI: Tenencia de la tierra y organización de un señorío.* Mexico City: Ediciones de la Casa Chata, 1984.

Medina Rubio, Aristides. *La iglesia y la producción agrícola en Puebla, 1540–1795.* Mexico City: El Colegio de México, 1983.

Meier, August and Elliot Rudwick. *From Plantation to Ghetto.* 3rd ed. New York: Hill and Wang, 1976.

Melville, Elinor. "Environmental and Social Change in the Valle del Mezquital, Mexico, 1521–1600." *Comparative Studies in Society and History* 32(January 1990):24–53.

———. *A Plague of Sheep: Environmental Consequences of the Conquest of Mexico.* Cambridge: Cambridge University Press, 1994.

Meyer, Michael. *Water in the Hispanic Southwest: A Social and Legal History, 1550–1850.* Tucson: University of Arizona Press, 1984.

Millon, René, Clara Hall, and May Díaz. "Conflict in the Modern Teotihuacán Irrigation System." *Comparative Studies in Society and History* 4(1963): 494–524.

Mintz, Sidney. *Sweetness and Power: The Place of Sugar in Modern History.* New York: Viking Books, 1985.

Moore Jr., Barrington. *Social Origins of Dictatorship and Democracy: Lord and Peasant in the Making of the Modern World.* Boston: Beacon Press, 1966.

Moreno Toscano, Alejandra. "Regional Economy and Urbanization: Three Examples of the Relationship Between Cities and Regions in New Spain at the End of the Eighteenth Century." In Schaedel, ed., *Urbanization in the Americas,* pp. 399–424.

Morin, Claude. *Michoacán en la Nueva España del siglo XVIII: Crecimiento y desigualdad en una economía colonial.* Mexico City: Fondo de Cultura Económica, 1979.

Murphy, Michael. *Irrigation in the Bajío Region of Colonial Mexico.* Boulder: Westview Press, 1986.

Musset, Alain. *De l'eau vive à l'eau morte. Enjeux techniques et culturels dans la vallée de Mexico (XVIe–XIXe s.).* Paris: Editions Recherche sur les Civilisations, 1991.

Nickel, Herbert. *Morfología social de la hacienda mexicana.* Trans. Angélica Scherp. Mexico City: Fondo de Cultura Económica, 1988.

Olivera, Mercedes. *Pillis y macehuales: Las formaciones sociales y los modos de producción de Tecali del siglo XII al XVI.* Mexico: Ediciones de la Casa Chata, 1978.

Ots Capedequí, J. M. *España en America: El régimen de tierras en la época colonial.* Mexico City: Fondo de Cultura Económica, 1959.

Ouweneel, Arij. "The Agrarian Cycle as a Catalyst of Economic Development in Eighteenth-Century Central Mexico: The Arable Estate, Indian Village and Proto-Industrialization in the Central Highland Valleys." *Ibero-Amerikanishes Archiv* 15(1989):399–417.

———. *Shadows over Anáhuac: An Ecological Interpretation of Crisis and Development in Central Mexico, 1730–1800.* Albuquerque: University of New Mexico Press, 1996.

Ouweneel, Arij and Catrien Bijleveld. "The Economic Cycle in Bourbon Central Mexico: A Critique of the *Recaudación del diezmo líquido en pesos.*" *Hispanic American Historical Review* 69(1989):505.

Paige, Jeffrey. *Agrarian Revolution: Social Movements and Export Agriculture in the Underdeveloped World.* New York: Collier Macmillan, 1975.

Palerm, Angel. "The Agricultural Basis of Urban Civilization in Mesoamerica." In Steward, et al., eds., *Irrigation Civilizations: A Comparative Study,* pp. 22–42.

———. *Obras hidraúlicas prehispánicas en el sistema lacustre del Valle de México.* Mexico: Instituto Nacional de Antropología e Historia, 1973.

Paredes Martínez, Carlos Salvador. *La región de Atlixco, Huaquechula y Tochimilco: La sociedad y la agricultura en el siglo XVI.* Mexico City: Fondo de Cultura Económica, 1991.

del Paso y Troncoso, Francisco. *Papeles de Nueva España.* Tomo III, Suplemento. 1569. Reprint, Mexico: Editor Vargas Rea, 1947.

de Pineda, Juan. "Carta al Rey sobre Cholula." In Pedro Carrasco, ed., *Tlalocan, Revista de Fuentes para el Conocimiento de las Culturas Indígenas de México,* pp. 176–92.

Powell, R. Daniel. "Centralization of Irrigation Systems: A Case on the Argentine Frontier." *Canadian Journal of Latin American and Caribbean Studies* 10(1985):55–80.

Prem, Hanns. "Early Spanish Colonization and Indians in the Valley of Atlixco, Puebla." In Prem and Harvey, *Explorations in Ethnohistory*, pp. 205–28.

—— and H. R. Harvey. *Explorations in Ethnohistory: Indians of Central Mexico in the Sixteenth Century.* Albuquerque: University of New Mexico Press, 1984.

Prem, Hanns. *Milpa y hacienda: Tenencia de la tierra indígena y española en la cuenca del Alto Atoyac, Puebla, México (1520–1650).* Wiesbaden: Franz Steiner Verlag, 1978.

Price, Barbara. "Prehispanic Irrigation Agriculture in Nuclear America." *Latin American Research Review* 6(1971):3–61.

Ramírez, Susan. *Provincial Patriarchs: Land Tenure and the Economics of Power in Colonial Peru.* Albuquerque: University of New Mexico Press, 1986.

Raymond, Joseph. "Water in Mexican Place Names." *The Americas* 9(1952–1953):201–05.

Robertson, Donald. "The Relaciones Geográficas of Mexico." *Proceedings of the 33rd International Congress of Americanistas* 2–3(1958):541–42.

Rojas Rabiela, Teresa and William Sanders, eds. *Historia de la agricultura prehispánica—siglo XVI.* Mexico City: Instituto Nacional de Antropología e Historia, 1985.

Rojas Rabiela, Teresa, Rafael A. Strauss K., and José Lameiras, eds. *Nuevas noticias sobre las obras hidráulicas prehispánicas y coloniales en el valle de México.* Mexico City: Instituto Nacional de Antropología e Historia, 1974.

——. *Las siembras de ayer: La agricultura indígena del siglo XVI.* Mexico City: Secretaría de Educación Pública, 1988.

——. "La tecnología agrícola mesoamericana en el siglo XVI." In Rojas Rabiela and Sanders, eds., *Historia de la agricultura prehispánica—siglo XVI,* pp. 9–52.

Roys, Ralph. *The Titles of Ebtun.* Washington, D.C.: Carnegie, 1939.

Ruiz de Velasco, Felipe. *Historia y evoluciones del cultivo de la caña en México hasta el año de 1910.* Mexico City: Editorial Cultura, 1937.

Sanders, William, Jeffrey Parsons, and Robert Santley. *The Basin of Mexico: Ecological Processes in the Evolution of a Civilization.* New York: Academic Press, 1979.

Schaedel, Richard, ed. *Urbanization in the Americas from its Beginnings to the Present.* The Hague: Mouton Publishers, 1978.

Scott, James. *Weapons of the Weak: Everyday Forms of Peasant Resistance.* New Haven: Yale University Press, 1985.

Sheridan, Richard. *Sugar and Slavery: An Economic History of the British West Indies, 1623–1775.* Baltimore: Johns Hopkins University Press, 1973.

Simmons, Marc. "Spanish Irrigation Practices in New Mexico." *New Mexico Historical Review* 47(1972):135–50.

Smith, Michael E. "New World Complex Societies: Recent Economic, Social and Political Studies." *Journal of Archaeological Research* 1(1993):5–41.

de Solano, Francisco. *Cedulario de tierras: Compilación de legislación agraria colonial (1497–1820).* Mexico City: Universidad Nacional Autónoma de México, 1984.

Spalding, Karen. *Huarochirí: An Andean Society Under Inca and Spanish Rule.* Stanford: Stanford University Press, 1986.

Spores, Ronald and Ross Hassig, eds. *Five Centuries of Law and Politics in Central Mexico.* Vanderbilt Publications in Anthropology, no. 30. Nashville: Vanderbilt University, 1984.

Spores, Ronald. *The Mixtecs in Ancient and Colonial Times.* Norman: University of Oklahoma Press, 1984.

Stephens, John Lloyd. *Incidents of Travel in Central America, Chiapas, and Yucatán.* London: John Murray, 1841.

Stern, Steven J. *Peru's Indian Peoples and the Challenge of Spanish Conquest: Huamanga to 1640.* Madison: University of Wisconsin Press, 1982.

Steward, Julian, et al., eds. *Irrigation Civilizations: A Comparative Study.* Washington, D.C.: Pan American Union, 1955.

Suárez, Clara Elena. *La política cerealera y la economía novohispana: El caso del trigo.* Mexico City: Ediciones de la Casa Chata, 1985.

Taggart, James. "Metaphors and Symbols of Deviance in Nahuat Narratives." *Journal of Latin American Lore* 3(1977):279–308.

Taylor, William. "Conflict and Balance in District Politics: Tecali and the Sierra Norte de Puebla in the Eighteenth Century." In Spores and Hassig, eds., *Five Centuries of Law and Politics in Central Mexico,* pp. 87–106.

——. *Drinking, Homicide, and Rebellion in Colonial Mexican Villages.* Stanford: Stanford University Press, 1979.

——. "Land and Water Rights in the Viceroyalty of New Spain." *New Mexico Historical Review* 50(1975):189–212.

——. *Landlord and Peasant in Colonial Oaxaca.* Stanford: Stanford University Press, 1972.

——. *Magistrates of the Sacred: Priests and Parishioners in Eighteenth-Century Mexico.* Stanford: Stanford University Press, 1996.

Thomas, William, ed. *Man's Role in Changing the Face of the Earth,* vol. 1. Chicago: University of Chicago Press, 1956.

Thomson, Guy. "The Cotton Textile Industry in Puebla During the Eighteenth and Early Nineteenth Centuries." In Jacobsen and Puhle, eds., *The Economies of Mexico and Peru During the Late Colonial Period,* pp. 169–202.

——. *Puebla de los Angeles: Industry and Society in a Mexican City, 1700–1850.* Dellplain Latin American Studies, no. 25. Boulder: Westview Press, 1989.

Trautmann, Wolfgang. *Las transformaciones en el paisaje cultural de Tlaxcala durante la época colonial.* Wiesbaden: F. Steiner, 1981.

Tutino, John. "Agrarian Social Change and Peasant Rebellion in Nineteenth-Century Mexico: The Example of Chalco." In Katz, ed., *Rural Social Conflicts in Mexico*, pp. 95–140.

Van Young, Eric. "The Age of Paradox: Mexican Agriculture at the End of the Colonial Period, 1750–1810." In Jacobsen and Puhle, eds., *The Economies of Mexico and Peru During the Late Colonial Period*, pp. 64–90.

———. *Hacienda and Market in Eighteenth-Century Mexico: The Rural Economy of the Guadalajara Region, 1675–1820.* Berkeley: University of California Press, 1981.

de Villa Sánchez, F. J. *Puebla Sagrada y Profana.* Puebla: Casa del Cuidadano José María Campos, 1835.

Viqueira Albán, Juan Pedro. *¿Relajados o reprimidos? Las diversiones públicas y vida social en la ciudad de México durante el siglo de las luces.* Mexico City: Fondo de Cultura Económico, 1987.

Völlmer, Gunter. "La evolución cuantitativa de la población indígena en la región de Puebla (1570–1810)." *Historia Mexicana* 23(1973):43–51.

Von Wobeser, Gisela. "El uso del agua en la región de Cuernavaca, Cuautla durante la época colonial." *Historia Mexicana* 32(1983):467–95.

Wauchope, Robert, ed. *The Indian Background of Latin American History: The Maya, Aztec, Inca, and Their Predecessors.* New York: Knopf, 1970.

Webre, Stephen. "Water and Society in a Spanish American City: Santiago de Guatemala, 1555–1773." *Hispanic American Historical Review* 70(1990): 57–84.

Wells, Hutchins C. "The Community Acequia: Its Origins and Development." *Southwestern Historical Review* 47(1972):85–112.

Wittfogel, Karl. "The Hydraulic Approach to Pre-Spanish Mesoamerica." In Johnson, ed., *The Prehistory of the Tehuacán Valley*, vol. 4, pp. 59–80.

———. "The Hydraulic Civilizations." In Thomas, ed., *Man's Role in Changing the Face of the Earth*, pp. 152–64.

———. *Oriental Despotism: A Comparative Study of Total Power.* New Haven: Yale University Press, 1957.

Wolf, Eric. *Peasant Wars of the Twentieth Century.* New York: Harper, 1969.

Woodbury, Richard and James Neely. "Water Control Systems of the Tehuacán Valley." In Johnson, ed., *The Prehistory of the Tehuacán Valley*, pp. 81–161.

Worster, Donald. *Rivers of Empire: Water, Aridity, and the Growth of the American West.* New York: Pantheon, 1985.

Index

193

About the Book and Author

What happened when native peoples and Spanish landowners in eighteenth-century Mexico competed for increasingly scarce water? In an unusual book that studies the interplay between the environment and colonial social institutions, Sonya Lipsett-Rivera examines the exercise of power by elites in colonial Puebla and how it brought ruin on Indian communities by denying them access to the water they needed to survive.

Because control over water was vested in the colonial bureaucracy rather than a local corps of guards, large landowners were able to manipulate the system in order to control access to water for irrigation, watering livestock, and other purposes. Not content to grow crops for local consumption, by the eighteenth century a creole elite emerged and, seeing an expanding and lucrative market for wheat, sugar (most of which was made clandestinely into cane brandy), corn, fruit, and livestock, they increased their production and therefore their irrigation. These owners of large haciendas and sugar refineries changed agriculture and, in so doing, disrupted the fragile ecosystem of a semi-arid environment. Their domination of water resources denied it to smaller users, resulting in the loss of crops and animals on which Indian communities depended.

As a first study in the ecology of water in Latin America, this book delineates the social and environmental consequences of power exercised to create a monopoly over irrigation.

"This is an outstanding piece of work, of considerable significance for both Mexican and environmental history."—Elinor G. K. Melville, author of *A Plague of Sheep: Environmental Consequences of the Conquest of Mexico*.

Sonya Lipsett-Rivera is a professor of colonial Latin American history at Carleton University and coeditor of *The Faces of Honor: Sex, Shame, and Violence in Colonial Latin America* (UNM Press).